FLORIDA STATE
UNIVERSITY LIBRARIES

JUN 2 0 2001

TALLAHASSEE, FLORIDA

HIERARCHY AND FLEXIBILITY IN WORLD POLITICS

*To my mother and father
for their love and encouragement*

Hierarchy and Flexibility in World Politics

Adaptation to shifting power distributions in the United Nations Security Council and the International Monetary Fund

PATRICK A. MC CARTHY
European University Institute

Ashgate
Aldershot • Brookfield USA • Singapore • Sydney

© Patrick A. Mc Carthy 1998

All rights reserved. No part of this publication may be reproduced, stored in a retrieval system or transmitted in any form or by any means, electronic, mechanical, photocopying, recording or otherwise without the prior permission of the publisher.

Published by
Ashgate Publishing Limited
Gower House
Croft Road
Aldershot
Hampshire GU11 3HR
England

Ashgate Publishing Company
Old Post Road
Brookfield
Vermont 05036
USA

British Library Cataloguing in Publication Data
Mc Carthy, Patrick A.
   Hierarchy and flexibility in world politics : adaptation to
shifting power distributions in the United Nations Security
Council and the International Monetary Fund
   1.United Nations. Security Council 2.International Monetary
Fund 3.Economic stabilization 4.Political stability
5.International relations 6.World politics - 1945-
I.Title
327.1'01

Library of Congress Cataloging-in-Publication Data
Mc Carthy, Patrick A.
   Hierarchy and flexibility in world politics : adaptation to
shifting power distributions in the United Nations Security Council
and the International Monetary Fund / Patrick A. Mc Carthy.
     p. cm.
   Includes bibliographical references.
   ISBN 1-84014-471-8 (hb)
   1. World politics--1945- 2. Political stability.
3. International relations. 4. International finance. 5. United
Nations. Security Council. 6. International Monetary Fund.
I. Title.
D843.M334 1998
341.23'23--dc21   98-35234
                                                                          CIP

ISBN 1 84014 471 8

Printed in Great Britain by The Ipswich Book Company, Suffolk

Contents

List of Figures   viii
Acknowledgements   ix

1   Introduction   1
     Of Firemen and Racing Drivers   1
     Overview of the Argument   3
     Overview of the Chapters   6

2   Confusing Stability with Peace and Status-quo   10
     Introduction   10
     The Trajectory of "Stability" in International Relations   12
     The Association of Stability with Peace   33
     The Association of Stability with Status-quo   38
     Revival of the Polarity Debate and
         Re-appraisal of Stability   39
     Conclusion   42

3   Stability as Process   46
     Introduction   46
     Gilpin on International Stability   47
     Some Short-comings of Gilpin's Approach   49
     The Status Inconsistency Approach to
         International Stability   53
     Towards a Dynamic Understanding of Stability   54
     An Alternative Definition of Stability   68
     Departures From Gilpin's Model   70
     Positioning the Theory of Stability   73
     Conclusion   77

4   Towards Testing the Hypotheses   79
     Introduction   79
     Specifying the Variables   80
     Delimiting the Universe   80

	Generating Predictions	81
	Operationalising the Central Concepts	81
	Choosing a Research Methodology	83
	Choosing the Cases	87
	Introducing an Additional Independent Variable	89
	Increasing the Number of Observations	90
	Postulating Causality	92
	Overview of Research Strategy	93
5	Hierarchy and Flexibility in the UN Security Council	95
	Introduction	95
	The Genesis of Security Council Hierarchy	95
	The Nature of Security Council Hierarchy	98
	The Genesis of Security Council Flexibility	105
	The Nature of Security Council Flexibility	108
	Conclusion	109
6	The 1965 Reform of the UN Security Council	114
	Introduction	114
	The Prelude to Reform	115
	The Geographic Impulse for Reform; Article 108	115
	The Constitutional Impulse for Reform; Article 109	118
	Soviet Opposition to Charter Amendment	120
	The Reversal of the Soviet Position	121
	Content of the 1965 Reform	123
	Conclusion	124
7	Positionality, Tension and Instability in the UN Security Council	127
	Introduction	127
	Upward Positionality	128
	Downward Positionality	141
	Tension	147
	Diffusing the Tension	156
	Conclusion	159
8	Hierarchy and Flexibility in the International Monetary Fund	163
	Introduction	163
	The Genesis of the IMF Hierarchy	163
	The Nature of the IMF Hierarchy	171

	The Genesis of IMF Flexibility	176
	The Nature of IMF Flexibility	177
	Conclusion	184
9	Positionality, Tension and Stability in the International Monetary Fund	187
	Introduction	187
	Upward and Downward Positionality in the IMF 1946-1995	188
	First Evidence of Positional Conflict	190
	The Demotion of China and the Promotion of Germany	198
	The De-coupling of German and French Quotas	200
	The Rise of Japan	201
	Unchanging Hierarchy	203
	A Hierarchy Transformed	208
	Conclusion	213
10	Reviewing (and Restating) the Hypotheses	216
	Introduction	216
	The Strategy of Analysis	216
	On Reorganisation and Institutionalisation	217
	On Differential Growth	220
	On Upward Positionality	220
	On Downward Positionality	223
	On Tension	228
	On Conflict	231
	Restating the Hypotheses	232
	Conclusion	233
11	Conclusion	235
Bibliography		245

List of Figures

Figure 1	A Simple Model of Tension Build-up	62
Figure 2	Tension Configuration of Opposing Positional Forces	64
Figure 3	A Simple Cycle of Change	67
Figure 4	The Theory-specific Variables	80
Figure 5	The Variables for Analysis	90
Figure 6	IMF Voting Power 1946-1995	191
Figure 7	IMF Voting Power 1946-1995 (Magnification 1)	192
Figure 8	IMF Voting Power 1946-1995 (Magnification 2)	193
Figure 9	IMF Voting Power 1946-1960 (Magnification 2)	194
Figure 10	IMF Voting Power 1960-1970 (Magnification 2)	195
Figure 11	IMF Voting Power 1970-1980 (Magnification 2)	196
Figure 12	IMF Voting Power 1980-1995 (Magnification 2)	197

Acknowledgements

The writing of this book was supported by grants from the Irish Government and from the European University Institute. Research was carried out at the European University Institute, Florence, the Cracow Academy of Economics, the Graduate Institute of International Studies, Geneva, the University of California, Berkeley, United Nations headquarters in New York and Geneva, and International Monetary Fund headquarters in Washington, D.C.

Throughout, the book has benefited from the input of a number of individuals. In particular, I would like to thank Alan Cafruny and Roger Morgan for their general guidance of the project, Czeslaw Mesjasz for his inspiration and interest, and Richard Rosecrance, Kenneth N. Waltz, Ernst B. Haas and Sir Brian Urquhart for important contributions and stimulating discussions.

For granting interviews, I would like to thank Vladimir Petrovsky, Director-General of the United Nations, Geneva, as well as officials of the permanent missions to the United Nations in New York of the United States, Britain, France, Russia, Germany, Japan and the European Union, who, by their own request, will remain anonymous. Likewise, for their assistance while conducting research at the International Monetary Fund, I am indebted to Pam Bradley, James Boughton, Alison Roth and Angie Snyder.

I thank the editors of *Global Governance* for allowing me to use materials from my article "Positionality, Tension, and Instability in the UN Security Council" published in Vol. 3, No. 1, 1997, pp. 147-169.

Finally, I would like to express my gratitude to all of my colleagues at the European University Institute whose friendship, interest and support made the production of this book such an enjoyable and enlightening experience and especially to Tom Lawton for encouraging me to publish my research in the form of this book and for facilitating the process. To all of you; thank you for helping make the years I invested in writing this book the most enjoyable of my life thus far.

1 Introduction

What do we mean when we say that an international system is stable? Do we mean that the system is characterised by continuity - i.e., by a distinctive lack of change - even though certain events threaten disruption every now and again, or do we mean that change takes place in the international system in a relatively harmonious and harmless way? Do we mean that war has not been observed in the system for a considerable period of time and/or is unlikely to be observed in the foreseeable future, or do we mean that, despite the occurrence of war, the international system maintains its essential characteristics? Do we mean that the state of the international system contributes to the achievement of certain common goals - order or repose, for example - or do we mean that the state of the international system contributes to the achievement of the specific goals of certain states? The answer seems to be that we mean all of these things, and more, when we speak, and write, of international stability.

There is no single, accepted definition of international stability that holds sway in the study of international relations. Agreement exists that stability is something positive, to be sought after and preserved once established, but that is as far as agreement stretches. Giovanni Sartori, the foremost advocate of the clarification and standardisation of social-scientific concepts, would not be impressed with the variety of interpretations of stability that exist in the discipline of International Relations. He would be even less impressed, however, by the lack of attention that has been devoted to rectifying this situation.

Of Firemen and Racing Drivers

In the natural sciences, where it enjoys wide currency, the concept of stability has been divided into various sub-categories, all of which have widely accepted, objective meanings. The simplest meaning of stability concerns the adherence of a system to an original equilibrium point despite the occurrence of disturbances that temporarily move the system away from that point. The greater the disturbances the system is able to withstand, and still return to its original equilibrium point, the greater is the stability of the system. Thus, a system represented by a golf-ball in an egg-cup is stable, but one represented by a golf-ball in a tea-cup is even more stable.

Why is it, then, that an apparently objective, concrete term such as stability - with such an unambiguous meaning in the harder sciences where it is widely employed - should have fallen prey to a range of sometimes conflicting interpretations in the discipline of International Relations? What is it about this concept that makes agreement upon its meaning in the social, rather than the natural, realm so difficult? The answer is provided, quite unintentionally, by a pioneer in the "hard science" of cybernetics, W. Ross Ashby, who attempts to show, by means of a number of examples, that stability need not necessarily be a good thing and may, in some instances, be downright undesirable. Ashby points out that:

> Stability is not always good, for a system may persist in returning to some state that, for other reasons, is considered undesirable. Once petrol is lit it stays in the lit state, returning to it after disturbance has changed it to "half-lit" - a highly undesirable stability to a fireman (Ashby, 1979 [1956]: 81).

Ashby correctly observes that the perfectly natural stability of lit petrol is not very desirable from the fireman's viewpoint. He fails to add, however, that this same stability may be perfectly desirable from other viewpoints - from that of racing-drivers, for example, who depend upon the stability of lit petrol to drive the engines of their cars in a smooth and responsive manner. What Ashby's example does, in effect, is to demonstrate how it is possible that, once transferred from a natural to a social setting, the concept of stability looses its clean, objective veneer and falls foul of contending interpretations. It is a short step from hard-scientific agreement on the stability of lit petrol to social-scientific disagreement (between the fireman and the racing-driver, for example) over whether lit petrol is desirable and, therefore, stable, or undesirable and, therefore, unstable.

Importing the concept of stability from the hard sciences for use in the significantly "softer" study of international relations, therefore, has the disadvantage of injecting normative content where none existed before and of introducing the possibility of varying interpretations across "view-points" or "perspectives" on international politics. Thus, an observer primarily concerned with the ravages inflicted by war equates the absence of war with stability while an observer mainly preoccupied with the preservation of the system's essential characteristics views wars as periodic tests of stability but not as proof of instability as such. Likewise, an observer satisfied with a particular configuration of an international system interprets the absence of change as a factor for stability whereas an observer particularly dissatisfied with the same configuration interprets the occurrence of change as harbinger of stability.

The problem with the concept of international stability, therefore, is not that it is always interpreted as something positive, but that what is positive for one observer may be negative for another. *The Doublespeak Dictionary for the 1990s* appropriately gives the meaning of stability as "political and economic conditions that satisfy *our* interests" (Herman, 1993; my emphasis). As long as interests vary among individuals, groups and states - i.e., as long as the possessive pronoun "our" has numerous possible referents - stability may be interpreted in myriad different ways.

One way of resolving this problem would be to make preferences constant across all observers. In this way, stability would come to be interpreted in a homogenous way, since what is positive for one would be positive for all. This solution is interesting only at a theoretical level, however, since, obviously, it will not be possible to convince all observers to trade in their existing set of preferences for another, homogeneous set. It would be difficult, for example, to convince the fireman to subscribe to the preferences of the racing-driver - or vice-versa - in order thereby to produce a standardised interpretation of stability with regard to lit petrol. A more realistic way of resolving the problem, however, would be to propose a conceptualisation of stability that has at least the possibility of being interpreted positively by all observers *at some stage*. For this to be possible, the preferences of observers must be capable of changing in such a way that all observers may periodically perceive as positive the conceptualisation of stability proposed. Since, in the realm of international politics, state preferences are not fixed but rather vary with changing circumstances, this solution offers the best chance of success.

Overview of the Argument

The purpose of this book is to construct a meaning of international stability that may be viewed by all observers - at one time or another - as being desirable and that does not give preference to any particular configuration of the international system or to the particular interests of any one state or group. I do not claim, of course, that such an interpretation of stability is without normative content. To do so would be to claim the impossible for a social-scientific concept. However, I do claim that its normative content is not linked to the preferences of any clearly defined set of observers and that the possibility exists that, in the long term, all observers - at different times, not all at once - may interpret the understanding of stability presented in this book in a positive manner.

A brief outline of the conceptualisation of stability presented in the following chapters serves to illustrate this point. I interpret international politics as being characterised by the interaction of two perennial phenomena; on the one hand, the tendency of states to institutionalise their relative influence over the governance of the international system and, on the other, the differential growth in capabilities of states. By governance, I mean the attempts made by powerful states to order and manage international relations primarily for their own benefit. By differential growth, I mean the spectacle of the rise and fall in state power that has been observed over centuries.

These two phenomena are potentially incompatible. The institutionalisation of relative influence over the governance of the international system may freeze in place a particular distribution of power that existed at one point in time. Frozen distributions of power are artificial and differ fundamentally from distributions of power in their natural, fluid form; continuously shifting as states grow and decline at different rates. Such an artificial freezing of relative influence over the governance of the international system may precipitate conflict when shifts in the distribution of power caused by continuing differential growth cause discrepancies to emerge between the distribution of influence frozen at a particular time and a new distribution of power that emerges subsequently.

Such discrepancies may lead rising states - those whose relative capabilities are growing faster than average - to become dissatisfied with the fact that the great increase in their capabilities has not been translated into greater influence over the governance of the international system. As a result of this dissatisfaction, rising states may attempt to increase their formal influence to an extent commensurate with their actual capabilities. Since governing states - those already exerting significant influence on the governance of the international system as a result of the institutionalisation of a now anachronistic distribution of power - are reluctant to cede influence, they will oppose these attempts by rising states even if they are aware that, in relative terms, their own capabilities have declined over time. The result of this conflict of interest is a kind of stalemate in which states seeking more formal influence are opposed by states unwilling to cede it.

The conceptualisation of international stability contained in this book revolves around whether or not - and, if so, how efficiently - states diffuse the tension that arises when such a stalemate occurs. Simply put, an unstable international system is one that is incapable of resolving the conflict of interest that exists between rising and governing states. In such a system, the dissatisfaction of rising states continues to increase along with the resolve and ability of governing states to maintain their own positions. A stable international system, on the other hand, is capable of resolving this conflict of interest, thereby decreasing the dissatisfaction of rising states. It may do so by granting rising states their desired increase in formal influence over the governance of the international system and/or by granting them some other forms of side-payments that reduce their dissatisfaction.

Let us return now to the question of allowing for the possibility that a conceptualisation of international stability may be viewed positively by all observers - in this case, states. It is obvious that the conceptualisation of stability briefly outlined above will be viewed positively by rising states, since it advocates that the extent of their dissatisfaction be reduced by ceding to them greater influence in the governance of the international system. It will most likely be viewed negatively, however, by governing states, since it advocates that they cede some of their formal influence over the governance of the international system when their relative capabilities decline. In the short-term, therefore, contending appraisals of this conceptualisation of international stability are possible. Rising states may view its preference for change and adaptation as being positive and desirable while governing states may view this same preference as being negative and repugnant.

However, while these contending interpretations are held by two opposing groups or *types* of states - rising and governing - they are not associated with opposing groups of *particular* states - i.e., Spain and Italy in one group and Norway and Greece in the other. The identity of the particular states that make up each type is not constant but, rather, is subject to variation over time. Spain and Italy, to use a random example, may during one period of time enjoy a relative increase in their capabilities and, therefore, be counted among the rising states but during a different period may experience a relative decline from a dominant position and, therefore, be counted among governing states. Accordingly, states' evaluations of the conceptualisation of stability outlined above will vary as they move between the groups of rising and governing states. As rising states, they will be positively disposed to this interpretation; as governing states, they will be negatively disposed to it. The important point is, however, that all states may be positively disposed to this conceptualisation of international stability, albeit at different times. Thus, there is hope for a more standardised response to the understanding of international stability set forth in this book for the same reason that, if firemen took frequent sabbaticals as racing-drivers, there would be hope for a more standardised interpretation of the stability of lit petrol.

The conceptualisation of international stability presented in this book is based, therefore, upon the recognition that change is perennially occurring in the international system. It is a dynamic conceptualisation and is to be distinguished from the more conventional equation of stability with stasis. It revolves around the potential for conflict that is created when particular distributions of power are frozen in place by processes of institutionalisation.

This understanding of international stability may be applied at numerous levels of specificity. At a quite broad level, it might be applied, for example, to the freezing of the post-Napoleonic Wars distribution of power that was achieved by creating and utilising a congress system to govern European affairs or, in general, to all such institutionalisations of relative influence that tend to take place following major international wars. At a less general level, it might also be applied to similar institutionalisations of relative influence that take place in specific issue-areas of international politics such as security, trade, money, services, etc.. Numerous possibilities exist, therefore, to test the conceptualisation of stability contained in this book.

An attempt will be made to test it using two examples drawn from issue-specific areas of international governance - security and money. These examples are chosen with various methodological considerations in mind that maximise the likelihood that the results obtained will be generalisable to other cases. They do not, however, exhaust the possibilities of subjecting the conceptualisation of stability presented in this book to systematic empirical analysis. In this respect, this book raises more questions than it claims to answer or, at least, makes more assertions than it claims to corroborate in full. It outlines an extensive research programme but only initiates the work thereon.

Overview of the Chapters

The book may be broadly divided into three parts. The first part, comprising chapters 2 through 4, sets the theoretical groundwork and prepares the way for the second part; the empirical analysis conducted in chapters 5 through 9. Finally, chapters 10 and 11 constitute the final part, where the empirical results of part two are compared and contrasted with the predictions generated by the theoretical considerations of part one.

Each chapter, however, serves a specific purpose in the overall plan of the book.

Chapter 2 seeks to undermine the conventional equation of stability with peace and/or the preservation of the status-quo in the international system. It does so by employing an innovative procedure introduced by David Collier in the area of comparative politics, a procedure best described as "concept tracing." It traces the trajectory of the concept of stability in the study of international relations from its incorporation from the fields of systems theory and cybernetics in the latter half of the 1950s to its widespread re-conceptualisation begun at the end of the Cold War in the early 1990s. In doing so, it strives to show that the meaning of stability in the study of international relations has varied greatly over time. At the outset, it was greatly influenced by systems theoretic and cybernetic thinking. In the mid-stage of its development, it fell under the influence of the Correlates of War project and became largely associated with the absence of war in the international system. More recently, great confusion has arisen around the concept of international stability, implying that a re-conceptualisation is needed in the wake of the Cold War.

The aim of chapter 2 does not extend beyond demonstrating that dominant modes of thought and particular configurations of the international system have exerted a strong influence on how stability has been conceptualised. It does not attempt to rank the various interpretations of stability that have existed over the past four decades in order of their closeness to a "true" meaning of stability. Indeed, it does not even begin from the assumption that such a true meaning exists. Instead, it aims to show that the meaning of stability in the study of international relations has been volatile and that numerous interpretations - some undoubtedly more useful than others - have existed. It argues that the end of the Cold War represents an opportunity to develop an alternative understanding of international stability that is more useful than those that have preceded it.

Chapter 3 constitutes the main theoretical contribution of the book to the development of such an understanding. Taking Robert Gilpin's theory of international political change and insights provided by status-inconsistency theory as starting-points, it develops a theory of international stability - in the form of a set of inter-related hypotheses - based on the occurrence of change in the international system. The theory developed begins with the observation that, following system-wide conflict, powerful states often establish systems of international governance that are sometimes broad-ranging, sometimes limited to specific issue-areas, but that always share the purpose of ordering and managing some aspect or aspects of post-war international affairs. The extent of the influence of individual states on this process of post-war reorganisation varies greatly, with more powerful states tending to have a greater say than less powerful ones. Furthermore, the differential influence of states on the process of post-war reorganisation tends to be institutionalised to an extent that may range from treaty obligations to fully-fledged international organisations. Whatever the extent of the institutionalisation, however, chapter 3 argues that the key determinant of the stability of an international system - either broadly defined or limited to a particular issue-area of governance - is its ability to adapt its hierarchy of influence in line with shifts in the international distribution of power precipitated by the differential growth of states.

The remainder of the book is concerned with testing these ideas against empirical evidence and with reflecting upon the results obtained. Chapter 4 reviews the methodological possibilities suitable for testing the hypotheses presented in chapter 3 and provides a justification for selecting particular methodologies - the complimentary methods of structured, focused comparison and process-tracing - and for selecting particular cases for analysis - the UN Security Council and the International Monetary Fund.

Chapters 5 through 7 apply a standardised set of research questions to a case study of the UN Security Council. Chapter 5 deals with the establishment of the Security Council. It investigates the origin of its hierarchical organisation and emphasises the differential influence exerted thereon by the most powerful states to emerge from World War II. It also expands upon the nature of the Security Council's hierarchical organisation, with special emphasis on the features of permanent membership, veto power, and the dominant position of the Security Council within the UN organisation as a whole.

Chapter 6 deals with the background and content of the 1965 reform of the Security Council. It identifies the sources of the reform impulse and chronicles the process by which dissatisfaction mainly among developing countries was successful in overcoming the opposition to reform displayed by some permanent members in order to add two extra non-permanent seats to the Security Council.

Chapter 7 constitutes the most important part of the Security Council case study. It deals with the current debate on reforming the Security Council that, unlike the debate that took place in the first half of the 1960s, has as its focus the addition of permanent seats to the Security Council. It examines in detail the attempt by Japan and Germany to gain permanent membership of the Council as well as the reactions of the current permanent members to these attempts.

Chapters 8 and 9 apply the same set of research questions to a case study of the International Monetary Fund. Chapter 8 is the counterpart of chapter 5. It examines the origin of the Fund's hierarchical organisation, emphasising once more the significant influence exercised by a small number of states on the design of the organisation and the important role played by political as well as economic considerations in determining which states would exercise most influence within it. It also describes in detail the nature of the IMF's hierarchical organisation, according to which a state's contribution to the monetary and gold reserves of the Fund determines the extent of its input in deciding on Fund policy.

Chapter 9 constitutes the most important part of the IMF case study. Unlike in the case of the Security Council, where the examinations of reform are concentrated over relatively short time-periods, chapter 9 spreads an analysis of the reform of the IMF over the course of its history; from 1946 until 1995. It traces the way in which the relative decision-making influence of states has varied over this period of time and the reactions that such variation has engendered from member states.

Finally, chapter 10 fits the empirical evidence generated by the case studies with the theoretical propositions set out in chapter 3. It finds that, on the whole, the fit is good, although some alterations need to be made.

2 Confusing Stability with Peace and Status-quo

Introduction

It is customary in the study of international relations for the concepts of "peace" and "status-quo" to be used interchangeably with the concept of "stability." Relatively peaceful systems - such as the Concert of Europe - are conventionally considered stable as are systems that do not drastically change over a long period of time - such as the Cold War international system. Also in the practice of international relations, the foreign policies of states are often shaped by expectations of how a particular policy will effect the "stability" of some other country or region by effecting the likelihood of war or change. The close association between the concepts of peace and status-quo on the one hand and the concept of stability on the other has become so ingrained in the study and practice of international relations, as well as in media reports of international events, that few have questioned its validity. This chapter does just that, however. It questions the validity of associating stability with peace and/or with the preservation of the status-quo.

The association of stability with peace and/or status-quo is misleading. It does not provide a satisfactory understanding of what constitutes international stability. Rather, it simply reflects a particular view of the world that prevailed during the Cold War. By plotting the trajectory of the concept of stability through almost forty years of IR literature, this chapter shows how the meaning of stability shifted from an association with change and the occasional necessity of war to an association with peace and status-quo that has come to characterise the conventional contemporary understanding of stability. The chapter identifies two processes that aided in this shift. First, the notion of stability became associated with peace as a result of the synthesis of two distinct debates; one of which sought to formulate a scientific meaning of stability that could be applied to the study of international relations and the other of which applied quantitative tools to the task of identifying regularities in the occurrence of war. The coalition of these two debates in the early 1970s narrowed the abstract theoretical meaning of stability to an association with peace. Second, the concept of stability came to be associated with the preservation of the international status-quo as a result of the realities of the bipolar Cold War order. The concept of stability was linked to the preservation of the bipolar structure, an alternative to which most scholars could not envision arising without the occurrence of major war. Furthermore, the chapter shows that the end of the Cold War has led many scholars to rethink what they mean by international stability; suggesting that the Cold war played a significant role in determining the contemporary meaning of stability but that it is no longer valid for thinking about international relations in the post Cold War world.

At this early stage, a few caveats are in order. By arguing, first of all, that we should be careful not to confuse the concepts of peace and stability, I do not wish to imply either that we are wrong to care about peace or that war is always compatible with stability. Rather, I wish to indicate that the concept of international stability is larger and more complex than simply the presence or absence of war. The same applies to the relationship between stability and the status-quo. By insisting that we should not confuse instability with change, I am not implying that static systems are always unstable. Rather, I am allowing for the possibility that dynamic systems may be stable. I wish to point out that it is overly simplistic and, more often than not, inaccurate to label a changing system unstable or to label an unchanging system stable.

The purpose of this chapter is to clear the way for the articulation, in chapter 3, of a more useful interpretation of international stability. This chapter is divided into four parts. The first part plots the trajectory of the concept of stability during what I call the "early theoretical debate" on stability; i.e., from its incorporation as an analytical concept into the study of International Relations in the late 1950s until the transformation of the debate on stability that began in the early 1970s. It identifies the "source fields" from which the concept was imported and points to the strong influence that these exercised on the early theoretical understanding of international stability. It shows how early theoretical formulations were biased towards equating stability with evolutionary change in the international system. Furthermore, it shows that, in these early formulations, war was even considered a tool that could be used under certain conditions to preserve stability.

The second part deals with the process by which the concept of stability came to be associated with peace in IR, describing the transformation of the debate on stability that began in the early 1970s. It recounts how the empirical questions raised by the theoretical debate on stability - especially the question of the relationship between stability and polarity - attracted the interest of a separate field of enquiry in IR that was exclusively concerned with employing quantitative methods in investigating the regularities underlying the occurrence of war in the international system. Furthermore, part two argues that the coalition of these two approaches to understanding and investigating stability had the effect of narrowing the abstract theoretical understanding of stability to an association with peace.

The third part focuses on the process by which the concept of stability became associated with the preservation of the international status-quo. It forwards two hypotheses as to why this association took place. The first posits that stability became associated with status-quo as a direct result of stability's association with peace and the desire to maintain peace in a bipolar world. The second hypothesis posits that the preponderant influence of U.S. scholars on the formulation of the meaning of stability aided in its association with the preservation of the status-quo.

The revival of the debate on stability caused by the demolition of the Berlin Wall and the decomposition of the Soviet Union is the focus of the final part of this chapter which also deals with the fundamental re-appraisal of stability inherent in that revival. It shows that since the revival of the debate, at least as much attention has been paid to re-thinking the meaning of international stability as has been paid to discussing stability in conventional terms.

The Trajectory of "Stability" in International Relations

In his article *Trajectory of a Concept: "Corporatism" in the Study of Latin American Politics*, David Collier (1995) pursues a line of enquiry not common in political science. He identifies the point at which the concept of corporatism entered the debate on Latin American politics and tracks its trajectory through the different stages of the debate. Furthermore, he assesses the impact that the concept of corporatism had, and continues to have, on the debate on Latin America. Collier's is by no means a standard analysis but its usefulness to a social science often plagued by myriad, vaguely defined concepts is becoming increasingly obvious.[1] Collier asserts that "scholars should occasionally step back and take stock of the major concepts with which they work" and that "it is useful periodically to assess the evolution of concepts and attempt a codification of what has been accomplished" (Collier, 1995: 135). His call that increased attention be paid to the concepts that we use in the political and social sciences constitutes strong intellectual encouragement for one of the main tasks of this chapter; namely, to critically analyse the trajectory of the concept of stability in the study of international relations.

Plotting the trajectory of stability through the early IR literature, serves a number of important functions. First, it identifies (1) whence the concept came; (2) the main formative influences on the meaning of the concept once it entered the realm of international relations; (3) the main definitions of the concept that were offered; and (4) how these definitions were thought to translate into stability in international systems. All of these points are crucial in answering the two central questions of the analysis; namely, (5) how did the early theoretical concept of stability relate to change and status-quo on the one hand and to (6) war and peace on the other? Furthermore, the exercise of plotting stability's trajectory through the early debate not only identifies the actual trajectory followed by the concept but also suggests other trajectories that might have been followed. This leads to the important question; why did the concept of stability plot the trajectory that it did in IR and not some other trajectory? Answering this question leads to important conclusions regarding the social construction of the concept of stability in IR.

The Incorporation of the Concept of Stability into IR

Before following the trajectory of the concept of stability in the study of international relations, however, it is necessary to determine whence it came; to find the point at which it entered the discourse on international politics and the route it took in order to do so. That done, it will be considerably easier to trace the concept's development and to understand why it developed in the way it did.

When discussing the incorporation of concepts, it is useful to speak in terms of "source fields," i.e., fields from which a discipline draws concepts for its own use. However, when speaking in terms of source fields, one should also be mindful of the fact that concepts may make their way through many fields before finally being incorporated into any particular discipline of study. In other words, when one identifies the field from which a particular concept has been incorporated into a particular discipline, one has identified the "source" field for that concept only in relation to the incorporating discipline. The fact is, the identified field may not be the "original source" for the concept in question and may have itself incorporated the concept from another field. Thus, it is possible to speak of a series of fields; each one acting as the "source" for the one it precedes.

With regard to the incorporation of the concept of stability into the study of international relations, a series of three source fields are of primary importance. They are, in descending order of relevance, systems theory, cybernetics and mathematics. Cybernetics incorporated the concept of stability from mathematics, especially from the stability theory of differential equations developed by Richard Bellman (1953) whose work drew on the ideas of mathematicians Lyapunov and Poincaré and "proved applicable in [the] mathematical modelling of automatic control systems. As a natural consequence stability became a key element of cybernetic terminology" (Mesjasz, 1993: 8).

Systems theory, in turn, incorporated the concept of stability from cybernetics. Cybernetics, or the study of 'automatic control systems,' includes within its research framework such useful concepts as positive and negative feedback, and a number of interesting variations on the theme of system stability such as invariant stability, state of equilibrium, cyclical stability and stable region (Ashby, 1956). Systems theory found these concepts invaluable in framing its research; especially in view of its preoccupation with describing system stability.

Finally, IR incorporated the concept of stability from both systems theory and cybernetics in about equal measure. The research projects of systems theory and cybernetics exerted a strong influence on the scientific community in the late 1950s. This influence extended also to students of international relations who were looking not only for a language with which to describe the fundamental changes that were occurring in the international system, but also for analogies that could help them understand these changes. Systems theory and cybernetics provided such a language and such analogies. They allowed students of international relations to speak of stability in complex and nuanced ways and to map system theoretical and cybernetic dynamics onto the contemporary dynamics of the international system. Thus, the source fields of the concept of stability for students of international relations were systems theory and cybernetics. For systems theorists the source field was cybernetics and for cyberneticists it was mathematics. The further one follows the genealogy of the concept of stability back in time, the "harder" become the scientific disciplines that constitute its source fields.

Influences on the Conceptualisation of Stability

Most scholars recognise 1964 as the birth-year of the polarity debate since in that year, two articles appeared that spurred the debate into full ferment. One was Kenneth Waltz's *Stability of a Bipolar World*, the other Karl W. Deutsch and J. David Singer's *Multipolar Power Systems and International Stability*. However, the roots of the ideas that permeate the debate may be traced back even further to the works of Morton A. Kaplan (1957a; 1957b) and George Liska (1957). Other scholars have recognised the significant early influence that these works exerted on the development of the polarity debate (Haas, 1970) and it is there that this analysis will begin.

Before proceeding, however, a general introduction to the major works to be analysed is in order. These works have been chosen on the basis of their influence on the debate on stability. Each dedicates much effort to understanding the new bipolar structure of the international system, to defining international stability and to commenting on how best stability may be maintained in the international system. Kaplan attempts to "chart the equilibrium conditions for six different models of international systems, the characteristic behavior of such systems, and the transformations which such systems undergo when the equilibrium conditions no longer hold" (Kaplan, 1957a: xviii). Central to his work is a consideration of equilibrium and a conceptualisation of stability. George Liska's *International Equilibrium*, also published in 1957, offers an abstract analysis of international stability, or equilibrium, and in the process formulates a theory of systemic equilibrium. Richard Rosecrance's influential study *Action and Reaction in World Politics* (1963) sets itself the task of identifying the "requisites for international stability" (Zinnes, 1964). It does so by identifying nine distinct international systems and by distilling out of them common observed characteristics of stability. Karl Deutsch and J. David Singer's *Multipolar Power Systems and International Stability* argued in favour of the stability of multipolar international systems while Kenneth N. Waltz, on the other hand, defended *The Stability of a Bipolar World*. If the works of Kaplan and Liska from 1957 may be considered to have initiated abstract discussion of what constitutes international stability and under what conditions it is displayed in the international system, these works by Deutsch & Singer and Waltz respectively may be viewed as the first to relate the concept of stability to international structure in a theoretically rigorous and systematic manner.

One of the most striking aspects of the early theoretical discussion of stability is the strong influence that was exerted on the meaning of stability by the disciplines of systems analysis and cybernetics, the source fields from which the concept was incorporated into IR. With one significant exception, - that of Kenneth Waltz - all of the works analysed display a debt to these disciplines. This is not unusual when one takes into consideration the popularity that the systems approach enjoyed among diverse scientific communities at the time. By the mid-1950s, general systems theory had been articulated in such a way as to make it applicable in many scientific fields (von Bertalanffy, 1950, 1955; Boulding, 1956). Its mode of analysis and its methods, along with those of cybernetics (Ashby, 1952, 1956), promised to transform the study of international politics from an intuitive into a scientific process (Rosenau, 1963).

Kaplan makes very specific the influences on his conceptualisation of stability. He points out that his analysis "is based upon a particular kind of theory; namely, systems theory" (Kaplan, 1957b: 684) and describes cyberneticist's Ross Ashby's work *Design for a Brain* (Ashby, 1952) as "a landmark in [systems-] theoretical research" (Kaplan, 1957b: 684, f.n. 3).[2] In doing so, Kaplan acknowledges his debt to the ideas and methodologies of systems theory and cybernetics. Furthermore, Kaplan's understanding of stability is based on the core cybernetic concept of "negative feedback."[3]

Likewise for Liska, cybernetics or "mechanics" (Liska, 1957: 11) constitutes the main source field from which Liska draws his analogies of stability. He is mindful, however, of the application of the concept of stability in economic theory. He is sceptical of the use in economic theory of variegated concepts of equilibrium such as "general and partial; unique and multiple; stable, neutral and unstable; long- and short-term; perfect and imperfect..." (p. 12). He is not convinced by the use of differentiated forms of equilibrium and prefers instead to invest time and effort "in defining the kind of equilibrium one is prepared to defend as operative in the investigated realm" (p. 12). Consequently, Liska devotes most of his efforts to defining the kind of equilibrium that is operative in his investigated realm; namely, the international system of states. Liska is not as comfortable as Kaplan, however, in importing a pure cybernetic understanding of stability directly into the social sciences. For the purposes of social scientific investigation, he considers the use of concepts of stability based on "automatic compensatory reactions to disturbances, restoring the original state" (cybernetic feedback) as useless. He argues that "[i]f such an unfailing equilibrium operates anywhere, it is certainly not in the social realm" (p. 12). Despite the fact that Liska rejects such a "maximalist" cybernetic understanding of stability, he embraces a more dynamic cybernetic interpretation; one that allows for the establishment of a *new* equilibrium after each disturbance to the system.

Also Rosecrance (1963) is heavily influenced in his conceptualisation of stability by cybernetics and systems theory and he is most explicit about this influence. He transfers "from the field of cybernetics to that of international politics the notions of disturbance and regulator and of an interplay between them within a more or less constraining environment" (Liska, 1963: 132). He conceptualises international systems as composed of "mechanistic elements" and follows "an analogy with formal systems analysis" (Rosecrance, 1963: 220).

Similarly, Deutsch & Singer's (1964) contribution to the polarity debate displays strong links to the thought patterns of systems theory and cybernetics despite the fact that they claim distance from a purely mechanistic understanding of the operation of the international system. At the outset, they distinguish their understanding of stability from that of Richardson (1960), which they recognise as being based on classical mechanics (Deutsch & Singer, 1964: 391). However, their own understanding of stability in the international system is based on a classic cybernetic property; the feedback loop. They state that:

> Our focus is on the degree to which the [international] system exhibits negative feedback as well as cross pressuring. By negative - as distinguished from positive or amplifying - feedback, we refer to the phenomenon of self-correction: [...] This is the self-restraining system, manifested in the automatic pilot, the steam-engine governor, and most integrated social systems, and it stands in contrast to the self-aggravating system as seen in forest fires, compound interest, nuclear fission, runaway inflation or deflation , and drug addiction (Deutsch & Singer, 1964: 393).

In any case, Deutsch & Singer consider their proposition that multipolarity supports stability to be "a special case of the general Richardson model" (p. 400). Thus, although Deutsch & Singer go to considerable lengths to draw attention to the distance between their model and Richardson's classical mechanical model, it is clear from their assumptions about the operation of the international system that the distance is not as great as they assert. Deutsch & Singer's approach to the operation of the international system is mechanistic insofar as it is based on the analogy of the cybernetic feedback loop. The influence of systems theory and cybernetics on their conceptualisation of international stability is unmistakable.

With regard to influences on the conceptualisation of stability during the early theoretical debate, however, Kenneth Waltz constitutes the exception to the rule. The influences of systems theory and cybernetics on Waltz's understanding of stability are not explicit in his work. Furthermore, Waltz denounces the "cumbrous mechanisms of compensation and realignment" (1964: 883) inherent in the multipolar system, suggesting his dissatisfaction with analogies drawn from the source fields of cybernetics and systems theory.

The fact that the source fields from which the concept of stability was drawn heavily influenced the early meaning of the concept in IR is not in itself surprising especially when one considers the wide cross-disciplinary popularity enjoyed by systems theory and cybernetics in the late 1950s and early 1960s. However, it is an important factor to be considered when analysing the trajectory of stability in IR since it leads to particular definitions of stability that take the first step towards relating pure systems theoretical and cybernetic notions of stability to the international system.

Definitions of Stability

The definitions of stability offered by the early theoretical debate demonstrate the ways in which abstract ideas drawn from the source fields of systems theory and cybernetics translated into definitional statements that could be applied to the international system. However, the analogies drawn from these source-fields did not produce uniform definitions of stability for the international realm. Instead, a variety of definitions of stability competed with one another in the early theoretical debate. This is due to the fact that a certain margin of interpretation surrounded the way in which "scientific" ideas about stability were applied to the international system. Particularly significant in this respect was the way in which scholars interpreted the operation of "negative feedback;" i.e., the way in which a system uses information about its present and desired states to keep it on track to its goal. As we shall see in the analysis to follow, some argued that negative feedback operated in the international system in such a way as to always return the system to its original equilibrium state after a disturbance had been experienced; others argued that negative feedback operated but did not always return the system exactly to its original equilibrium position; and still others argued that negative feedback did not operate at all in the international system and that, instead, the system moved repeatedly from one equilibrium state to another.

Kaplan's definition of stability involves many steps and is highly complex. He first distinguishes between the concepts of stability and equilibrium. Equilibrium and stability, he argues, "are not the same concepts, for an equilibrium may be unstable. The stable equilibrium is the equilibrium that fluctuates within given limits" (1957: 6). He asserts that the concept "stability" may refer either to a state of equilibrium of a system or to the system itself; i.e., to its *ability to find an equilibrium*. Thus, Kaplan distinguishes between two levels of, or two ways of thinking about, stability. First, one may describe a system as being stable if the system is capable of finding an equilibrium. Second, one may then look more closely at that equilibrium and determine whether it in turn is stable; i.e., whether or not it "fluctuates within given limits." In other words, one may not imply the stability of a system's equilibrium simply by determining that the system itself is stable but one may deduce that a system is stable if one knows that its equilibrium is stable (or even if one knows that an equilibrium exists). For Kaplan, a stable system is a necessary but not a sufficient condition for the existence of a stable equilibrium. On the other hand, a stable equilibrium is a sufficient but not a necessary condition for the existence of a stable system.

Kaplan argues that a system in equilibrium will remain there until disturbed. If, however, a disturbance of sufficient magnitude to move the system away from its equilibrium point does not exist or is not likely to occur, then one may conclude that the system's equilibrium is stable. If such a disturbance does exist "but its effects are dependent upon its strength, the equilibrium has local stability" (1957: 8). If a system *is* disturbed, it will either change its equilibrium or, if it fails to do so, will cease to exist. If a system manages to find a new equilibrium point; i.e., if it manages to execute "equilibrium change," it is "ultrastable" (1957: 8; 1957a, f.n. 5).[4] If, when the disturbance subsides, the original equilibrium is not restored in the system, the system has undergone "system change" - as opposed to equilibrium change. Such a system is also ultrastable but it has the characteristic of having been irreversibly altered.

Kaplan also identifies another type of stability which he calls "steady state" or "homeostatic" stability (1957: 6; 1957a, f.n. 5). This type of stability is maintained thanks to the fluctuation of certain variables in order keep other system variables within certain limits. This type of stability is epitomised by systems characterised by negative feedback. Political systems such as the international system of states, according to Kaplan, are the epitome of systems displaying homeostatic stability. The international system is homeostatically stable because "it acts selectively toward states of its internal variables and rejects those which lead to unstable states" (1957a: f.n. 5). Homeostatically stable (political) systems display "regulation" and have a "capacity." By regulation Kaplan means "the process by means of which a system attempts to maintain or preserve its identity over time as it adapts to changing conditions" (1957: 89). The capacity of a system, on the other hand, is the "measure of the responses a system is able to make that compensate for potential disturbances of the system's equilibrium" (ibid.).

A discussion of Kaplan's definition of the concept of stability could lapse into more and more detail about the complex way that he understands the concept and the specialised jargon he employs in order to communicate his ideas about it. However, such detail would not serve the purpose of this analysis. What I have attempted to demonstrate is that his grasp of the complex nuances underlying his understanding of stability is clearly aided by his reliance on technical concepts drawn from systems theory and cybernetics. The concepts of feedback, disturbance, equilibrium, equilibrium change, system change, regulation, capacity and the numerous variations on the theme of stability - local stability, ultrastability, and static state stability - are all concepts that Kaplan drew from these two source fields.

Liska, as we have already seen, distances himself from the maximalist cybernetic conceptualisation of stability but does not abandon the cybernetic framework of thought in formulating his definition of stability. He offers what he considers to be a more realistic view of stability in the social realm; one that centres more on the primacy of change over status-quo. He considers that "[m]ore realistic and at the same time "dynamic" is the view of the equilibrium mechanism as a state of relative temporary stability, uniquely or recurrently upset by factors precipitating change and replaced eventually by a new temporary equilibrium" (Liska, 1957: 12). He does not accept that social systems, the international system included, operate according to classical cybernetic causality - i.e., state of equilibrium followed by disturbance followed by the operation of negative feedback culminating in the restoration of the original equilibrium of the system. Rather, he argues that negative feedback is not operative in the social realm and that the original equilibrium is not restored after a disturbance is experienced by the system. Instead, the system continually moves to new equilibria after each disturbance.

Rosecrance (1963) defines stability in a way consistent with the influences on his approach. A system aiming at stability, he argues, is comprised of four essential elements; (1) a source of disturbance (input), (2) a regulator that undergoes change as a result of disturbance, and (3) environmental constraints which translate the disturbance and regulator into (4) outcomes. A disturbance to the system is acted upon by the regulator and constrained by the environment to produce outcomes which may be either stable or unstable. Rosecrance associates stability with "the ratio of disturbance over regulatory forces; a system is stable as long as the ratio is less than unity but unstable when it exceeds unity" (Zinnes, 1964: 303). In other words, a system is stable when the regulator is always capable of offsetting the disturbance. But how is one to determine by reference to the outcomes whether the ratio was lesser than or greater than unity? The answer is provided by Rosecrance himself, who asserts that an international system is stable "if its outcomes fall within limits generally "accepted" by the major participants in the system" (Rosecrance, 1963: 231).

Deutsch & Singer (1964) are explicit in their definition of

stability. They offer a *probabilistic* definition of *political* stability as:

> The probability that the system retains all of its essential characteristics; that no single nation becomes dominant; that most of its members continue to survive; and that large-scale war does not occur. [...] A more stringent definition of stability would require also a low probability of the actors' becoming engaged even in limited wars (Deutsch & Singer, 1964: 390-91).

As well as being probabilistic, this definition is highly problematic. In short, it is vague and does not lend itself to unambiguous application to some international system. Deutsch & Singer fail to elaborate on what the "essential characteristics" of the international system actually are, whether "dominance" is to be understood in the imperialistic, hegemonic or world leadership sense (or in some other sense), and what criteria we are to use in determining whether a war is "large-scale" or "limited." Without these refinements to the definition, it is difficult to imagine a concrete international system that conforms to Deutsch & Singer's conceptualisation of stability. However, it is at least clear that their understanding of stability encompasses three distinct and, presumably, equally essential elements - retention of essential characteristics, deterrence of hegemony, and the absence of large-scale war - and that the absence of even one of these elements would denote instability in the system.

Waltz (1964) offers a specific definition of international stability although it is necessary to refer to some of his later work in order fully to comprehend it. In his first treatment of the matter, he suggests that international stability should be measured in terms of "the peacefulness of adjustment within the international system and by the durability of the system itself" (Waltz, 1964: 881). It is initially unclear, however, exactly what Waltz means by 'adjustment' in this definition. At least two meanings of the term are possible. On the one hand, adjustment may mean change in response to exogenous stimuli, leading to evolution. On the other hand, it may mean the adjustment necessary in order to move the system back to its original state of equilibrium after a disturbance has been experienced. Obviously, these two understandings of "adjustment" have their roots in fundamentally different interpretations of how the international system operates, or *should* operate if it is to be stable.

The former interpretation suggests an understanding of stability akin to that of Liska (1957) according to which the international system is continuously undergoing a process of changing from one equilibrium to another and, in doing so, is evolving in ways that reflect underlying shifts in social forces. The latter interpretation, on the other hand, evokes a conceptualisation of stability similar to the more status-quo oriented understanding forwarded by Kaplan (1957) according to which negative feedback operates to restore the original equilibrium of the system after the effects of a disturbance have subsided. To which interpretation of "adjustment" does Waltz subscribe? The answer may be found in his 1967 article; *International Structure, National Force, and the Balance of World Power*, in which he defines stability as "the perpetuation of that structure [defined as "the pattern according to which power is distributed"] without the occurrence of grossly destructive violence" (Waltz, 1967: 229, f.n. 18). This definition accords with the latter meaning of "adjustment" outlined above; namely, the reinstatement of the original equilibrium after disturbance in order to maintain an existing balance or structure. From this one may deduce that Waltz's conceptualisation of stability is closer to Kaplan's status-quo conceptualisation than it is to Liska's evolutionary approach (see also Ostrom & Aldrich, 1978: 747).

Whether the definitions of stability forwarded by those involved in the early theoretical debate on stability envision stability as lying primarily in the preservation of the status-quo or in the facilitation of evolutionary change depends on the particular interpretation of negative feedback contained in the definitions. Kaplan, Rosecrance, and Deutsch & Singer, agree that negative feedback operates in the international system. However, they disagree on its outcomes. Kaplan suggests that negative feedback may or may not return the system to its original state after a disturbance. If it does, the system is ultrastable but underwent temporary equilibrium change. If it does not, but the system finds a new equilibrium point, the system is still ultra-stable but has undergone system change. Rosecrance argues that for a system to be stable, negative feedback must always operate to return the system to its original equilibrium state. Deutsch & Singer base their definition of stability on negative feedback but envision its operation in a multipolar international environment where the likelihood of restoring an original equilibrium state after a disturbance is low. Liska, on the other hand, rejects the operation of negative feedback outright, arguing that it does not operate, at least in its strong Rosecrancian interpretation, in social systems. Finally, although Waltz does not deal directly with the concept of negative feedback, his definition of stability reads as if he believed negative feedback to be operative in the international system.

Stability in the International System

Beyond providing abstract definitions of stability, scholars engaged in the early theoretical debate also applied those definitions to the international system in order to deduce the best possible way of preserving stability there. Again, the results of their efforts differ from one another; often dramatically. Indeed, it was the controversy generated by the competing hypotheses regarding stability in international systems that was ultimately to lead to the transformation of the meaning of stability in IR.

Kaplan is an ardent proponent of the view that international structure strongly determines stability. "An important condition for stability" he argues, "concerns the number of essential national actors" (1957a: 689). He argues strongly in support of the thesis that international stability is best preserved by an international system displaying multipolar characteristics. He bases this argument squarely on his definition of stability. A system is more likely to be stable, he reasons, the better it is able to accommodate disturbances to its equilibrium. Thus, in an international system characterised by two major groupings (bipolarity), "any rapid change in military capabilities tends to make [the] system unstable" (1957a: 692). In an international system of three essential actors, "the probability that two would combine to eliminate the third is relatively great" (1957a: 689). When more than three essential actors compose the system, however, disturbances caused by mistakes and failures of the system members or by changes of or additions to alliances can be accommodated more easily and without serious detriment to the system.

Liska's dynamic understanding of stability is reflected in the way he sees stability displayed in the international system. He approaches the problem of international stability from an institutional perspective, seeing the participation of states in routinised sets of interactions as the criteria by which international stability or instability may be established. His understanding of institutional stability centres on the correspondence that must exist between the influence exercised by individual states within an institution and their actual capabilities relative to other members of the international system:

> A composite organization is in structural equilibrium if there is an overall correspondence between the margins of restraints it imposes on members and their willingness to tolerate them; if the ratios between the influence exercised by individual members and their actual power are not too unequal; and if the respective powers of the different organs correspond to the composition of their membership (Liska, 1957: 13).

Liska assumes that states pursue levels of security, welfare, and prestige that are in excess, whenever possible, of their share as suggested by their relative power position in the international system. However, in an international system characterised by effective systems of international organisation, a state's prestige and influence are determined not primarily by competition under anarchy but by "an authoritative distribution of the coveted values" by international institutions (p. 15). When all states feel that the current distribution of "coveted values" (security, welfare and prestige) corresponds with their relative position in the system, the system is in "an ideal state of equilibrium" (p. 15). Thus, according to Liska, the laws governing the authoritative distribution of prestige within international institutions play a major role in determining the stability of the institution and of the system within which the institution operates. When these laws create a hierarchy of prestige within the institution that corresponds broadly with the hierarchy of capabilities actually in existence in the international system, they provide for an ideal state of equilibrium. However, just as the laws operating in institutions can provide for the stability of the institution, they can also provide for its instability. Liska argues that "when formal law fails to keep in touch with changing social forces, the result is a legal disequilibrium which makes the law dubiously normative and ineffective" (p. 18). The result of this disequilibrium is "lawless evasion" of the institution by states dissatisfied with their position within it.

Rosecrance focuses on four abstract characteristics of the international system and identifies them as the main determinants of stability. First, elite attitudes to international politics determine the "direction" of the system and whether it is oriented to preservation or reform of the status-quo. Second, the strength of the factors that effect the elite's exercise of power determine the "control" in the system; i.e., the extent to which the elite is free to follow its direction. Third, the base upon which control is exercised in the system constitutes the system's "resources." Finally, the ability of the system to contain disruption is its "capacity."

Deutsch & Singer argue that stability (as they have defined it) is best preserved in a system with multiple essential actors. They present "two distinct - but related - lines of formal, semi-quantitative, argument as to why the diffusion-stability relationship should turn out as the theoretician has generally assumed and as the historian has often found to be the case" (p. 390); i.e., why multipolarity should support stability. Their first line of argument focuses on "interaction opportunities" and runs as follows. The greater the number of independent actors in the international system, the higher will be the number of possible pair-wise interactions (dyads). When these interactions display cross-cutting tendencies and tend to undermine deep lines of cleavage, as would be the case in a normally functioning multipolar system, negative feedback will function to provide for stability through flexibility of interaction (pp. 392-396). Their second line of argument centres on the allocation of attention between independent actors in the system. Based on the assumption that a certain, relatively large, percentage of one actor's attention - the critical attention ratio - needs to be focused on another actor before a conflict between them can escalate, they argue that the more actors exist in the system, the less attention any one actor can afford to direct at any one other actor. As a result of the reduction in the average attention ratio below the critical attention ratio, fewer conflicts will escalate (pp. 396-400). In short, their argument is based on the assertion that stability is causally linked to the quantity, diversity and qualities of interaction opportunities.

Waltz's (1964) contrary argument that bipolar international systems best preserve stability hinges on four points. First, in a bipolar world there are no peripheries and, consequently, "a loss to one [superpower] could easily appear as a gain to the other" (p. 882). Second, not only are geographical peripheries non-existent, so are issue area peripheries since "the range of factors included in the competition is extended as the intensity of the competition increases" (p. 883). Third, due to the resulting "constant presence of pressure and the recurrence of crises," (p. 883), limited wars may be avoided. Waltz thus adds the maxim; "[r]ather a large crisis now than a small war later" (p. 884) as a preliminary note to the Machiavellian maxim that "there is no avoiding war, it can only be postponed to the advantage of others" (Machiavelli, 1961: 40). Finally, because of the extent to which "attention is focused on crises by both of the major competitors" (p. 884), the limits of international politics are clearly defined and a strong emphasis is placed on the effective management of crisis situations.[5]

Rosecrance (1963) deals specifically with the contributions of Deutsch & Singer (1964) and Waltz (1964) analysed above. After outlining and critiquing both hypotheses, he offers an alternative "relevant utopia" to that of bipolarity or multipolarity. Drawing on the best elements of each system, he outlines what he considers to be the most stable international structure; bi-multipolarity - a system in which two almost preponderant powers exist in an external multipolar environment. This system is stable, according to Rosecrance, because of the fact that "[t]he two major states would act regulators for conflict in the external areas; but multipolar states would act as mediators and buffers for conflicts between the bipolar powers" (Rosecrance, 1966: 322).

As in the case of defining stability, there is little agreement also on how stability is best preserved in the international system. Liska approaches the problem from an institutional perspective arguing that stability will be best maintained when the "coveted values" authoritatively distributed by institutions remain in line with the ever-changing de facto distribution of capabilities in the system. Rosecrance concentrates on the domestic standing of elites and their attitudes towards the status-quo as well on the resources available in the system and its ability to offset disturbances to its equilibrium. Kaplan, Deutsch & Singer, and Waltz, on the other hand, all agree that system structure is the main determinant of stability; although they disagree fundamentally on which structure makes for most stability. Kaplan and Deutsch & Singer defend the thesis that multipolarity best preserves stability. Waltz argues the opposite; that bipolarity is most stable. The questions raised by these contending hypotheses regarding the requisites for stability in the international system led to the "polarity debate;" the debate regarding the optimal international structure for the preservation of stability.

The Relationship of Stability with Change and Status-quo

A defining characteristic of the early theoretical debate on stability is the way in which stability is related to change and status-quo. Interestingly, it is more common for stability to be equated with some dynamic or evolutionary process of the international system than with its status-quo state.

Clearly, Kaplan's understanding of stability is not dominated by considerations of the preservation of a status-quo equilibrium. True, Kaplan's understanding of stability is underpinned by the concept of negative feedback and equilibrium but this does not lead him to argue that in all cases stability is displayed by a system when it successfully resorts to its original equilibrium state after a disturbance has displaced it from that state. Remember that Kaplan includes under his definition of ultrastability the concept of "system change;" i.e., what happens when a system is displaced from its original equilibrium as a result of a disturbance but does not return to the original equilibrium once the disturbance subsides. In such a case, the original equilibrium is not preserved due to the fact that the system has been irreversibly altered. Furthermore, Kaplan also refers to stability as being analogous with flexibility (1957: 99) and states that in undertaking his analysis he is mainly concerned with "the requirement for stability or equilibrium - *whether to maintain or to restore an old equilibrium or to establish a new equilibrium*" (1957: 247; emphasis added). It is clear from this that

Kaplan's conceptualisation of stability includes, but is not restricted to the requirement that a system maintain its status quo by continually restoring its original equilibrium after each disturbance has subsided. Kaplan includes within his conceptualisation of stability the possibility that a system display evolutionary change by not returning to its original equilibrium state after a disturbance has subsided but rather by remaining at the equilibrium state to which the system was displaced at the time of disturbance. Kaplan's conceptualisation of international stability accepts the possibility, even the necessity, of international change.

      Liska accepts the usefulness of cybernetic analogy in describing international stability but rejects the maximalist version of mechanical stability that requires that the original equilibrium be restored after disturbance is experienced. He interprets social stability in an essentially dynamic way, arguing that a displacement of one equilibrium will lead to the establishment of another. He transposes this interpretation onto the international system, characterised by functioning international organisation, by arguing that the rules governing the authoritative distribution of prestige within institutions create an equilibrium when these rules broadly correspond with the de facto distribution of capabilities existing in the international system. When a disturbance in the system occurs, such as a change in the de facto distribution of capabilities (change in the underlying social forces), a new equilibrium must be established within the institution in question if stability is to be maintained. This dynamic understanding of international stability is based on a recognition of the inevitability of social or international change and on a conviction that stability will best be preserved when actual state power is reflected by institutional influence. For Liska, attempting to preserve an institutional status quo may be detrimental to the preservation of stability if changes have taken place at the level of the international system that make the hierarchy of an institution anachronistic. In short, Liska does not equate stability with the preservation of the status-quo but rather with the flexible management of inevitable change. We have already seen that Kaplan incorporates two mechanisms of stability into his understanding of the concept; one that uses negative feedback to restore the original equilibrium after a disturbance has been experienced and another that allows for the promulgation of the new equilibrium to which the system was displaced after a disturbance. Liska's understanding of stability, on the other hand, incorporates only the latter mechanism.

      It is clear from two separate perspectives, on the other hand, that Rosecrance's understanding of stability is tightly linked to the preservation of the status-quo. The first perspective has its roots in his particular use of cybernetic analogy and the second in the importance he attaches to the satisfaction of major powers in the international system. First, his free use of cybernetic analogy leads him to equate the functioning of a stable international system with that of a pendulum which consistently reinstates the original equilibrium after a disturbance is experienced. His understanding of stability is strongly influenced by the importance he attaches to the re-establishment of the original equilibrium or to "the ability of a regulator to cope with disturbances threatening to undermine an existing power distribution" (Haas, 1970: 99). Second, the weight he apportions to the satisfaction of major powers in the international system also orients his understanding of stability to a preference for the status-quo. The outcome of a disturbance, after it has been acted upon by the regulator and effected by the environment, is deemed to be stable or unstable by reference to the opinions that the major powers hold regarding it. If the major powers approve of the outcome, it is stable; if not, it is unstable. It is reasonable to suspect that the major powers would not approve of any outcome that undermined their position in the system by altering the status-quo. Therefore, by this reckoning also, Rosecrance's conceptualisation of stability is tightly linked to the status-quo.[6]

In contrast, Deutsch & Singer's conceptualisation of stability paints a picture of fluidity and automatic adjustment that is not necessarily linked to the preservation of the status-quo. Their ideal of stable multipolarity is one in which more than five[7] independent actors interact with one another in a variety of cross-cutting ways so that no divisive cleavage is allowed to develop that might polarise the system into two opposing blocs. The operation of such a system implies constant change in alliances patterns as a result of the changing relative power of system members.

While it is not possible to assert that Waltz's understanding of stability is influenced by systems theory and cybernetics to the same degree as is the work of other scholars analysed thus far, it seems reasonable to argue that his understanding of stability places more emphasis on the preservation of the status-quo than on the facilitation of evolutionary change (Ostrom & Aldrich, 1978: 747). His conceptualisation of stability is based on the premise that the system be able to preserve an existing power distribution despite disturbance and without experiencing "grossly destructive violence."

The early theoretical debate did not link the concept of stability exclusively to the preservation of the status-quo. Granted, for Rosecrance and Waltz, the concept of stability was synonymous with the preservation of some status-quo state. Rosecrance believed the preservation of the status-quo was conducive to stability because of the weight he attached to the operation of negative feedback in the international system which always returned the system to its original equilibrium state. Also, like Waltz, he was especially concerned with the importance of preserving the existing distribution of power or, to paraphrase Waltz, the structure by which power is distributed. However, it was just as common for the concept of stability to be articulated in a way that allowed for the occurrence of evolutionary international change or, indeed, in a way that made the occurrence of such change the main prerequisite of stability. The work of Kaplan, and especially that of Liska, is characteristic of this genre of thinking. Both recognise that the status-quo of a social or political system is at best temporary and at worst precarious and that a system that does not have the means for its own evolution built into itself is bound to fail.

The Relationship of Stability with War and Peace

In the early theoretical debate on stability, the strong association between stability and the absence of war - characteristic of contemporary thinking on international stability - does not exist. Although this link is made in some instances, it is much more common for stability to be associated with factors other than the occurrence of war. Indeed, the theoretical debate tends more in the direction of interpreting war as a tool that may, in some instances, be used in preserving international stability.

Under Kaplan's scheme of things, war plays both a positive and a negative role in preserving international stability. Both the resort to war and the abstention from it preserve stability in different situations. For Kaplan, the stability of an international system is determined by the system's adherence to six essential rules the content of which both proscribe and prescribe war:

> (1) increase capabilities but negotiate rather than fight; (2) fight rather than fail to increase capabilities; (3) stop fighting rather than eliminate an essential actor; (4) oppose any coalition or single actor which tends to assume a position of predominance within the system; (5) constrain actors who subscribe to supranational organizational principles; and (6) permit defeated or constrained essential national actors to re-enter the system as acceptable role partners, or act to bring some previously inessential actor within the essential actor classification. Treat all essential actors as acceptable role partners (Kaplan, 1957b: 686).

Under some circumstances Kaplan advises that war be avoided and under other circumstances that it be resorted to in order for stability to be maintained. War is in some cases detrimental to stability; as when a state chooses to wage war rather than to negotiate or to continue waging war at the risk of eliminating an essential actor. However, war may also be used as a tool to preserve stability; as when a state chooses to wage war rather than cease to increase its power, when it opposes by any means necessary a state or coalition that strives for hegemony, and when it applies restraint to states with a preference for supranational organisation. War, for Kaplan, is a tool whose use is in some cases detrimental and in other cases conducive to the preservation of international stability.

For Liska, on the other hand, stability is associated with peaceful change (Liska, 1957: 187). The international system is in equilibrium if the distribution of security, welfare and prestige is such that it could not be significantly improved for individual states by resort to force. However, this is just a snapshot of a stable system that offers only a partial insight into Liska's understanding of stability. Liska recognises that a particular hierarchy of capabilities does not remain intact for long and that such hierarchies are continually being eroded and re-shaped as a result of the differential growth of states. The main cause of instability, according to Liska, is the failure of institutional hierarchies to keep pace with de facto hierarchies. Instability occurs when states recognise that the security, welfare and prestige that is authoritatively distributed to them by institutions is below the level they may expect by reference to their share of the international distribution of power. When states translate their dissatisfaction with their institutional position into the realisation that their position may be improved by resort to violence, the system is unstable. Central to Liska's understanding of stability is the ability of institutions to keep their hierarchies in line with those existing in the international system. If institutions are able to fulfil this task, states will remain more or less satisfied and the system will remain stable. If they are not up to the task, some states will attempt to increase their allocation of security, welfare and prestige by resorting to war. Thus, Liska's conceptualisation of stability involves one key mechanism - institutional flexibility. Its main outcome is peaceful change.

From his description of how stability is portrayed by the international system, Rosecrance takes the step of linking instability to war following the logic that "[c]atastrophic conflict or international chaos are almost certain to be deleterious to some major actor; hence these outcomes are almost always unstable or unacceptable" (Rosecrance, 1963: 231). By this reasoning, however, to the extent that wars are not "deleterious to some major actor," they are compatible with international stability. It is not difficult to imagine situations in which wars and their outcomes could be beneficial to major actors in the international system;

for example when wars are waged in defence of a status-quo with which the major powers are satisfied. Thus, Rosecrance's understanding of stability does allow for the occurrence of some war in the international system, provided it is not detrimental to some major power. Although he utilises the occurrence of interstate war as an indicator of stability, for Rosecrance war is not a *sufficient condition* of instability. Rather, it is an indicator of instability *only* when by nature of its extent or its type it causes dissatisfaction among the major powers.

Consistent with Deutsch & Singer's weaker definition of the term, stability in the international system is compatible with a level of war below that of "large-scale" war. Their stronger definition of stability proscribes even limited war but Deutsch & Singer do not forward the stronger definition as their main definition. Taking the other elements of their definition into account - the retention of the system's essential characteristics and the deterrence of hegemony - shows why some level of war may be necessary in order to preserve stability as Deutsch & Singer understand it. Their definition demands that only *most* of the system members continue to survive. Since it is unlikely that even the most insignificant system members would cease to exist without some level of violence, this aspect of Deutsch & Singer's definition allows for the occurrence of some level of war in the international system. Furthermore, in order to ensure that one state does not become dominant in the system, it may be necessary to oppose, by violent means, a state set on achieving hegemony.

This brings us to the consideration of the role of war in Waltz's (1964, 1967) understanding of stability. Presumably, stability as Waltz defines it would still exist if adjustment caused the system to experience levels of violence not substantial enough to merit the description "grossly destructive." Although Waltz's definition suggests that the less violence a system experiences the more stable it is likely to be, it does not preclude the occurrence of some level of destructive violence if that is the price the system has to pay for preserving the structure by which power is distributed, thereby demonstrating the system's stability. Indeed, Waltz admits that his early understanding of stability bundled together too many outcomes under the heading of stability and suggests that "peacefulness" was one of those largely superfluous outcomes (Waltz, 1979: 161).

In his second contribution to the debate, Rosecrance (1966) posits a markedly different relationship between stability and war than he did in his 1963 attempt. Instead of continuing to allow for some occurrence of war as he originally did, he equates his later conceptualisation of stability directly with peace or with a low level of conflict in the international system. His alternative model of stability is intended to provide "general solutions to basic conflicts in the contemporary international system" (p. 314) and to limit violence "to far smaller proportions than does either bipolarity or multipolarity" (p. 324). In his grand scheme of things, "peace," or a reasonable approximation thereto, "is the objective" (p. 324).

The association between international stability and peace is not strong in the early theoretical debate on stability. Although Liska and Rosecrace's later contribution both link stability to the absence of war, they are alone in doing so. For Kaplan, war is sometimes to be avoided and sometimes to be resorted to in order to preserve stability. The early Rosecrancian view sees war as detrimental to stability only when it is detrimental to the major powers in the international system. Finally, Waltz considers peace to be a largely superfluous outcome in a stable international system.

The Early Theoretical Understanding of Stability

This section has plotted the trajectory of the concept of stability through the early theoretical debate on stability in IR. It traced its incorporation from the source fields of systems theory and cybernetics and demonstrated the strong influence that these disciplines exerted on early theorising about stability. It showed that, despite its common roots in these source fields, contending hypotheses emerged regarding the correct definition of international stability and the optimal international structure required to preserve it. Furthermore, it demonstrated that, in the early theoretical debate, no strong link existed between the concept of stability on the one hand and the concepts of status-quo and peace on the other.

On the contrary, a variety of interpretations surrounded the concept of stability, most of which tended to associate it with a process of evolutionary change in which the occurrence of war was regarded as either insignificant or analogous to a tool to be selectively used in the preservation of stability. Therefore, the fact that in the latter half of the 1960s Zinnes could report that there were two definitions of international stability present in the IR literature - one associated with peace and the other with the status-quo (Zinnes, 1967: 271) - raises an important question: Why did stability become strongly associated with peace and status-quo when, first of all, so many other possible associations existed and, second of all, the associations that did exist with peace and status-quo were in competition with other, quite opposite, associations?

The Association of Stability with Peace

The association of stability with peace has gone largely unquestioned by IR scholars. Referring to the modifications that the scientific meaning of stability has undergone since its incorporation into IR, Robert Axelrod points out that:

> In strategic usage stability usually refers to the maintenance of peace, rather than any other possible state of the system. Thus, in political usage the concept takes on a positive connotation: stability is assumed to be a good thing. This connotation is so strong that often the meaning of the term gets lost and the word is simply used to indicate approval of a policy by saying that it promotes stability (Axelrod, 1990).[8]

Focusing on the metaphorical character of the concept of stability in the study of international relations, Mesjasz asserts that the concept of stability in international relations was *killed* - i.e., transformed from a *dormant*- into a *dead* metaphor (1993: 25)[9] - precisely because of the fact that it was equated with peace in the international system. He points out that the concept of stability incorporated into IR from its hard scientific source fields has lost most of its original connotations due to the fact that "[m]ost authors followed rather more Richardsonian views and narrowed the meaning of stability to the absence of war" with the result that the notion of stability became a kind of "homologue of perpetual peace" (Mesjasz, 1993: 25).

However, although the association of stability with peace has come under some scrutiny, it has not been sufficiently questioned or analysed to wrest it from the realm of accepted truth. Nor has the process by which stability came to be associated with peace been elucidated in a satisfactory manner. Axelrod goes no further than to point out that "[t]he concept of stability has carried over into political and strategic usage with two important modifications" (Axelrod, 1990: 248). Mesjasz does offer a tentative explanation for the association, suggesting that:

> Perhaps the word "peace" was too emotionally loaded, or perhaps it was the concept of "positive peace" that motivated scientists to use another, more "precise" and "neutral" term. Maybe the abuses of the word "peace" in the Soviet anti-Western propaganda was also one of the reason[s] for search[ing] for another term depicting the absence of war (Mesjasz, 1993: 25).

This section aims to fill this gap in understanding by outlining the process by which the concept of stability came to be associated with that of peace.

By doing so, it hopes to stimulate a critical re-appraisal of the association.

In the study of international relations, the concept of stability became associated with peace as a result of the coalition between the early theoretical debate on stability, outlined above, and the quantitative-empirical research project on the occurrence of war, outlined below. The coalition took place largely as a result of the interest shown by the quantitative project on war in the questions raised by the theoretical debate on stability. As a result, the concept of stability in IR moved decidedly towards an association with peace. I will briefly outline the origin and content of the quantitative project before offering an account of how the debates coalesced and the meaning of stability was transformed.

The Quantitative Project on the Occurrence of War

War and peace have long been the main focus of interest for students of international relations. However, it was not until the middle of the twentieth century that a systematic quantitative-empirical approach to studying war emerged to take its place alongside the traditional intuitive-theoretical approach that had dominated IR since Thucydides. The emergence of this quantitative approach to studying war ultimately led to IR's second "great debate," in which advocates of traditional realism vied with "scientific man" for the accolade of becoming IR's dominant paradigm (Morgenthau, 1946).

Systematic quantitative-empirical interest in war was sparked by Quincy Wright's *The Study of War* (Wright, 1942). Before that time, the study of war had been largely the realm of intuitive speculation based on insights drawn from various theoretical standpoints and from an intimate knowledge of diplomacy and the interests of states. Says Singer of Wright:

> If Georges Clemenceau is noted for pointing out that the *conduct* of war is too important to be left to the militarists, it is Quincy Wright who reminds us that the *analysis* of war is too important to be left to the intuitionists. After years and volumes of literary speculation on the causes of international war, it was he who undertook the first systematic search for those empirical regularities which might shed some light on the origins of war among nations (Singer, 1970).

Other important contributions to this empirical research project on war offered formal analyses of arms races between states and detailed data on the occurrence of war (Richardson, 1960, 1960a); of the relationship between alliance aggregation and war (Singer & Small, 1968); and of the relationship between the occurrence of war and polarity in international sub-systems (Haas, 1970).

It is imperative to understand from the outset that this research project aimed to apply quantitative-empirical research tools to the task of understanding the regularities that underlie the occurrence of war in the international system. The project's dependent variable is clearly war and not stability as such; except when stability is defined as the absence of war in the international system. The use of the term stability does permeate the empirical debate precisely because stability *is* defined as the absence of war. Richardson (1960), for example, links his mechanistic understanding of stability[10] directly with war, arguing that if an arms-race does not escalate and war is avoided, stability is served.[11] Singer & Small (1968) seek to correlate alliance aggregation with the onset of war and thus to comment on the relative stability of various alliance formations. Finally, Haas (1970) uses the occurrence of war as an indicator of the effect of polarity on stability in international sub-systems.

The definition of stability employed by this debate is formulated by exclusive reference to war. Simply put, the occurrence of war in the international system denotes instability; the absence of war suggests that the system is stable. However, this project does not explore the concept of stability as such. Rather, it takes its meaning as given. What those who engage in it set out to measure is the occurrence of war in the international system. The terms 'stable' and 'unstable' simply provide convenient short-hand ways of referring to the absence or presence of war in the international system, nothing more.

A Coalition of Debates

By now the essential differences between the empirical project on the occurrence of war and the theoretical debate on the meaning of stability should be clear. The empirical project posited war as its dependent variable and utilised the term stability only as a convenient way of referring to the absence of war. The theoretical debate, on the other hand, delved deeply into the meaning of international stability and provided definitions of stability that ranged from associations with peace and status-quo on the one hand (Zinnes, 1967) to associations with change and war on the other. In the empirical project, stability was utilised as a descriptive term that was convenient for labelling a particular state of non-war. In the theoretical debate, stability was investigated as a complex concept with nuanced meanings that were in most cases not necessarily tied up with the preservation of the status-quo or, for that matter, with the absence of war.

Beginning in the 1970s, however, the empirical research project on war began to take an interest in the questions being raised by the theoretical debate on stability. From that point onward, the clear gap between the two approaches to international stability began to narrow and blur. The result was a fundamental change in the way in which the theoretical concept of stability came to be understood.

The first move towards the coalition of the empirical and theoretical debates was made by Michael Haas in 1970 with his work *International Subsystems; Stability and Polarity*; a quantitative work in the tradition of Wright that addresses itself directly to the theoretical questions raised by the likes of Waltz and Deutsch & Singer in the theoretical debate. It is the first work that spans the divide between the empirical and theoretical approaches to understanding international stability. Haas points to the "intriguing hypotheses so eloquently raised by Kaplan, Waltz, Deutsch, Singer and Rosecrance" and points out that they "have remained largely unexamined" (Haas, 1970: 98). His aim is to apply quantitative methodology in answering what had become the central question in the theoretical debate; which is more "stable," a bipolar or a multipolar international system? In pursuing this aim, however, he overlooks the complex and sometimes counter-intuitive way in which stability had come to be understood in the theoretical debate. He makes the error of mapping onto the theoretical debate on stability the meaning of stability that had long existed in the empirical tradition; i.e., that "[i]nstability... is empirically defined as the number of wars of various types" (Haas, 1970: 100).[12] In doing so, Haas blurs the distinction between the two debates on stability and lays the foundations for similar future work.

Following in Haas' footsteps came a stream of quantitative studies on the relationship between polarity and stability in the international system. Some of these analyses were primarily concerned with operationalising the independent variable; polarity (De Mesquita, 1975); others were interested in analysing the relationship between polarity and stability by measuring polarity in terms of alliance polarisation (Wallace, 1973) or in terms of systemic polarisation (De Mesquita, 1978). The *Correlates of War* (COW) project led by J. David Singer grew out of respect for the quantitative tradition that Quincy Wright had initiated and the desire to apply that tradition to solving the puzzle of the relationship between polarity and stability (Singer, 1979, 1980; Singer et al., 1979) and numerous other studies found inspiration in a similar problematique (De Mesquita, 1981; Sabrosky, 1985; Thompson, 1986; Vasquez, 1987; De Mesquita & Lalman, 1988; Mansfield, 1988; Scarborough, 1988; Zinnes & Muncaster, 1988). All of these quantitative studies have two elements in common, however. They all set out to use quantitative methods in analysing the relationship between polarity and stability and they all define stability as the absence of war in the international system.

The theoretical understanding of stability was greatly effected by the fusion of the empirical and theoretical approaches. The operationalisation of stability as the absence of war in the international system filtered through to the theoretical discussion of stability with the result that the notion of stability *in abstracto* became strongly associated with peace. In their review of the controversy surrounding the polarity debate, Ostrom and Aldrich (1978) side with Zinnes (1967) in agreeing that two notions of stability existed in the literature; one associated with peace and the other with the status-quo. However, even after reviewing the various abstract definitions of stability in the literature and especially those provided by Waltz (1964) and Deutsch & Singer (1964), they chose "to focus on a definition which equates stability with a low probability of war in the international system" (Ostrom & Aldrich, 1978), despite the fact that the definitions they reviewed included, as has been shown above, some that incorporate war as a necessary mechanism of stable systems.

A similar approach to the theoretical understanding of stability to that of Ostrom & Aldrich pervades the literature from the 1970s onward. To a large extent, the abstract and sometimes highly complex conceptualisations of stability from the theoretical debate's formative period gave way under pressure from the new empirical research project to conceptualisations of stability that linked it to peace in the international system. To cite some important examples, Zinnes focuses on stability as a manifestation of peace when she addresses the question: "Is Polarization a Precondition for War?" (Zinnes, 1980: 331; Zinnes & Muncaster, 1988). Others point to the relative peacefulness of the Cold War system as the main evidence of that system's stability (Gaddis, 1986; Finkelstein, 1989; Saperstein, 1991). Likewise, important formal work on the stability of international systems has taken for granted that stability may be conceptualised as the peacefulness of the system (Niou, Ordeschook & Rose, 1989; Niou & Ordeschook, 1990). Finally, the majority of even the most recent theoretical contributions to the debate on the relationship between stability and polarity retain the conviction that stability may be usefully measured by reference to various war indicators (Hopf, 1991, 1993; Midlarski, 1993).

The Association of Stability with Status-quo

The association of stability with status-quo is perhaps even more ingrained in the minds of students of international relations than is the association of stability with peace. This is evidenced by the widespread use by political scientists and politicians alike of "stability" as the antithesis of "change."[13] Here again, however, the validity of this association has not gone completely unchallenged. Axelrod (1990: 248) points out that "the scientific usage [of stability] does not imply a lack of change, but only the ability to restore the system after a perturbation" and that "[i]n political usage this distinction is often blurred." This section forwards a number of hypotheses as to why the concept of stability came to be associated with status-quo in IR.

Two main hypotheses may be forwarded to explain why the concept of stability became associated with the preservation of the international status-quo. The first posits that the association came about as a result of the combination of two factors; first, the association of stability with peace, outlined above, and second, the stark realities of the Cold War international system. Despite the various definitions of stability offered by the early theoretical debate, many scholars used the bipolar system as their main reference-point in defining stability. For them, the bipolar structure was best suited to preserving peace in a world dominated by two superpowers. For this reason, stability would be best served by preserving the bi-polar structure, thereby ensuring the continuation of peace. In this way, the association of stability with peace led, under conditions of bipolarity, to the association of stability with the preservation of the status-quo.

The second hypothesis, which is complementary to the first, has its roots in the sociology of knowledge. It posits that the concept of stability in IR became associated with the preservation of the status-quo also because IR is "an American social science" (Hoffman, 1977) and that the preservation of the bipolar order was in the interest of the United States during the Cold War. It is not beyond the realms of possibility that the world-views of these scholars might have been influenced by the fact that bipolarity from a U.S. perspective was a largely satisfactory state of affairs and that this led them to view international stability in terms of the preservation of the bipolar status-quo.

It is most likely that some combination of the latter and former hypotheses explains why stability came to be associated with status-quo in IR. If these hypotheses hold any kernel of truth, it would be reasonable to expect that thinking on international stability would undergo some kind of revision after the end of the Cold War. And, indeed, it has. Beginning in

1989, there has been renewed interest in the relationship between stability and polarity and, significantly, a palpable move towards re-appraising the meaning of stability.

Revival of the Polarity Debate and Re-appraisal of Stability

As already mentioned, the debate surrounding the relationship between polarity and stability lost much of its momentum in the 1980s due, understandably, to the fact that, despite voluminous amounts of theoretical and empirical scholarship, no progress had been made towards finding an answer to the puzzle.[14] However, the fall of the Berlin wall in 1989 and the decomposition of the Soviet Union in 1991 caused a revival of interest in the relationship between polarity and stability. Just as the structural upheaval caused by the genesis of the Cold War had sparked the first serious interest in the topic, the comparable upheaval caused by its demise rekindled that interest. Furthermore, contained within this revival of interest in the relationship between polarity and stability is a strong push toward re-appraising the meaning of stability itself.

The demise of the bipolar system predicated by the dissolution of the Soviet Union lead scholars of international relations to re-examine the supposed relationship between structure and stability. For those satisfied both with the conventional equation of stability with peace and with the thesis that bipolarity best preserves stability, the end of bipolarity was the source of much concern and even nostalgia (Mearsheimer, 1990a, 1990b; Saperstein, 1991). For those of a more optimistic bent who, despite conceptually linking stability with the absence of war, claimed to recognise sources of stability in factors other than the bipolar structure, on the other hand, the transition from bipolarity to multipolarity was not considered a significant threat to international peace (Van Evera, 1991). Following this line of argument, Kegley and Raymond (1992) pose the rhetorical question; *Must we Fear a Post-Cold-War Multipolar System?* They challenge the conventional wisdom that the Cold War system was stable; referring to the division of the globe into antagonistic blocs, the fact that the system was chronically crisis-ridden, that the bipolar structure "diminished the superpowers' perceived security and exacerbated their perception of threats." They conclude that the "cold war "stability" was fragile and constantly on the brink of collapse," and that "[i]t is surely mistaken to equate bipolarity with stability" since "the phrase "bipolar stability" [is] an oxymoron (Kegley & Raymond, 1992: 576-7).

For others, however, the re-appraisal of the relationship between polarity and stability brought on by the end of the Cold War involves deeper considerations that challenge not only the conventional assumption of bipolar stability but also the meaning of stability itself. One of the earliest attempts to revise the theoretical meaning of international stability comes from Patrick James & Michael Brecher (1988) who are dissatisfied with the intractable nature of the polarity debate and set out to reformulate it in such a way as to make its resolution possible. This involves a re-statement not only of the debate's independent variable - polarity - but also of its dependent variable - stability. In offering a reformulation of the dependent variable, they are the first to suggest that the empirical measurement of stability as the absence of war may be invalid. They assert that "[a]lthough war is the gravest type of disturbance to system tranquillity, it is not synonymous with instability" (James & Brecher, 1988: 38). They also point out that the contending results of various empirical studies purporting to measure the stability of different historical periods should lead one to consider that "the measurement of instability is invalid" (f.n. 13).

However, their re-formulation of stability does not go far in achieving their aim of reformulating the debate. Rather than abandoning the equation of instability with war, they simply widen the measurement of conflictual inter-state relations to include not only war but also inter-state crises. Rather than focusing on determining factors of stability outside of the conventional conceptual framework, they simply widen the range of measurement of stability within the already existing conceptual framework. This does not move the debate on stability along new innovative paths. Rather, it entrenches it more deeply in its conventional place.

Furthermore, James & Brecher's treatment of stability is highly problematic. In their re-appraisal of the polarity debate, James & Brecher (1988) equate instability with "cost" in terms of "frequency and intensity of disruptive interaction" (p. 35). In this way, the degree to which the system is costly to its members reflects international instability insofar as it reflects "a lack of agreement over the allocation of existing political, economic and military resources" (p. 35). This operationalisation of international instability is problematic, however, since it does not measure stability but only a manifestation of it that does not occur in all cases when instability is present. The fact that they find that instability in a bipolar world is less costly than instability in a multipolar world does not substantiate their conclusion that bipolarity is more stable than multipolarity. Rather, it simply shows that the occurrence of a particular amount of instability in a bipolar system is less costly than the occurrence of the same amount of instability in a multipolar system. While this may be a useful finding in itself, it tells us nothing about the likelihood of instability arising in either type of system in the first place.

Nevertheless, James & Brecher's contribution is significant for at least two reasons: First, it at least questions the conventional empirical conceptualisation of stability and the theoretical understanding that follows naturally from it and, second, it clearly demonstrates fundamental confusions surrounding the relationship between stability and war. They offer conflicting accounts of the relationship between instability and war. They move from a consideration of war as a *reflection* (p. 35) and *litmus test* (p. 38) of international instability to a consideration of war as the *source* of international instability (p. 38). The relationship between war and instability must be either one or the other; it cannot be both. This inconsistency raises the fundamental question of how war is to be understood in the context of stability/instability in the international system; i.e., is war is to be understood as constituting instability or as reflecting it? If war constitutes instability, then obviously the best way to combat instability would be to attempt to eradicate war directly. If, on the other hand, war simply reflects instability, then we cannot combat it until we first seek out the source of instability that war is reflecting and find a way of dealing with it. Thus, James and Brecher's contribution is more significant for the questions it begs than for the analysis it offers. Nevertheless, it is the first major attempt, followed shortly by a similar one (Brecher & Wilkenfeld, 1989), to at least test the foundation supporting the conventional understanding of stability.

In examining *The Concept of Stability in the Context of Conventional War in Europe*, Robert Axelrod takes the important step of reviewing the meaning of stability and tracing the path it followed in finding its way into international relations studies. He points out that "the concept of stability has carried over into political and strategic usage with... important modifications" (Axelrod, 1990: 248). His is the first serious attempt to initiate a reformulation of the concept of stability by reference to the strong normative influences on its meaning. He concludes that conventional analysis of stability and balance of power have lead researchers to attend to the wrong variables and to ask the wrong questions.

Also around this time, a strong deconstructivist critique of the conventional conceptualisation of stability began to form. One strand of this critique argued that the concept of international stability was "ideologically loaded... representing the views of those who pretend to preserve a status quo" (Mesjasz, 1990: 6; 1992, 1993). After the Cold War, it became obvious that it had been wrong all along to equate stability with tight security structures and unchanging frameworks of action and that it was necessary to rethink the meaning of international stability in such a way as to relate it to political evolution (Rossbach, 1992). A second strand focused on the discursive aspects of the polarity debate and on the way in which various pairs of concepts - such as bipolarity / multipolarity; certainty / uncertainty; cautious / non-cautious foreign policy; stability / instability - were manipulated in the polarity debate in order to support contradictory arguments (Huysmans, 1992). Finally, as if to demonstrate the speed and intensity with which scholars of international relations were critically reviewing their ideas on the Cold War, one scholar went as far as to pose the question; *What was Bipolarity?* (Wagner, 1993).

Also, one of the key players in the early theoretical debate on stability, Kenneth Waltz, has begun to rethink the meaning of international stability in light of the end of the Cold War. On the association between stability and peace in particular he asserts that:

> The conflation of peace and stability is all too common. The occurrence of major wars is often identified with a system's instability. Yet systems that survive major wars thereby demonstrate their stability. The multipolar world was highly stable, but all too war-prone. The bipolar world has been highly peaceful, but unfortunately less stable than its predecessor (Waltz, 1993: 45).

From the end of the Cold War until the present day, interest in the relationship between structure and stability has increased markedly. Some of this interest has confined itself to already established frameworks of analysis and to the conventional understanding of stability that emerged as a result of the coalition of the early theoretical and empirical debates on stability. An increasing amount of attention, however, is being currently focused on re-appraising the meaning of international stability itself. The end of the Cold War seems to have acted as a catalyst for this phenomenon, suggesting that the Cold War played an important role in establishing the conventional meaning of stability in IR.

Conclusion

When the concept of stability was incorporated into the study of international relations, it had a relatively low level of normative content. True, stability was considered a good thing, worthy of pursuit and preservation once obtained, but the good inherent in stability was not immediately associated with the welfare of any one state or the preservation of any particular type of international structure. Initially, students of international relations indulged in *scientism* (Hayek, 1952), slavishly imitating the methods and language of systems theory and cybernetics in order to establish a meaning of stability applicable to the study of international relations. The conceptualisations of stability that emerged from the early theoretical debate tended to associate stability with change and evolution rather than with the preservation of some status-quo state of the international system. Furthermore, as well as being associated with the preservation of peace, stability was also made compatible with the presence of some amount of war in the international system.

The concept of stability in IR, therefore, was not associated from the outset with the preservation of peace and of the status-quo. Rather, it became so as a result of a process of meaning transformation that took two forms. First, the concept of stability became associated with peace as a result of the coalition of two distinct research projects - the quantitative project on the occurrence of inter-state war and the theoretical project on the meaning of international stability. When applying its quantitative methods to solving the questions raised by the latter, the former failed to take account of the complex ways in which the meaning of stability was being analysed and instead operationalised international stability by reference to war indicators. This had the effect of narrowing the meaning of stability to the absence of war also in the theoretical debate.

Second, international stability came to be associated with the preservation of the status-quo international structure as a result of the constraints inherent in the Cold War system. From an interest in the preservation of peace flowed an interest in preserving the Cold War bipolar structure, since any change in that structure, it was believed, would lead to international unrest and war. A further factor in this equation was the preponderant role of U.S. scholars in formulating the meaning of stability. It is not implausible that these scholars were influenced in their formulation by the relatively favourable position that the United States held in the bipolar world order.

This chapter's argument is borne out by the strong interest that has emerged after the Cold War in rethinking the meaning of international stability. The conventional meaning of stability simply does not compute in the post-Cold War international system. It is becoming clear to more and more scholars that the association of stability with peace and status-quo is artificial and non-viable. It is misleading, therefore, to associate international stability exclusively either with peace or with the preservation of some status-quo state and it is certainly erroneous to equate it with a combination of the two. It is as misleading to do so now as it was during the Cold War. A more useful meaning of stability may only be developed by first de-coupling the concept of stability from the interests of certain states in the preservation of a certain order of things. It is the purpose of the next chapter to attempt such a decoupling and, in doing so, to develop a more useful understanding of international stability.

Notes

1. See also Collier & Levitski (1994) for a detailed analysis of the many forms of the concept of democracy and Collier & Mahon (1993) for a discussion of conceptual "stretching."
2. Significantly, Ashby is also the author of the influential work *An Introduction to Cybernetics* (Ashby, 1956) which builds on the ideas of his 1952 work and which also played an important role in the development of the concept of stability in International Relations.
3. Feedback is negative when it operates in the opposite direction to the input; thus maintaining the system's original equilibrium in much the same way as does a aeroplane's automatic pilot. Feedback is positive when it operates in the same direction as the input thereby distancing the system from its original equilibrium in ever increasing spirals as is the case when the printing of money is chosen as a strategy to combat inflation (Kaplan, 1957).
4. With regard to the concept of "ultrastability," Kaplan once more acknowledges his debt to W. Ross Ashby's *Design for a Brain* (1952). On ultrastability, see also Ashby (1956).
5. Note that this emphasis on the extent to which the superpowers apportion attention to one another in a bipolar situation runs directly contrary to the argument of Deutsch & Singer (1964) who stress that the lower the attention apportioned to any one dyadic relationship, the lower will be the likelihood that conflict in that relationship will escalate.
6. This argumentation contradicts that of Zinnes who argues that, in Rosecrance's scheme of things, "a stable system could have the same propensity for change as an unstable one" (Zinnes, 1964:304). However, in making this argument Zinnes overlooks the role of cybernetic analogy in Rosecrance's analysis and the weight he attaches to the satisfaction of major powers.
7. "Until N reaches five, there is an insufficient number of possible dyads, ... beyond that level the stability-enhancing increment begins to grow very sharply" (Deutsch & Singer, 1964:395).
8. Ironically, Axelrod's interpretation of the political/strategic meaning of stability is similar to that contained in the *Doublespeak Dictionary for the 1990s* in which the meaning of stability is given, only half jokingly, as "political and economic conditions that satisfy our interests" (Herman, 1993).
9. "Live" metaphors, according to Mesjasz, are "substitutes for literal utterances... [that] particularly lend themselves to further conceptual development" (1993:6). "Dead" metaphors, on the other hand, "have become so familiar and so habitual that we are not aware of their metaphorical nature and use them as literal terms. [...] ...their meanings usually are shifted either by association with live metaphors or by interpretations in different contexts" (1993:7).

10   "The words stable and unstable are used, in a defined sense, as adjectives qualifying equilibrium, in accordance with the usage long established in the science of mechanics" (Richardson, 1960:22).

11   For an interesting challenge of Richardson's analysis, see Intrilligator & Brito (1986) who argue that arms-race stability and stability against the outbreak of war are analytically different. They assert that the escalation of an arms race between states acts as a deterrent to the outbreak of war. In this way, arms-race instability is conducive to stability against the outbreak of war.

12   Interestingly, however, Haas also defines stability on a more abstract level as being equivalent to behavioural *change* over time (Haas, 1967, 1970). See Mesjasz (1993), however, for a criticism of attempts to define stability as being equivalent to change.

13   Works that counterpose the concepts of stability and change are countless. Consider the following examples: *Change and Stability in Foreign Policy* (Goldmann, 1988); *Regarding Politics: Essays on Political Theory, Stability and Change* (Eckstein, 1992); *Stability and Change in Africa* (Nyerere, 1974); *Stability and Change in American Politics* (Delli Carpini, 1986); *Stability and Change in Australian Politics* (Aitkin, 1977).

14   Ostrom & Aldrich succinctly describe the far from consensual state of the polarity debate at the end of the 1970s. In the theoretical literature they find support for the following hypotheses; that "the greater the size of the system, the more stable it will be...; the smaller the size of the system, the more stable it will be...; and that stability is not related to the number of actors..." In the empirical literature they encounter equal disarray; they "find support for propositions which suggest that size and stability are related positively.., negatively.., curvilinearly.., and not at all" (Ostrom & Aldrich, 1978:743). By the mid 1980s this situation had, if anything, worsened.

3 Stability as Process

> To establish methods of peaceful change is ... the fundamental problem of international morality and of international politics (Carr, 1964 [1946]).

Introduction

Contemporary theories of international relations are not very helpful in suggesting ways of solving what Robert Gilpin has described as the fundamental problem facing the discipline; "the problem of peaceful adjustment to the consequences of the uneven growth of power among states" (1981: 230). As a result, "the question remains for us to grapple with: under what conditions will adaptations to shifts in power, in available technologies, or in fundamental economic relationships take place without severe economic disruption or warfare?" (Keohane, 1989: 65). John Burton is sceptical about the ability of the discipline to deal effectively with this question. He argues that:

> The outstanding feature of reality is the dynamic nature of International Relations. No general theory is appropriate which cannot take into consideration the rapidly changing technological, social and political environment in which nations are required to live in peace one with the other. But the only device of fundamental change which is possible in the context of power politics is that of war, for which reason war is recognized as a legitimate instrument of national policy. It is not surprising that International Relations has tended to be discussed in static terms, and that stability has tended to be interpreted in terms of the maintenance of the *status quo*. A dynamic approach to International Relations would immediately confront the analyst with no alternative but to acknowledge war as the only available mechanism for change (Burton, 1965: 71-72).

This chapter addresses the fundamental problem of peaceful change in an inherently dynamic international system and seeks to show that, while Burton is correct in his general appraisal of the discipline of IR, he is incorrect in arguing that a dynamic approach to the study of international relations has no alternative but to accept war as the only mechanism of change in the international system. It argues that there is another mechanism - the incremental adjustment of "hierarchies of influence" as a result of the differential growth of states - that constitutes an alternative to war as an agent of change in the international system. This mechanism constitutes the core of this chapter's definition of international stability.

Morton Kaplan has correctly pointed out that "the concept of stability has meaning only in relation to the questions the investigator puts to his data" and that, therefore, "[t]here is no such thing as stability in and of itself" (Kaplan, 1967: 151, 153). This chapter specifies a set of questions by which the stability of international systems may be recognised. Its purpose is to articulate a testable and, therefore, falsifiable theory of stability that centres on the incremental adjustment of hierarchies of influence. The aim is to develop a theory that is more useful than conventional understandings of stability insofar as (1) It is generally applicable to the study of international relations regardless of the "type" of system being analysed (bi-polar, multi-polar, balance of power, hegemonic, etc.), (2) it takes for granted the perennial presence of change - in the form of the differential growth in power of states - in the international system, and, most important, (3) it allows for the elaboration of means by which human ingenuity and creativity may be employed in the improvement of international stability.

In doing so, this chapter will rely a great deal on the ideas set forth by Robert Gilpin in his seminal work *War and Change in World Politics* (1981) in which he develops a theory of international political change based on cycles of war, organisation, and differential growth. In formulating a theory of international stability, however, this chapter refines many aspects of Gilpin's analysis, rejects others and greatly expands on others. The result is a theory that owes a great debt to Gilpin's work but that independently provides an original and useful means of thinking about international stability.

Gilpin on International Stability

Robert Gilpin's (1981) theory of international political change provides an ideal starting-point for articulating a dynamic theory of international stability. Change in the international system - mainly in the form of the differential growth in power among states[1] - stands prominently at the centre of Gilpin's theory For present purposes, his most significant contribution lies in the specification of a cycle of international political change and its division into the following distinct stages of development:

Gilpin's Cycle of International Political Change

First, following system-wide war, "the dominant powers... organize and control the processes of interactions among the elements of the system" (1981: 29). In other words, the most powerful states to emerge from major conflict impose their wills on the governance of the post-war international system by advancing "particular sets of political, economic, of other types of interests" (1981: 9). Since these powerful states occupy the upper echelons of what Gilpin terms "the international hierarchy of power and prestige" (1981: 29), their governance is accepted as legitimate by less powerful states.

Second, the differential growth of states causes power to be redistributed in the international system. As a result, a disjuncture emerges between the hierarchy of prestige through which the post-war system was ordered and the new distribution of power in the international system:

> On the one hand, the hierarchy of prestige, the division of territory, the international division of labor, and the rules of the system remain basically unchanged; they continue to reflect primarily the interests of the existing dominant powers and the relative power distribution that prevailed at the time of the last systemic change. On the other hand, the international distribution of power has undergone a radical transformation that has weakened the foundations of the existing system (Gilpin, 1981: 14).

Third, this weakening of the foundations of the international system precipitates a "crisis" therein. Those states that benefit from the re-distribution of power caused by differential growth come to perceive an advantage in changing the international system to suit their interests:

> [When] economic, political, and technological developments have increased considerably the potential benefit or decreased the potential costs to one or more states of seeking to change the international system [...,] [f]orestalling one's losses or increasing one's gains becomes an incentive for one or more states to attempt to change the system (Gilpin, 1981: 14).

Finally, the crisis is resolved through another system-wide war. A new period of reorganisation occurs whereby a new set of major powers establishes a new hierarchy of prestige and seeks once more to impose its will on the governance of the post-war international system. And the cycle begins once more from the beginning.

Some Short-comings of Gilpin's Approach

Because of its focus on states' reactions to changes in the international distribution of power, Gilpin's theory of international political change provides a useful starting-point for developing a dynamic theory of international stability. It has three main short-comings, however, that need to be highlighted before advancing. First, Gilpin prefers a static over a dynamic understanding of international stability. Second, his theory of international political change asserts that war is the main mechanism of change without devoting sufficient attention to the analysis of the conditions under which alternative mechanisms of change may operate. Finally, his theory has weak policy relevance since it does not provide any insights into how the stability of the international system might be improved.

The Dominance of a Static over a Dynamic Understanding of Stability

Gilpin offers two definitions of international stability, the first of which describes the static configuration by which the existence of stability may be recognised and the second of which describes the dynamic process by which this configuration may be maintained.

Stability as a Static Configuration Gilpin identifies the necessary conditions for international stability as follows:

> An international system is in a state of equilibrium [is stable] if the more powerful states in the system are satisfied with the existing territorial, political, and economic arrangements (Gilpin, 1981: 11).[2]

In other words, the international system is stable when net satisfaction obtains. Taken in the context of Gilpin's overall approach to change in the international system, stability, so defined, can only exist during the period between post-war reorganisation of the international system by the major powers and the time at which the power underlying dissatisfaction comes, as a result of differential growth, to surpass the power underlying satisfaction. The international system can be stable, therefore, only during a certain period of its development since the inevitable occurrence of differential growth ensures that net satisfaction will not obtain for long.

This understanding of stability is static because it counterpoises stability with change in the international system. According to this definition, a system is most stable in the period immediately following post-war reorganisation since at this time all of the major powers are satisfied with "the existing territorial, political, and economic arrangements" in the international system. They are satisfied with them because they themselves determined these arrangements. As soon as the differential growth of states begins to re-distribute power among states, however, the stability of the international system begins to decrease. Stability disappears altogether when differential growth causes the power underlying dissatisfaction to surpass that underlying satisfaction. In short, the occurrence of change undermines stability.

Stability as a Dynamic Process Gilpin also identifies a dynamic process by which the necessary conditions for stability may be maintained despite shifts in the distribution of power. He argues that:

> The relative stability of the system is... largely determined by its capacity to adjust to the demands of actors affected by changing political and environmental conditions (1981: 13).

In other words, the international system is stable when it is capable of maintaining net satisfaction *despite* the occurrence of differential growth. This understanding of stability is dynamic because it equates stability with the management of change in the international system. Stability is understood not as the temporary presence of a particular state of affairs - net satisfaction, for example - but as a constant *process* of adaptation whereby the demands of rising states are accommodated within the system. Gilpin refers to this type of stability as "homeostatic or dynamic equilibrium" (1981: 12).

Gilpin argues that dynamic equilibrium is subject to two important limitations, however. First, it only operates when minor discrepancies emerge between the hierarchy of prestige and the distribution of power; i.e., only "in the absence of large potential net benefits from change" (1981: 13). The operation of dynamic equilibrium, therefore, results in the *incremental* adjustment of the system to *small* shifts in the distribution of power. It does not operate, according to Gilpin, when larger power-shifts occur.

Second, dynamic stability is not capable of adapting the governance of the international system. Although Gilpin argues that "territorial, political, and economic adjustments among states in response to conflicting interests and shifting power relationships function to relieve pressure on the system," he adds that, rather than thereby also adjusting the governance of the system, these adjustments serve to preserve the system "intact" (1981: 46; see also 1981: 47 Table 3).

These qualifications of the operation of dynamic equilibrium beg two important questions: First, why does dynamic stability only operate when small disjunctures emerge between the hierarchy of prestige and the distribution of power? What factors prevent it from functioning when larger discrepancies emerge? Second, if dynamic stability is incapable of adjusting the governance of the international system, how are the demands of rising states accommodated so that "pressure is relieved" in the system? Since Gilpin does not provide answers to these questions, his treatment of dynamic stability is underdeveloped and inconsistent.

Preferring Statics to Dynamics Another shortcoming of Gilpin's analysis is his preference for a static over a dynamic understanding of stability. Instead of investigating the *process* that ensures the preservation of net satisfaction in the international system, he focuses instead on the static configuration necessary for stability to exist in the first place. His preference is determined by two factors; first, by his argument that dynamic equilibrium only operates when small disjunctures emerge between the hierarchy of prestige and the distribution of power and, second, by the historical observation that "the principal mechanism of change throughout history has been war" (1981: 15). For Gilpin, dynamic equilibrium only operates at the fringes of international politics whereas the violent adjustment of systemic disequilibrium through war has been a more consistent and visible phenomenon. For this reason, he focuses most of his attention on rationalising the occurrence of war and significantly less on explaining why the operation of dynamic equilibrium is not more prevalent in the international system.

Focus on War as the Main Mechanism for Re-establishing Stability

Instead of investigating the conditions under which the international system may adapt without the occurrence of war, Gilpin is preoccupied with arguing that war is the main mechanism for restoring stability to the international system once differential growth has re-distributed power and generated dissatisfaction. He argues that war fulfils this function both in international systems in which a dynamic equilibrium is operative as well as in those in which it is absent.

In international systems in which a dynamic equilibrium is operative, the incremental adjustment involved in order to accommodate the demands of rising states *may* involve the use of coercive force. Gilpin argues that the "gradual evolution of the international system is characterized by bargaining, coercive diplomacy, and warfare over specific and relatively narrowly defined interests" and, therefore, takes the form not only of "peaceful accommodation" but also of "limited conflicts at the level of interstate interaction" (1981: 45). It is possible, therefore, to make a distinction in Gilpin's analysis between *belligerent* and *peaceful* dynamic equilibrium. Belligerent dynamic equilibrium operates when war is used as a mechanism of minor adjustment in the international system. Peaceful dynamic equilibrium, on the other hand, operates when mechanisms other than war are used to appease dissatisfaction in the system.

In the absence of either type of dynamic stability, war is the only means through which shifts in the distribution of power may come to be reflected in the hierarchy of prestige. War destroys the old hierarchy and allows the most powerful states to emerge from it to create a new hierarchy of prestige that better corresponds to the actual distribution of power in the international system.

In sum, Gilpin elaborates at length on the role war has played in correcting systemic disequilibrium in the past but eschews an examination of the conditions under which peaceful correction of systemic disequilibrium is possible. This is a major shortcoming of Gilpin's book. Although it sets out to study war and change, it does not contribute to the task of specifying the conditions under which the latter is possible without the former.

Weak Policy Relevance

Despite the fact that Gilpin does not make any claims as to the policy relevance of his theory of international political change, it is worth pointing out that because he does not elaborate on the conditions under which peaceful change may be possible, his model cannot be used as the basis of action designed to improve international stability. As Robert Keohane has correctly pointed out; "after one puts down *War and Change*, the question of how institutions and rules can be developed *within* a given international system, to reduce the probability of war and promote peaceful change, looms even larger than it did before" (Keohane, 1989: 52).

Gilpin's analysis is practically useful only insofar as it supports the historical observation that war has been the main mechanism for restoring stability to international systems. In this way, it clearly indicates that, historically, the odds have been stacked against the effective functioning of peaceful dynamic equilibrium. Since it does not specify why this has been the case, however, Gilpin's analysis is akin to the approach of realism in general - it "helps us determine the strength of the trap, but does not give us much assistance in seeking to escape" (Keohane, 1989: 66).

The theory of international stability developed below uses Gilpin's analysis as a basis on which to build. In doing so, it attempts to rectify the three main shortcomings of Gilpin's approach outlined above. Specifically, it favours a dynamic over a static understanding of international stability, it investigates the conditions under which systemic disequilibrium may be resolved without the occurrence of war and, finally, it attempts to outline means through which human ingenuity and creativity may be brought to bear on the improvement of international stability.

The Status Inconsistency Approach to International Stability

Gilpin's approach to understanding international stability is very similar to that used in status inconsistency theory which posits that a state suffering from a disjuncture between its *achieved status* - its actual capabilities - and its *ascribed status* - the prestige accorded to it by other states - leads it to "evidence a strong desire to change the status-quo, and failing to do so, to engage in conflict and violence" (Volgy & Mayhall, 1995: 68).

An important distinction may be made, however, between these two approaches. On the one hand, Gilpin focuses mainly on the cost/benefit calculations made by states in deciding upon the utility of changing the status-quo to suit their interests. The perception of status inconsistency is what leads states to make such calculations. However, action is taken primarily on the basis of the cost/benefit calculations and not solely on the basis of recognised status inconsistency. As such, Gilpin's approach is grounded in economic rationality. Status inconsistency theory, on the other hand, posits that the very existence of status inconsistency may lead states to pursue aggressive foreign policies. As such, this approach is grounded more in the kind of irrationality associated with pride.

Status inconsistency theory, like Gilpin's theory of international political change, also offers insights that are useful for developing a dynamic theory of international stability. It transposes a sociological understanding of stratification - the "structure of social inequalities manifested via differences in prestige, power and/or economic rewards" (Noel, 1976) - onto the international system where, it argues, states are ranked in accordance with their level of prestige and thereby exercise differential influence on the governance of the international system. From this assertion the theory argues that:

> When a strong incongruence exists between a certain level of achievement and the recognition accorded to that achievement (i.e., status inconsistency), foreign policy makers will come to see the incongruence as an important indicator of all that is wrong with the international system, and may take steps to change the status quo. Such steps will most likely lead to conflicts, and perhaps international violence, all other things being equal (Volgy & Mayhall, 1995: 68).

This theory has been subjected to numerous empirical tests using the statistical method (e.g., East, 1971; Wallace, 1972, 1973; Midlarsky, 1975; Tomlin & Buhlman, 1977; Gochman, 1980) all of which have found a causal relationship between the degree of status inconsistency in the international system, on the one hand, and patterns of international violence, on the other. As Wallace (1972: 63) has concluded: "Regardless of which indicators we use, the effects of status inconsistency on both the dependent and intervening variables remain strong."

Gilpin's theory of international political change and status inconsistency theory will be used as touchstones for the development of a dynamic theory of international stability. Aspects of each will be combined in order to produce a theory of stability that is based both on the cyclical evolution of the international system and on the role of status inconsistency in influencing state behaviour. While a great deal of emphasis will be placed on these two approaches, the theory of stability developed below will not limit itself to them. Rather, new concepts and variables will be introduced that do not exist in the respective frameworks of these approaches. The aim is to develop a theory of international stability that is strongly grounded in existing theory but that also transcends it.

Towards a Dynamic Understanding of Stability

The theory of stability developed below follows Gilpin in identifying a pattern of evolution in the international system that is generally cyclical and, therefore, repeats itself with some degree of regularity. Like Gilpin, it divides this pattern up into different "stages" of development; (1) reorganisation and institutionalisation, (2) differential growth, (3) tension and, *under certain circumstances*, (4) war. These stages are largely identical to those identified by Gilpin. I elaborate on each one in an original way, however, and approach the transition from stage 3 to stage 4 in a completely different way than does Gilpin.

Reorganisation and Institutionalisation

Hypothesis 1
The most powerful states to emerge from system-wide conflict establish and institutionalise a hierarchy of influence atop which they install themselves and through which they attempt to govern the post-war international system.

The cycle of change in the international system is anchored by a period of reorganisation that occurs after each system-wide war. This reorganisation is orchestrated by the most powerful states to emerge from the conflict in question. Responsibility for "the governance of the system, the rules of the system, the recognition of rights, etc." (Gilpin, 1981: 10) is taken over collectively by these states who, between them, attempt to order the post-war international system in such a way as to avoid a repeat of the type of conflict just experienced (Holsti, 1991).

Before advancing, it is necessary to emphasise a few points regarding the concept of international governance. Gilpin correctly points out that "when we speak of control over the international system, this term must be understood as "relative control" and "seeking to control" (1981: 28). International governance is, therefore, a relative concept. States and groups of states have been more or less successful in governing post-war international systems but "no state has ever completely controlled an international system" (Gilpin, 1981: 28). Governance does not imply the subjugation of the international system of states under a "common power" (Lieber, 1991) or leviathan that mitigates the effects of anarchy. Equating domestic governance with international governance in this way misinterprets the meaning of the concept. The concept of governance used here may be defined as the *attempt* by powerful states to order and manage international relations. Once understood in this way, it becomes evident that governance has taken place throughout the history of the modern state system.

Institutionalisation In order to facilitate the governance of the post-war international system, the great powers establish a "hierarchy of influence"[3] which divides states into two broad categories; those powerful enough to have exerted a significant influence on the organisation of the post-war international system and those not powerful enough to have done so. The states who create this hierarchy of influence invariably place themselves on top of it, creating at its zenith an exclusive club of powerful states who take it upon themselves to govern the post-war international system.

The hierarchy of influence thus created tends to be institutionalised; i.e., to have embodied within itself a certain level of formalised practice, be it in the form of treaty obligations, regular meetings of the great powers, international regimes, or full-blown international organisations. The institutionalisation of the hierarchy of influence formalises relations among the major powers as well as between the latter, on the one hand, and the remaining states in the system, on the other. In short, it freezes the configuration of power that exists during the reorganisation stage.

Since the major powers establish the hierarchy of influence and since they place themselves in the uppermost echelons thereof, a close correspondence exists at the end of the reorganisation period between the hierarchy of influence and the distribution of power in the international system.

Reorganisation and Institutionalisation in the Modern State System The first hypothesis is lent some support by a brief examination of the behaviour of relatively powerful states following the cessation of the major conflicts that have punctuated the history of the modern state system: The Thirty Years War, the War of the Spanish Succession, The Napoleonic Wars, World War I and World War II. Such an examination also reveals a trend towards the increased institutionalisation of hierarchies of influence.

At the end of the Thirty Years War, Sweden and France emerged as the most powerful states in the then burgeoning international system of states, having, through their alliance, gotten the better of the Hapsburg family complex. In the treaties of Münster and Osnabrück that made up the "Peace of Westphalia" of 1648, Cardinal Richelieu and Gustav Adolph, acting for France and Sweden respectively, set forth their ideas on the management of the post-war system. These ideas were heavily influenced by their respective interpretations of what had caused the war in the first place (Holsti, 1991: 30-31).

Following the defeat of Louis XIV in the war of the Spanish Succession, the bi-lateral treaties that made up the Peace of Utrecht of 1713 formalised relations between the most powerful states to emerge from that conflict - Great Britain, France, Holland and the Austrian Empire - and led to the formation, in 1718, of the Quadruple Alliance, "an organization of the powers devoted to upholding the Utrecht settlements against the revisionist policies of Spain" (Holsti, 1991: 75).

The Peace of Westphalia and the Settlements of Utrecht, therefore, were composed exclusively of bi-lateral and multi-lateral treaties and, as such, did not establish a highly institutionalised hierarchy of influence. They did, nonetheless, impose the will of the great powers on the design of their respective post-war systems and established these powers as the guardians of the post-war peace.

At the Congress of Vienna of 1814, Britain, Austria and Russia, in the persons of Viscount Castlereagh, Prince Von Metternich and Tsar Alexander respectively, decided amongst themselves how best to manage the international system that had been thrown into turmoil by Napoleon. In contrast with the Settlements of Utrecht, the great powers opted to supplement treaty arrangements with regular, formal meetings of the representatives of the major powers to discuss issues that threatened to upset the order established at the end of the Napoleonic wars. This "Concert of Europe" formally installed the great powers at the zenith of the hierarchy of influence and introduced an institutionalised element into their post-war collusion.

In the peace conference of Paris in 1919, following the defeat of Germany in World War I, Britain, France and the other conference participants followed the United States' lead in agreeing to establish a League of Nations, a formal international organisation charged with the task of transforming the conduct of international diplomacy so as to avoid future wars.

Likewise, in San Francisco in 1945, members of the United Nations coalition that had defeated the Axis powers in World War II gathered to sign the Charter of another formal international organisation; the United Nations. The draft Charter had been produced by the United States in conjunction with Britain, Russia and China. A Security Council of the five biggest powers of the time (actual and potential) was created to lead the organisation and to manage the post-war system of international security.

The great-power collusion that followed the end of both the First and Second World Wars extrapolated the trend towards increased institutionalisation of hierarchies of influence, begun by the Concert of Europe, to its logical conclusion insofar as it resulted in the establishment of full-blown international organisations with personnel, buildings and budgets. The hierarchies of influence created by the League of Nations, on the one hand, and the United Nations, on the other, differ greatly from one another, however. The organisation of the League of Nations was based squarely on the principle of the sovereign equality of states and, as such, did not result in the creation of a clearly defined hierarchy of influence. Although certain privileges were granted to the major powers of the immediate post-World War I period - permanent membership of the League Council, for example - these were largely diluted by the fact that every League member held a veto over the decisions of the organisation.

The hierarchy of influence created by the United Nations organisation, on the other hand, is much more clearly defined. Although still based strongly on the principle of one-state-one-vote, the organisation of the UN grants significant privileges to the major powers of the immediate post-World War II period. They enjoy permanent representation on the Security Council - the body charged with maintaining peace and security in the international system - and only they hold a veto over the decisions of the organisation.

A Trend Towards Increased Institutionalisation In the period 1648-1945, the hierarchies of influence created by major powers following system-wide war have tended to become more and more institutionalised. The Peace of Westphalia and the settlements of Utrecht institutionalised the hierarchy of influence only insofar as it established a complex web of treaty obligations that imposed the will of the major powers on the management of the post-war international system. The Concert of Europe, on the other hand, constituted the first attempt made by major powers in the history of the modern state system to formally institutionalise the management of a post-war international system through means that went beyond treaty obligations. Since then, there has been a marked trend towards establishing formal institutions for the management of post-war systems - the League of Nations, the United Nations, the International Monetary Fund and the World Bank being examples. When referring to the post-war orderings that have taken place since the Settlements of Utrecht, therefore, it is useful to refer to the creation of "*institutionalised* hierarchies of influence."

In the reorganisation and institutionalisation stage of the evolutionary cycle of the international system, therefore, two processes are worthy of note: First, the most powerful states to emerge from system-wide conflict collude in creating a hierarchy of influence on top of which they install themselves and through which they attempt to order and manage the post-war international system. Second, these states overlay this hierarchy of influence with an institutionalised layer, freezing relations among the major powers of the immediate post-war period, on the one hand, and between the major powers and the remaining states in the international system, on the other.

Differential Growth

Hypothesis 2
The differential growth of states causes inconsistencies to emerge between the distribution of power in the international system and the hierarchy of influence created following system-wide war.

Even before the reorganisation and institutionalisation of the post-war international system is completed, a fundamental force is already at work rendering obsolete the configuration of power upon which it is based. This fundamental force is the differential growth in power of states.

On Differential Growth The factors that cause states to grow and decline at different rates has been the subject of much interesting research (for example, Lenin, 1978 [1917]; Olson, 1982; Kennedy, 1987). Various explanations have been offered as to why it occurs, most focusing on the uneven impact of environmental factors, the application of newly-available technology, improvements in the knowledge-base of societies or the ease with which societies may overcome collective action problems. There is widespread agreement, however, that, whatever the causes, differential growth is constantly occurring in the international system. Lenin (1978 [1917]) even refers to this phenomenon as "the law of uneven development." For this reason and for the additional reason that an understanding of the determinants of differential growth is not required by the theory of stability being presented here, I treat differential growth as an exogenous variable and do not attempt to add to the understanding of why it occurs.

Keohane (1989) has criticised Gilpin (1981) for failing to *account* for the rise of hegemons and for failing to *explain* why particular states emerge as hegemons and not others (Keohane, 1989: 51). Such a criticism is ill-placed regarding Gilpin's analysis and it would be equally ill-placed regarding this one. Research on the factors that determine differential growth contributes significantly to our understanding of change in the international system and takes the important step of introducing domestic processes into the analysis of international change. However, such a research programme is complimentary to, but not necessary for, an analysis of international change concerned primarily with the perennial occurrence of differential growth and with its effect on the behaviour of states. For the analysis undertaken in this chapter, it is enough to know that the differential growth of power among states is an ever-present factor in international relations. It is not necessary, although it is a worthwhile project in its own right, to be able to account for the occurrence of differential growth or to be able to explain why certain states grow faster than others.

The Emergence of Discrepancies The essential factor in explaining why discrepancies emerge between the hierarchy of influence and changing distribution of power is the *institutionalisation* of the hierarchy of influence that takes place during the reorganisation stage. Institutionalised arrangements tend to adapt more slowly than do arrangements that are not institutionalised. For this reason, a hierarchy of influence that is institutionalised will not adapt very quickly to changes in the distribution of power. In fact, if the hierarchy of influence is highly institutionalised - in a formal international organisation, for example - it may not adapt at all to the changing distribution of power.

Build-up of Tension

Hypothesis 3
Dissatisfaction caused by inconsistencies between the hierarchy of influence and the distribution of power lead rising states to seek to improve their position in the hierarchy of influence (upward positionality).

Hypothesis 4
Attempts by rising states to improve their position in the hierarchy of influence are opposed by states whose position therein is threatened by these attempts (downward positionality).

Hypothesis 5
As a result of the interplay of upward and downward positionality, tension is generated in the international system. Significantly more tension is generated when the hierarchy of influence is rigidly institutionalised than when it is flexibly institutionalised.

Because the hierarchy of influence is institutionalised, inconsistencies emerge between it and the actual distribution of power once a certain amount of differential growth has taken place. These inconsistencies produce dissatisfaction mainly among those states not originally involved in the ordering of the post-war system but whose relative power is growing fastest. As a result, these states seek to exert more influence on the governance of the international system by improving upon their position in the hierarchy of influence. I refer to this type of behaviour as "upward positionality."

Upward Positionality Upward positionality results from a desire to move upward in the hierarchy of influence. It is normally displayed by states experiencing higher than average rates of growth whose power is beginning to approach that of the original orderers of the post-war system. It results from the simultaneous perception by rising states that (1) they are growing faster than most states in the system, even those who created the post-war hierarchy of influence, and (2) increases in their capabilities are not being matched by increased influence in the formal management of international affairs. Upward positionality finds expression in a growing dissatisfaction with the configuration of the status-quo hierarchy of influence and in actions designed to increase influence upon the management of international affairs. These actions may have the aim of breaking into the exclusive club that originally reorganised the international system or of simply improving upon the position already occupied within the hierarchy of influence.

An upwardly positional state strives to occupy the highest possible position in the hierarchy of influence given the extent of its resources. It may display its upward positionality in various intensities ranging from simply making its dissatisfaction with its position in the hierarchy of influence known to other states, on the one hand, to actively seeking to increase its influence on the formal governance of the international system, on the other.

Downward Positionality The upward positionality of rising states engenders a negative response from those states occupying the upper echelons of the hierarchy of influence. Such states are loath to undermine their dominant position by granting increased influence in the governance of the international system to additional states. Their opposition to the upward positionality of rising states is based on their own determination not to be relegated in the hierarchy of influence. I refer to this type of behaviour as "downward positionality."

Downward positionality, therefore, results from an aversion to moving downward in the hierarchy of influence. It is a tendency displayed by states satisfied with the configuration of the hierarchy of influence; i.e., those states who ordered the post-war international system and placed themselves atop said hierarchy. Even though they may be aware that other states in the system are growing faster than they and that, therefore, their position in the hierarchy of influence may no longer be justified by reference to their relative power alone, they are loath to see

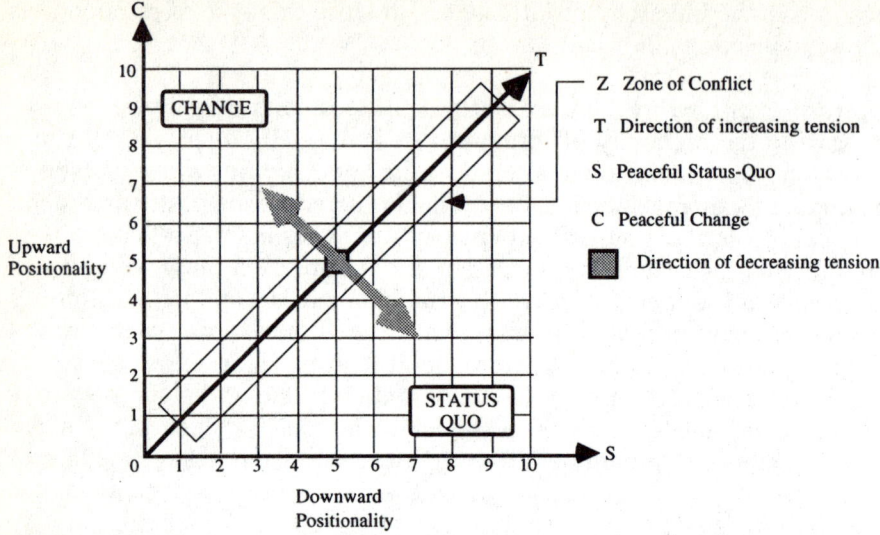

Figure 1   **A Simple Model of Tension Build-up**

their privileged position undermined by allowing additional states a larger say in the formal management of international affairs. Downward positionality finds expression in a refusal to consider the admission of additional members to the club of powerful states and in the rejection of claims made by upwardly positional states to increased influence in international affairs.

Tension Build-up "Tension" is generated when the forces of upward and downward positionality oppose one another; i.e., when some states seek greater formal influence in the governance of the international system and others refuse to grant it to them, preferring instead to retain all such influence for themselves. Tension is generated irrespective of the relative magnitude of each tendency; i.e., both when the amount of upward positionality exceeds that of downward positionality and vice-versa. Different levels of tension and, indeed, different outcomes may, however, be expected to result from different combinations of opposing positional forces.

Figure 1 graphically represents the interaction of upward- and downward positionality and charts the resulting levels of tension generated by this interaction. The strength of both tendencies is allowed to fluctuate between the nominal values of zero and ten inclusive. The points of intersection on the grid represent all the possible interactions of upward and downward positionality.

There are two lines in figure 1 along which no tension is generated since either upward or downward positionality is absent. One is the line S, along which the value of upward positionality is zero. This line represents the total absence of dissatisfaction in the international system. All states are satisfied with the configuration of the hierarchy of influence. Powerful states are satisfied with their respective shares of international governance and less powerful states are willing to defer to their governance. Line S, therefore, represents the peaceful status-quo.

The other line along which tension is completely absent is the line C, along which the value of downward positionality is zero. This line represents an international system in which states do not object to being relegated in the institutional hierarchy of governance. States govern the system as long as their power qualifies them to do so. Once their power wains relative to that of other states, they willingly cede a greater say in the governance of the system to rising states. Line C, therefore, represents peaceful change.

On the remaining one hundred intersections of the grid, however, tension is generated to some degree since both upward and downward positionality are present. Different levels of tension exist at different points of intersection, however. The line T represents the convergence points of all equal and opposite positional forces and, therefore, is the line along which maximum tension is generated. The direction of its extension represents the direction of increasing tension since tension increases as the magnitude of equal and opposite positional forces grows.

The bi-directional shaded line D represents the directions of decreasing tension. Such a line must have its origin somewhere on the line T and must run perpendicular to T. Tension decreases along any such line as it moves away from T in either direction since as opposing positional forces become more asymmetrical, the amount of tension generated decreases. Tension disappears when the line D cuts either S or C.

All these inferences may be made from the model without having to take into consideration the possibility of change occurring in the hierarchy of influence, the possibility of conflict occurring in the international system, or the effect that the institutionalisation of the hierarchy of influence has on the generation of tension. Introducing these three factors adds to the model in the following ways.

Change in the Hierarchy of Influence For change to be possible in the hierarchy of influence, upward positionality must exceed downward

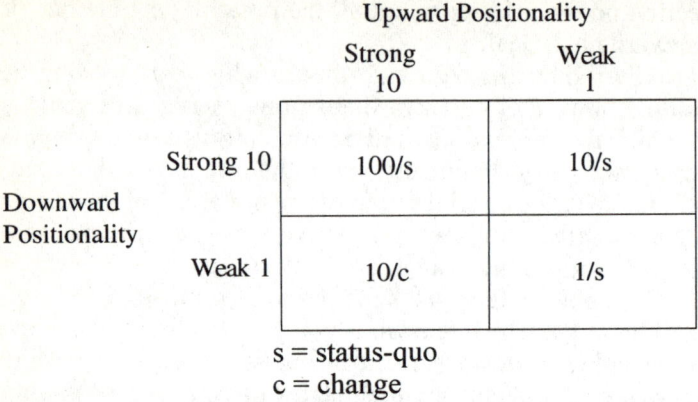

Figure 2   **Tension Configuration of Opposing Positional Forces**

positionality. In figure 1, therefore, change may only occur above the line T since only here does upward positionality always outweigh downward positionality. We may refer to the area above the line T, therefore, as the "zone of change."

The configuration of opposing forces at all points below the line T, on the other hand, is such that change in the hierarchy of influence may not occur since at all points below T, downward positionality is stronger than upward positionality. We may refer to the area below the line T, therefore, as the "zone of the status-quo."

There is an important distinction to be made, therefore, between the interplay of strong upward positionality and weak downward positionality, on the one hand, and the interplay of weak upward positionality and strong downward positionality, on the other. In the former case, change occurs but in the latter case it does not. This distinction is represented in figure 2 which, for the sake of convenience, denotes strong positionality with the value 10 and weak positionality with the value 1. The numbers in the table denote the amount of tension generated by the interaction of the positional forces.

Conflict in the International System   The presence of tension in the international system introduces the possibility of conflict. Conflict is possible, therefore, on all intersections of figure 1 except those that fall on the lines S or C - since, on these lines, no tension exists. Conflict is more likely to occur on some parts of figure 1 than on others, however.

Conflict is most likely to occur on or around the line T for two reasons: First, the highest levels of tension are generated in this region and the greater the amount of tension generated, the greater is the likelihood that conflict will occur. Second, in the area surrounding the line T, the forces underlying the opposing tendencies of upward and downward positionality are almost symmetrical, thus increasing the likelihood of preventative and pre-emptive conflicts. A preventative conflict is one initiated by a downwardly positional state or group against an upwardly positional state or group in order to prevent being overtaken in the hierarchy of influence. A pre-emptive conflict, on the other hand, is one initiated by an upwardly positional state or group that fears the imminent outbreak of a preventative conflict but prefers instead to make the most use of surprise and initiative by pre-empting such a conflict with an aggressive act of its own. For these reasons, we may refer to area surrounding the line T as the "zone of conflict."

Some Effects of Institutionalising the Hierarchy of Influence So far, we have assumed that change in the hierarchy of influence will occur when upward positionality outweighs downward positionality and that change will not occur when the opposite is true. Introducing an additional consideration - the way in which the hierarchy of influence is institutionalised - necessitates a refinement of these assumptions.

Generally speaking, the hierarchy of influence may be institutionalised in one of two ways - rigidly or flexibly. A hierarchy of influence may be said to be rigidly institutionalised when no institutional provisions exist to initiate and govern its amendment and/or when the ultimate decision to amend it lies in the hands of those states that occupy its upper echelons. A hierarchy of influence may be said to be flexibly institutionalised, on the other hand, when institutional provisions do exist to initiate and govern its amendment and when the ultimate decision to amend it does not lie exclusively in the hands of those states that occupy its highest levels. The way in which the hierarchy of influence is institutionalised may seriously distort the outcomes expected from particular combinations of positional forces.

On the one hand, if the hierarchy of influence is rigidly institutionalised, the downward positionality of those states occupying its uppermost strata is bolstered. Under such conditions, even when the nominal value of upward positionality is greater than that of downward positionality, downward positionality is likely to prevail. When the hierarchy of influence is rigidly institutionalised, therefore, the status-quo may be preserved under conditions where change would normally be expected to occur.

The rigid institutionalisation of the hierarchy of influence has important implications for the levels of tension generated in the international system. Since it reinforces downward positionality by assisting downwardly positional states in holding out against nominally stronger upwardly positional forces, it tends to encourage the generation of very high levels of tension - even higher than those generated along the line T in figure 1. In the absence of rigid institutionalisation, tension rises as the strength of upward positionality grows but tends to dissipate after upward positionality becomes predominant and change in the hierarchy of influence begins to occur. In the presence of rigid institutionalisation, however, tension rises as before but continues to rise even after the nominal level of upward positionality has become predominant.

If the hierarchy of influence is flexibly institutionalised, on the other hand, the downward positionality of those states occupying its upper strata is undermined. Not only do these states not have recourse to institutional rules that support their position in the hierarchy of influence, but the legitimacy of their position therein is also regularly brought into question by institutional provisions that stipulate the regular revision of the hierarchy of influence and provide solid guidelines for such revisions. As a result, flexibly institutionalised hierarchies of influence tend to be adjusted to relative power realities even when downward positionality outweighs upward positionality. In other words, the flexible institutionalisation of the hierarchy of influence facilitates change under conditions where none would normally be expected to occur.

The flexible institutionalisation of the hierarchy of influence also has important repercussions for the generation of tension in the international system. Since it undermines downward positionality - and, as a direct consequence, supports upward positionality - it tends to dissipate tension before it reaches critical levels; i.e., even before the level of upward positionality reaches that of downward positionality.

The build-up of tension in stage three of the evolutionary cycle of the international system results, therefore, from the interplay of two fundamental forces; upward positionality - the desire of rising states to improve upon their position in the hierarchy of influence - and downward positionality - the aversion of other states to being relegated therein. Tension in the system tends to reach higher levels when the hierarchy of influence is rigidly institutionalised than when it is flexibly institutionalised.

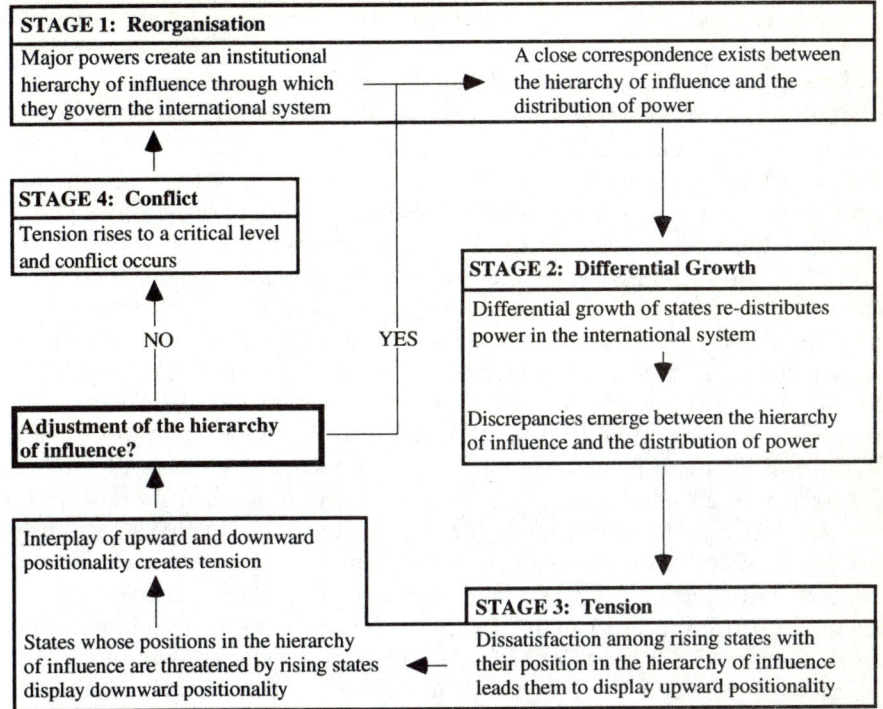

Figure 3   A Simple Cycle of Change

Conflict

Hypothesis 6
If the tension generated by the interplay of upward and downward positionality is not diffused but continues to increase, conflict is likely to occur.

If the tension generated in the international system by the interplay of upward and downward positional forces is allowed to increase to a critical level, it likely that conflict will occur sooner or later. The dissatisfaction of rising states caused by discrepancies between their actual capabilities and their influence on the governance of the international system turns to disillusionment at their failure to improve upon their position in the hierarchy of influence. Finally, on the initiative of either upwardly or downwardly positional states, the system degenerates into conflict following which a new stage or reorganisation begins.

An international system that reaches this stage in its evolutionary cycle is likely to have a hierarchy of influence that is rigidly institutionalised and, therefore, allows for the build-up of very high levels of tension. A system whose hierarchy of influence is flexibly institutionalised, on the other hand, is less likely to reach this stage of its evolutionary cycle since, in such a system, the hierarchy of influence tends to be adjusted at lower levels of tension making conflict less likely to occur. Figure 3 synopsises all of the hypotheses made thus far.

A vital juncture in the cycle of international change, therefore, occurs between stage 3 (tension) and stage 4 (conflict). The progression between these stages is not automatic. Rather, the possibility exists to bypass the conflict stage. The most important factor in determining how the international system will develop after tension has been generated within it is the way in which the hierarchy of influence is institutionalised. If it is rigidly institutionalised, tension in the system will be allowed to rise to very high levels and the system is likely to move from tension to conflict. If, on the other hand, the hierarchy of influence is flexibly institutionalised, it may be adjusted at relatively low levels of tension to conform with the new distribution of power in the international system caused by differential growth. In this way, the system may bypass the conflict stage and move directly to a situation in which symmetry is re-established between the hierarchy of influence and the distribution of power. This line of reasoning leads to the final hypothesis:

Hypothesis 7
An international system in which the hierarchy of influence is flexibly institutionalised is less likely to experience conflict than is an international system in which the hierarchy of influence is rigidly institutionalised.

An Alternative Definition of Stability

These hypotheses allow us to formulate a definition of stability: A stable international system is one which is capable, at low levels of tension, of adjusting its hierarchy of influence to conform with the shifting distribution of power in the international system. It is characterised by a flexibly institutionalised hierarchy of influence that strengthens upward positionality and undermines downward positionality. Rising states find it easy to translate their increasing power into greater influence in the governance of the international system while the ability of declining states to resist being demoted in the hierarchy of interest is undermined. In this way, shifts in the international distribution of power are consistently reflected in the hierarchy of influence according to which the international system is governed.

An unstable international system, on the other hand, is exactly the opposite. It is incapable of adjusting its hierarchy of influence in line with changes in the distribution of power among states. It thus allows tension to rise to very high levels. It is characterised by a rigidly institutionalised hierarchy of influence that undermines upward positionality and strengthens downward positionality. Rising states find it extremely difficult to translate their increasing power into greater influence in the governance of the international system while the ability of declining states to resist demotion in the hierarchy of influence is strengthened. In this way, shifts in the distribution of power among states remain independent of the hierarchy of influence according to which the international system is governed.

Relaxing the Single Hierarchy Assumption

For the sake of simplicity in formulating the theory, up to now I have implicitly assumed that a single hierarchy of influence forms the basis on which the entire international system is governed. This assumption is by no means necessary for the effective functioning of the theory, however. As well as being applicable to international systems governed by single hierarchies of influence, it is also applicable to international systems governed by multiple, issue-specific hierarchies of influence. Such systems emerge when powerful states distinguish sharply between the issue-areas of international politics - security, trade, development, etc. - over which they wish to exert influence. Governance then becomes issue-specific with distinct hierarchies of influence existing in each "system of international governance."

The question of whether hierarchies of influence are identical across systems of international governance is dependent upon the *fungibility* of power, a great deal of disagreement over which exists in the theoretical literature. Neo-realism asserts that states - especially the most powerful ones - can make their power in one issue area count in many other issue areas as well (Waltz, 1979). For neo-realists, in other words, power is fungible across issue-areas. Neo-liberal institutionalism, on the other hand, asserts that "power resources are differentially effective across issue-areas, and the fungibility of a given set of resources depends on the "policy-contingency frameworks" within which it must be employed" (Keohane, 1989 : 62). For neo-liberal institutionalists, therefore, power is not so fungible across issue-areas and a state that is powerful in one area may find it difficult to exert a lot of influence in another.

The question of the fungibility of power may, therefore, be examined as a consequence of testing our hypotheses. This can be achieved, however, only if we examine more than one system of international governance existing at the same time in the same international system. In this way, it will be possible to investigate a number of important questions: First, are issue-specific hierarchies of influence more or less identical or do major differences exist between them? In other words, do the same states exert most of the influence within all the systems of international governance examined or do some states exert more influence in some issue-areas and other states more influence in others?

Second, as shifts in the distribution of power occur, is the influence of rising states reflected equally in the hierarchies of influence of all systems of international governance? Of course, this is a question of stability as much as of the fungibility of power. Nevertheless, the stability of various international systems of governance impinges upon the fungibility of power in the international system. If the hierarchies of influence of some systems of governance are more flexibly institutionalised than others, it is likely that the fungibility of power will be inhibited since rising states will find it easier to exert influence in some issue-areas and more difficult to exert influence in others.

Departures From Gilpin's Model

Although the theory of international stability presented above is based squarely on Gilpin's analysis of international political change, it differs from Gilpin's approach in three important respects:

Adjustment of the Hierarchy of Influence

First, it does not exclude the possibility that incremental adjustment to small shifts in the distribution of power among states may also adjust the governance of the international system. On the contrary, the definition of stability presented above is based on the causal relationship between incremental adjustment to differential growth, on the one hand, and the adjustment of the governance of the international system, on the other.

The Role of War in Maintaining Stability

Second, whereas Gilpin argues that war may act as an adjustment mechanism under conditions of homeostatic equilibrium in much the same way as is does when such conditions do not exist, the definition of stability presented here posits that war is less likely to occur when the international system is stable since tension will not be allowed to reach critical levels.

This does not mean, however, that by simply measuring the occurrence of war we may induce the stability of the international system. Stability does not allow itself to be so easily quantified. If, for example, one were to measure the occurrence of war during the second stage of the system's cycle of development - when the hierarchy of influence largely corresponds with the distribution of power in the system - one would induce that the system were stable. Since little tension exists during this stage, little conflict occurs. To conclude that the system is, therefore, stable, would be to give a partial, and inaccurate, answer, however. Likewise, if one were to measure the occurrence of war over two cycles of international political change, it is possible that the analysis would also be distorted. If, for example, the international system during the first cycle failed to adapt its hierarchy of influence and, as a consequence, conflict occurred, one would have to conclude that the international system in the period being examined was unstable - even though the system might have commenced, during the second cycle, to adapt its hierarchy of influence to shifts in the distribution of power among states.

Two things are needed, therefore, before a definitive pronouncement may be made on the stability of an international system. First, distinct cycles of international political change must be identified. Second, these cycles must be examined in isolation in order to ascertain how they have advanced after tension has been generated within them by the interplay of upward and downward positional forces. If it is found that tension was allowed to reach high levels as a result of the rigid institutionalisation of the hierarchy of influence, one may conclude that, during the period of that cycle, the international system was unstable. If, on the other hand, it is found that tension was diffused at relatively low levels as a result of the flexible institutionalisation of the hierarchy of influence, one may conclude that, during the period of that cycle, the international system was stable.

The Role of Human Ingenuity in Maintaining Stability

Finally, the theory of international stability presented above is potentially more policy relevant than is Gilpin's analysis of international political change. It identifies the existence of strong downward positionality as the main cause of instability in international systems of governance. The key to improving the stability of such systems, therefore, is to undermine downward positionality.

Downward positionality may not be undermined directly, however. It would be pointless, for example, to appeal to the better judgement of the leaders of declining states in order to persuade them to acquiesce in being demoted in a hierarchy of influence simply for the sake of preserving international stability. This is the case because downward positionality is an inherent characteristic of state behaviour that has its roots both in the culture of national pride that constitutes the context for the actions of statesmen and in the natural aversion that all states have to conceding anything in international politics when they do not perceive an immediate advantage to themselves in doing so. The presence of downward positionality is likely to remain a perennial factor in international relations for as long as states exist in a self-help system.

For this reason, the only hope for improving the stability of systems of international governance is to undermine downward positionality indirectly. This may best be achieved, as has been indicated in the above presentation of the theory, by ensuring that the hierarchies of influence created to govern various issue-areas of international affairs are flexibly institutionalised - i.e., capable of diffusing tension at relatively low levels and thereby adapting to shifts in the international distribution of power without risking the breakdown of the system of governance in question or the occurrence of conflict. Since hierarchies of influence are designed and established not by inanimate systemic forces but by living, breathing individuals, human foresight, creativity and ingenuity may play a critical role in indirectly undermining downward positionality and, consequently, in improving international stability.

Since the individuals that design hierarchies of influence are affiliated with those states that emerge victorious from system-wide conflicts, the question presents itself: Why should such individuals create flexibly institutionalised hierarchies of influence if they know that doing so could undermine their own country's attempts to maintain its position therein at some time in the future? This is not an easy question to answer. It is possible, however, to suggest a plausible reason as to why they might decide to do so.

First, the main driving force behind the reorganisation of post-war international systems is the desire of major powers to address the factors that led to the war in the first place in order to avoid the occurrence of a similar war in the future (Holsti, 1991). Knowledge of the causes of wars, therefore, plays a major role in post-war reorganisation. A few examples illustrate this point. The great powers of the Concert of Europe saw the origin of the Napoleonic wars mainly in the French revolution. As a result, they took it upon themselves to suppress revolution wherever it threatened. The designers of the post-World War II international system recognised the important role that the suppression of Germany following World War I played in precipitating the war. As a result, they took steps to re-integrate Germany into the international system as soon as possible. Also, the recognition that the League of Nations failed mainly because it did not take adequate account of the differences of power among states influenced the decision to grant the major powers greater influence in the Security Council.

In a similar vein, if the differential growth of power among states is recognised as an important source of conflict, statesmen may take action to ameliorate its effects by designing systems of governance that adapt to shifts in relative power caused by differential growth. It is likely that the desire to provide for the longevity of a system of governance in the throes of creation will be strongest during the period immediately following the collapse of the previous system of governance. During this period, therefore, it is possible that, in their hierarchy of preferences, states will rank the general good of the system of governance being created above concerns about being able to maintain their position therein in the future. Under such conditions, the designers of post-war international systems may undertake to undermine downward positionality indirectly by flexibly institutionalising the hierarchies of influence of the systems of governance they create.

Positioning the Theory of Stability

In order to make explicit the theoretical foundations of the theory of stability developed in this chapter, the following sections focus on positioning the theory first within the field of International Relations theory and then within the general debate on international stability reviewed and criticised in the previous chapter.

Between Realism and Institutionalism

In the field of International Relations theory, the theory of international stability presented here falls somewhere between two stools; one represented by Realism and the other by Neo-liberal Institutionalism. Although the theory bears characteristics of both theoretical approaches, neither approach fully encompasses it. In this regard, this theory of stability would demonstrate, if supported by empirical evidence, that there is ample room for compromise and synthesis between the Realist and Neo-liberal Institutionalist approaches to International Relations (Mc Carthy & Alexopoulos, 1995).

The theory is, however, more Institutionalist than it is Realist insofar as it argues unconditionally that institutions *do* make a difference. International institutions are key intervening variables that modify the effect of upward and downward positionality on the stability of international governance. However, the theory stretches the Institutionalist approach somewhat when it argues that all institutions are not created equal and that badly (rigidly) designed ones can actually do more harm than good; that, instead of being "systems of peace," they may actually become "causes of war" or conflict (Betts, 1992). Thus, it modifies the Institutionalist approach by arguing that, while institutions definitely do make a difference, whether this difference is positive or negative with regard to international stability depends on the internal design of the institutions themselves. These characteristics of the theory, while not placing it squarely in either the Institutionalist or the Realist camp, position it a good deal closer to the former than to the latter.

Also from other perspectives, the position of the theory between Realism and Institutionalism may be discerned. The classic Realist/Institutionalist debate regarding relative and absolute gains is one important case in point. The main argument forwarded by Realists such as Grieco (1993) and Powell (1993) is that states do not like to engage in mutually beneficial institutionalised cooperation since, even though they may themselves gain absolutely from such cooperation, they are more concerned with the fact that other states may gain relatively more. The theory of stability presented here argues that states retain a preoccupation with relative gains even *after* they have begun to engage in institutionalised cooperation.

Thus, on the one hand, the theory does not completely fit the Realist approach since it implies that being concerned with relative gains cannot be a sufficient excuse for not participating in institutionalised cooperation if states may in any case protect their relative position within the institution itself. On the other hand, the theory also does not completely fit the Institutionalist approach since it implies that a concern with relative gains not only exists but actually persists even after states have begun to engage in institutionalised cooperation.

The distance, but not complete detachment, of the theory from Realism is demonstrated by comparing the general Realist view of institutions with that contained in the theory. Realists argue that international institutions are ineffective since they simply reflect the relative power of their members. The theory of stability presented here argues that realists are, in one sense, partly correct and, in another sense, completely wrong in this assertion. They are partly correct insofar as international institutions, at the time of their creation, do tend to reflect the relative power of their members. As time goes on and differential growth takes place, however, this reflection of capabilities becomes more and more distorted. They are completely wrong, on the other hand, insofar as the theory argues that, for international institutions to be *effective*, they must (continually) reflect the (shifting) relative power of their members.

A Liskian Interpretation of International Stability

The interpretation of international stability developed in this chapter is very similar to that promulgated by George Liska during the early theoretical debate on stability in the 1950s and 1960s. Like Liska, the theory rejects a purely cybernetic approach to conceptualising stability based on the necessity of re-establishing the original equilibrium following its displacement through disturbance. In this regard, the theory follows Liska in avoiding a "maximalist" cybernetic understanding of stability and in embracing a more dynamic interpretation - one that postulates the establishment of a new equilibrium following each disturbance of the system and that, therefore, accepts change as inevitable.

The theory does not, however, have its theoretical roots in cybernetics or systems theory as such. I agree with Liska that "if... an unfailing equilibrium operates anywhere, it is certainly not in the social realm" (Liska, 1957: 12). On the contrary, the theory is based on the acceptance of change as a perennial characteristic of international politics and on the conscious attempt not to interpret stability through the lens of any particular state-centred set of interests. Even the term "disturbance" - used in cybernetics to characterise a change that moves a system away from its equilibrium point - is incompatible with the thrust of the theory presented here. Change is not characterised as a "disturbance" in the sense of being unexpected and unwanted. Rather, it is characterised as an ever-present reality that we must learn to manage creatively.

Thus, Liska's interpretation of international stability, like that of the theory outlined in this chapter, centres on the primacy of change over the preservation of the status-quo. For him, stability is, at best, temporary, "uniquely or recurrently upset by factors precipitating change and replaced eventually by a new temporary equilibrium" (Liska, 1957: 12). The theory of stability presented here, however, differs in an important respect from this interpretation. It does not consider international stability itself to be a temporary phenomenon but rather to be permanently present when the international system is characterised by regularly shifting equilibrium points. In this respect, it makes a clear distinction between the concepts of "equilibrium" and "stability." An international system is in equilibrium, on the one hand, when the relative influence of states on the governance of the international system is more or less equivalent to the relative power or each. An international system is stable, on the other hand, when such equilibria may be re-established, albeit at different points, following the occurrence of differential growth.

Also like Liska, the theory approaches the problem of international stability from an institutional perspective. The participation of states in routinised sets of interactions is the criterion by which the existence of international stability or instability is established. International institutions, according to Liska, are in the business of authoritatively distributing coveted values such as security, welfare and prestige. If states consider that their share of these values is broadly in line with their relative power in the international system, they will not attempt to increase their share through a resort to violence. In other words, "if the ratios between the influence exercised by individual members and their actual power are not too unequal" an institution is in "structural equilibrium" (Liska, 1957: 13). The theory of stability outlined in this chapter applies identical reasoning to systems of international governance, of which institutions form an important part.

The theory of stability presented here is not only based on an association between stability and change, however. More precisely, it is based on an association between stability and *peaceful* change. This does not mean, as I have argued under 7.2 above, that international stability may be measured simply by reference to the amount of war occurring in the system. The cycle of change outlined above, although simple, suggests that a more nuanced analysis is necessary in order to determine the stability of a given international system.

Thus, the theory outlined in this chapter has more in common with the earliest theoretical ideas about international stability, especially those promoted by George Liska, than it does with later empirical notions of stability. Notwithstanding this, however, it is presented in such a way as to facilitate its application to the empirical analysis of international relations, a task that will be undertaken by the remainder of the book.

Conclusion

This chapter has outlined a dynamic theory of international stability that, I contend, is more useful than conventional understandings of stability in that it is applicable to many different types of international system, takes for granted the inevitable occurrence of change in the form of the differential growth of states, and provides hints as to how human ingenuity and foresight may be applied to the task of improving international stability. The theory owes a large debt to Robert Gilpin's approach to analysing international political change which it modifies, expands and combines with the insights provided by status inconsistency theory.

The theory is composed of the following set of inter-related hypotheses: The most powerful states to emerge from system-wide conflict establish and institutionalise a hierarchy of influence atop which they install themselves and through which they attempt to govern the post-war international system. The differential growth of states, however, causes inconsistencies to emerge between the distribution of power in the international system and the hierarchy of influence created following system-wide war. Dissatisfaction caused by inconsistencies between the hierarchy of influence and the distribution of power lead rising states to seek to improve their position in the hierarchy of influence (upward positionality). These attempts are opposed by states whose position therein is threatened by the ambitions of rising states (downward positionality). As a result of the interplay of upward and downward positionality, tension is generated in the international system. Significantly more tension is generated when the hierarchy of influence is rigidly institutionalised than when it is flexibly institutionalised. If the tension generated by the interplay of upward and downward positionality is not diffused but continues to increase, conflict is likely to occur. Therefore, an international system in which the hierarchy of influence is flexibly institutionalised is less likely to experience conflict than is an international system in which the hierarchy of influence is rigidly institutionalised.

Notes

1. Gilpin argues that "the most destabilizing factor is the tendency in an international system for the powers of member states to change at different rates because of political, economic, and technological developments" (1981: 13).
2. Gilpin uses the terms "(state of) equilibrium" and "stability" interchangeably. It is interesting to note that this definition of stability resembles very closely the cynical definition given in the *Doublespeak Dictionary for the 1990s* in which stability is defined as "Political and economic conditions that satisfy our interests" (Herman, 1993).
3. As we have already seen, Gilpin refers in this context to the creation of a "hierarchy of *prestige*." I prefer to use the term "hierarchy of *influence*" for two reasons: First, the fact that some states emerge from major war with a significant amount of their resources intact and thereby come to possess a certain amount of prestige does not tell the entire story. What is more important is how they use this prestige in influencing other states for the purpose of ordering the post-war international system. Second, Gilpin himself uses the term "prestige" to denote authority or influence. He argues, for example, that "prestige is the functional equivalent of the role of authority in domestic politics" and that prestige functions "to ensure that the lesser states in the system will obey the commands of the dominant state or states" (1981: 30).

4 Towards Testing the Hypotheses

> The best methodologies of qualitative and quantitative research have come from those engaged in active research in which methodology has been subordinated to the ardent desire to know and communicate something significant about human social life (Orum, Feagin & Sjoberg, 1991: 23).

Introduction

Having outlined a theory of international stability, it is now time to focus attention on testing it against empirical evidence. The purpose of this chapter is to lay the methodological groundwork in this respect. It specifies the research strategy used in moving from a set of hypotheses to a set of empirical results.

This chapter begins by laying the groundwork upon which the research strategy will be constructed. It defines the variables specified by the theory, delimits the universe to which the theory applies, makes specific the predictions generated by the theory, and, finally, operationalises the theory's central concepts. Having completed this preliminary work, it then moves on to the important task of outlining the reasons for choosing a particular research methodology - the method of structured, focused comparison - and the reasons for choosing particular cases - the UN Security Council and the International Monetary Fund. Finally, it deals with some specific problems caused by the selection of the research methodology and the cases: As a result of the particular cases that have been chosen for analysis, and in the interest of the internal validity of the overall research project, it includes an additional independent variable for consideration in the empirical analysis. It postulates a causal relationship between the independent and dependent variables and, as a consequence, chooses an additional research technique - process tracing - in order both to increase the generalisability of the empirical findings and to strengthen the causal inferences made.

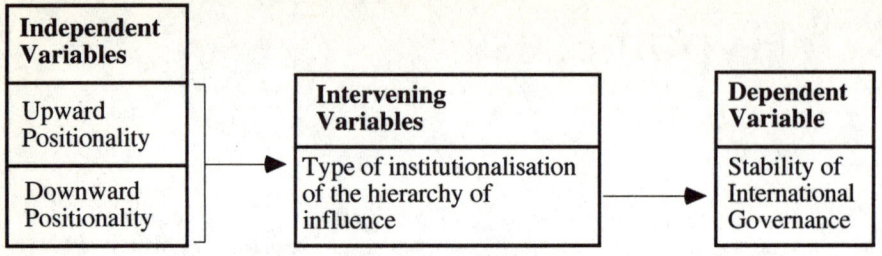

Figure 4   **The Theory-specific Variables**

Specifying the Variables

The theory of stability presented in chapter 3 postulates a relationship between the existence of upward and downward positionality in the international system (independent variables) and the stability of international governance (dependent variable), understood as the ability of such a system to adapt to shifts in the relative power of its members. The theory also postulates the existence of an intervening variable - the "type" of institutionalisation of the hierarchy of influence - which moderates the effect of the independent variables on the dependent variable. In short, if the "type" of institutionalisation is rigid, the stability of international governance will be adversely affected by the existence of upward and downward positionality. If, on the other hand, the "type" of institutionalisation is flexible, the stability of international governance will be strengthened. The postulated inter-relationship of these variables is presented in figure 4.

Delimiting the Universe

In order to strengthen the external validity of the research design, it is necessary to define the universe to which the research findings may be applicable (Yin, 1994: 35-6; George, 1979: 55). This universe is necessarily identical to that to which the theory of stability is held to apply; namely, to all contemporary or historical systems of international governance that are or were hierarchically organised - i.e., that distribute or distributed formal decision-making influence asymmetrically among their members - and that exist or have existed in the modern state system - i.e., since 1648. The theory does not apply to flatly organised systems of governance - those that attribute formal decision-making influence equally among all members regardless of power[1] - or to systems of governance that have existed outside of the modern state system - i.e., before 1648.

Generating Predictions

The hypotheses that constitute the theory of stability contain specific predictions that are amenable to empirical testing. These predictions may easily be deduced from the individual hypotheses themselves (see chapter 3). The more general predictions inherent in the over-all theory of stability may be stated as follows: A rigidly institutionalised hierarchy of influence will bolster downward positionality while undermining upward positionality, will allow tension to rise to high levels and will inhibit the incremental adaptation of governance to shifts in the international distribution of power thereby increasing the likelihood that the system of governance in question will break down. A flexibly institutionalised hierarchy of influence, on the other hand, will undermine downward positionality while bolstering upward positionality, will diffuse tension - even at relatively low levels - and will facilitate the incremental adaptation of governance to shifts in the international distribution of power thereby increasing the likelihood that the system of governance in question will persist.

Operationalising the Central Concepts

The central concepts of the theory of stability are "upward positionality," "downward positionality," "tension," and "diffusion." Only upward and downward positionality may be empirically observed. Tension and diffusion, on the other hand, may only be deduced from the magnitude of opposing positional forces. They are not directly observable as such. Tension is assumed to exist when both upward and downward positionality are detected in the same system of governance. Logically, the presence of both strong upward- and downward positionality in the same system is linked to higher levels of tension than is the presence of weak opposing positional forces. Also, higher levels of tension may be assumed to exist in systems where the presence of opposing positional forces has been detected over a long period of time than in systems where such forces have existed for only a relatively short period. The diffusion of tension, on the other hand, is assumed to have occurred when a decrease in the level of either upward- or downward positionality, or both, is detected in the system.

Upward and downward positionality, while observable, do not lend themselves as well to quantitative measurement as they do to qualitative measurement. This does not present a problem, however, since measuring positionality using qualitative techniques is more compatible with the conceptualisation of positionality used in the theory. Both upward and downward positionality are conceptualised as being tendencies and no particular importance is attached to the exact level of positionality that obtains in a particular system of governance. For this reason, it is sufficient to determine that one or the other obtains in a particular system and to give an indication of whether a relatively strong or weak version exists thereof. Therefore, as well as being more practical, it is also more suitable to measure upward and downward positionality in qualitative rather than in quantitative terms.

How, then, may upward and downward positionality be operationalised in qualitative terms? King, Keohane & Verba allow quite a lot a leeway in operationalising abstract concepts such as positionality. They state that:

> The choice of the specific indicator of the more abstract concept is justified on the grounds that it is observable. Sometimes it is the only thing that is observable (for instance, it is the only phenomenon for which data are available or the only type of historical event for which records have been kept). This is a perfectly respectable, indeed usually necessary, aspect of empirical investigation (King, Keohane & Verba, 1994: 110).

The best available qualitative measure of positionality are explicit statements made by senior state representatives regarding their satisfaction or dissatisfaction with the positions of their respective countries in the hierarchy of influence of a particular system of international governance. Upward positionality, therefore, may be measured by reference to explicit statements made by state representatives to the effect that they are dissatisfied with their country's position in the hierarchy of influence and wish to improve upon it.

Downward positionality, on the other hand, may be measured by reference to explicit statements made by state representatives to the effect that either (1) they do not support the promotion of states located below them in the hierarchy of influence (especially when such a promotion is likely to directly jeopardise their position) or (2) that they are unwilling to allow their country to fall in the hierarchy of influence.

A variety of research techniques may be used to measure both types of positionality. Of particular utility in this regard are (1) interviews of senior state representatives (when possible) and reviews of (2) official government documents, (3) the contemporary press, and (4) the historical literature.

Choosing a Research Methodology

The theory of stability presented in chapter 3 is ideally suited to being tested using either the case-study method or the comparative method. The statistical method is less suitable in this regard mainly because of the difficulties associated with operationalising the theory's central concepts in quantitative terms. Also, not enough cases of hierarchically organised systems of international governance exist to sustain traditional large-N quantitative analysis. A residual factor that also does not recommend the statistical method, even if one were to apply new quantitative techniques to a relatively small number of cases, is that more time and resources would be needed to test the theory using the statistical method than are currently available. In this respect, Lijphart has argued that "given the inevitable scarcity of time, energy, and financial resources, the intensive comparative analysis of a few cases may be more promising than a more superficial statistical analysis of many cases" (Lijphart, 1971: 685). Even if the theory of stability in its present form were more conducive to being tested using the statistical method, there would still be a strong case to be made for employing either the case study or the comparative method since either can serve as a useful first step before the commencement of more costly and time-consuming statistical analysis (Lijphart, 1971).[2]

For these reasons, the analysis will be focused to a small number of cases. There are significant advantages inherent in this choice. First, focusing the analysis makes it possible to provide a "thick description" of the cases in question and, in this way, to develop a detailed, interpretative understanding of them (Geertz, 1973). Second, a focused analysis is less likely to be prone to what Sartori terms "conceptual stretching" (Sartori, 1970; 1984) - the distortion of meaning that often occurs when concepts are applied to a broad range of cases but do not fit each one in a uniform manner. Given the abstraction of the concepts that constitute the theory of stability to be tested, this would be a real danger if the analysis were applied to a large number of cases. In this respect, Lijphart summarises the advantages of small N studies as follows:

> When one analyzes a relatively small number of cases, one can be more thorough and more attentive to details that are likely to be overlooked in

statistical analysis: one can make sure that concepts are not stretched, that the data are as reliable as possible, that the indicators are valid, and that the cases are really independent (Lijphart, 1975: 172).

Finally, it is widely accepted that the case study method is particularly useful in testing new and, therefore, under-developed theory. Hartley, for example, points out that "[c]ase study methods... are likely to be better able to adapt to and probe areas of original but also emergent theory (Hartley, 1994: 210). Eckstein argues more generally that "[c]ase studies... are valuable at all stages of the theory-building process..." (Eckstein, 1975: 80).

The next decision to be made, therefore, concerns the exact number of cases to be examined. The first choice to be made here is between the classical case-study method - focusing on the analysis of a single case - and the comparative method - extending the analysis to a small number of cases. This choice will determine the methodology to be used and the range of auxiliary research tools that will be available to aid the analysis.

Persuasive arguments have been made against the utility of conducting single case studies despite the fact that, given the same amount of effort, a richer analysis can be achieved by focusing on one case than by spreading the analysis across numerous cases. The main source of dissatisfaction with the classical case study methodology lies in the lack of generalisability of the findings generated by it. Sidney Verba was one of the first to raise this issue, complaining that single case studies are "idiosyncratic in style,... [that] they cannot test hypotheses... [and that] they do not easily add up" (Verba, 1967: 112-13). Likewise, Lijphart has argued that single case studies "cannot directly result in empirical generalisations and cannot even be used to test hypotheses (Lijphart, 1975: 160). These are harsh criticisms indeed and many researchers in the social sciences would not go so far in condemning the classical case study method. Nevertheless, even in a volume that collects exemplary single case studies and is designed to extol the virtues of the traditional case study method, the authors admit that "some of our best research studies have involved a small number of case studies conducted in a comparative framework" (Orum, Feagin & Sjoberg, 1991: 2).

As an alternative to the "configurative-ideographic" approach (Eckstein, 1975) of the single case study method, Verba (1967) makes a convincing case for exactly this type of "disciplined configurative" approach to empirical research that applies standardised procedures and hypotheses to more than one case. Such an approach is "based on general rules, but on complicated combinations of them. Explanations may be tailored to the specific case, but they must be made of the same material and follow the same rules of tailoring" (Verba, 1967: 115). The disciplined configurative approach, according to Verba, results in the greater generalisability of findings and lends itself well to testing theory.

Verba's preference for disciplined configurative research is shared by a large body of social science researchers. Yin, for example, points out that "[t]he evidence from multiple cases is often considered more compelling, and the overall study is therefore regarded as being more robust" (Yin, 1994: 45). Also, with regard to the generalisability of the results of case studies, Orum et al. argue that "[o]ne strategy to buttress assessing the results of one case study is to use several case studies in a comparative framework..." (Orum, Feagin & Sjoberg, 1991: 16). This widespread preference for the generalisability of results has even translated into a move to make single case studies more configurative than ideographic. Recent innovations in the single case study method - using such tools as pattern matching and process tracing, for example - has made it possible to identify multiple observations within single cases, thereby significantly increasing the generalisability of the findings as well as the utility of comparing them with the predictions of a theory (Collier, 1993).

Despite these relatively recent developments, Verba's warnings against the utility of the single case study, along with those of numerous other methodologists, will be heeded in testing the theory of stability. A disciplined configurative approach will thus be preferred to a configurative-ideographic one. Whether this choice involves a change in research methodology or simply a shift within a single research methodology is a contested question, however.

Some methodologists make a sharp distinction between the classic case study method - i.e., that using only one case - and the comparative method.[3] In his "typology of scientific methods," for example, Lijphart clearly distinguishes between the two, classifying the comparative case study method under the heading of comparative method and the classical case study method under the heading of the case study method (Lijphart, 1975: 162; see also Lijphart, 1971). Yin, on the other hand classifies the comparative case study method under the heading of the case study method arguing that "the choice between single- and multiple-case designs remains within the same methodological framework." He makes "no broad distinction... between the so-called classic (that is, single) case study and multiple-case studies. The choice is considered one of research design, with both being included under the case study strategy" (Yin, 1994: 45). Such classificatory differences are of marginal significance to the present analysis, however.

Having opted to extend the analysis to a small number of cases, considerable advantages may be gained by following the "valuable advice" (King, Keohane & Verba, 1994: 46) offered by such people as Arend Lijphart and Alexander George on how best to approach the comparative analysis of a small number of cases. The strategies outlined by both methodologists are designed to help overcome the "many variables, small N" problem that afflicts all comparative research when the number of explanatory variables approaches the number of cases to be examined. The strategies of both Lijphart and George focus on reducing the number of variables that have to be taken into account; a strategy that often leads to further reducing N.

Lijphart outlines a *comparable-cases strategy* that aims at compensating for a small N by focusing the analysis on "cases that are similar in a large number of important characteristics, but dissimilar with regard to the variables between which a relationship is hypothesised" (Lijphart, 1975: 159). This strategy makes it possible to achieve a large measure of "control" between cases and thereby reduces the number of variables that have to be measured. The difficulties inherent in finding cases that are sufficiently similar, however, usually lead to the further reduction of the number of cases available for analysis (Lijphart, 1975: 167).

Likewise, George extols the virtues of what he terms "the method of structured, focused comparison" (George, 1979) - basically Lijphart's comparable-cases strategy couched in different terms.[4] The type of research advocated by George is structured because "it employs general questions to guide the data collection and analysis" and focused because "it deals selectively with only certain aspects of the... case" (George, 1979: 61-62).[5] The strategies suggested by Lijphart and George are identical with regard to the way in which they attempt to overcome the "many variables, small N" problem.

In an appraisal of the state of the comparative method written in 1993, Collier notes that the method of "systematic comparison of a small number of cases... has been reinforced" by the completion of numerous successful research projects using the method originally advocated by Lijphart (Collier, 1993: 116). The method of structured, focused comparison, therefore, has proven to be effective in generating findings from a small number of cases that are both generalisable and useful for testing theory. It is an ideal methodology to employ in testing the theory of stability presented in chapter 3.

Choosing the Cases

Choosing the research methodology of structured, focused comparison necessitates restricting the analysis to a small number of comparable cases. For optimal results, it is necessary that the cases selected be similar in certain respects but dissimilar in others. Specifically:

> The desideratum that guides the selection of cases in the controlled comparison approach is not number but *variety*, that is, cases belonging to the same class that differ from each other. Thus, the investigator in designing the study will either seek cases in which the outcome of the dependent variable differed or cases having the same outcome but a different explanation for it (George, 1979: 60).

The essential criterion for case selection, therefore, is that cases should "differ in one or a few of the variables of theoretical interest" while at the same time being "instances of the same class or universe" (George, 1979: 59, 55). The aim is to maximise the ratio between the amount of variance of the operative variables - which should be as large as possible - and the amount of variance of the control variables - which should be as close as possible to zero (Lijphart, 1975: 163). This is not an easy thing to do. Achieving a high ratio usually requires that the number of cases examined be further restricted.

Another factor to be borne in mind when choosing cases for examination by the method of structured, focused comparison is selection bias. This occurs when "the nonrandom selection of cases results in inferences, based on the resulting sample, that are not statistically representative of the population" (Collier, 1995a: 2). Lijphart advises in this regard that "the amount of variance of the dependent variables should not be a consideration in the choice of cases because this would prejudge the empirical question (Lijphart, 1975: 164). Selection bias usually occurs, therefore, when the cases selected are grouped around either a high or a low value of the dependent variable - a phenomenon known as "truncation."

Selection bias can best be avoided by choosing cases that display a wide range of variation on the dependent variable; i.e., by following the advice of King et al. who stress that one should "not select observations based on the dependent variable so that the dependent variable is constant." (King, Keohane & Verba, 1994: 108). This advice is intended to shape research designs that are capable of conducting "theoretical replications;" that is, of examining cases that display "contrasting results but for predictable reasons" (Yin, 1994: 46).

Collier, on the other hand, is more sympathetic to research projects that group cases around one value of the dependent variable arguing that "at the outer limit, when variance on the dependent variable disappears and the investigator focuses on only one outcome on that variable, a shift to a different kind of research design has occurred" (Collier, 1995a: 4). He identifies three comparative techniques that have proven useful in dealing with such groups of cases - J.S. Mill's method of difference (Mill, 1974 [1843]), the "most different systems" design (Przeworski & Teune, 1970), and the technique of counterfactual analysis (Fearon, 1990). Notwithstanding the usefulness of these techniques in dealing with cases with no variance on the dependent variable, Collier concedes that "by not utilizing the comparative perspective provided by the examination of negative cases, the researcher gives up a lot. In general, it is productive to build in a comparison of contrasting outcomes" (Collier, 1995a: 4). In sum, it would seem that the most benefit may be gained by choosing cases that display a broad range of variance on the dependent variable.

For all of these reasons, I choose two contemporary systems of international governance as case studies against which to test the theory of stability presented in chapter 3 - the United Nations Security Council and the International Monetary Fund (IMF). These cases fulfil all of the criteria outlined above. First, a great deal of control is made possible by the fact that these systems of governance are similar in many respects: Both were established immediately following World War II and have developed in the same international environment. This fulfils Diesing's requirement that comparable cases should have common histories (Diesing, 1971). Also, both have large memberships and govern significant issue-areas of international politics - the Security Council being concerned with the maintenance of international peace and security and the IMF with the maintenance of international liquidity. The selection of these cases, therefore, serves to increase control by minimising variance between background variables.

With regard to the dependent variable - the adaptability of the hierarchy of influence - however, the cases exhibit considerable differences. The hierarchy of influence of the UN Security Council is relatively rigid and, apart from a slight revision in 1965, has not undergone significant change since it was created in 1945. The hierarchy of influence of the IMF, on the other hand, is relatively flexible. It has been revised at least every five years since its creation with the nominal aim of conforming with the relative economic capabilities of its members. Thus, these cases display considerable variance with regard to the dependent variable.

The selection of the Security Council and the IMF as case studies is mainly justified, therefore, by the fact that they maximise the ratio between the variance of the operative variables, on the one hand, and the variance of the background variables, on the other. Another important, although subsidiary, factor that supports the selection of these cases is the quality of the data that is available on them. It is an accepted methodological practice that the quality of the data that is accessible for each case under consideration may be a factor in choosing case studies (Lieberson, 1992: 116; Lijphart, 1975: 171). Because both the UN Security Council and the IMF are long-standing but contemporary systems of international governance, it is possible to collect more detailed data on them than it would be, for example, if two historical systems of governance had been chosen. Decisive in this respect is the fact that the interview may be used as a research-tool for collecting qualitative data on both cases. The use of the interview will greatly increase the quality of the data collected on each case and, thus, increase the quality of the overall research project.

Introducing an Additional Independent Variable

Although a great deal of control of background variables is achieved with these cases, one variable that is not controlled for is the degree of technicality of the activities undertaken by each system of governance. It is plausible that this difference between cases could account for some, if not all, of the variance on the dependent variable. An alternative explanation of this variance based on the degree of technicality of the issue-areas chosen might run as follows:

The IMF, on the one hand, deals with the highly technical issue-area of international liquidity within which mathematical formulas and general economic indicators may be employed to determine the relative economic capabilities of members. Upward and downward positionality therefore, do not play a large role in the IMF since promotion and demotion in the hierarchy of influence is objectively determined by the results of mathematical calculations. It is the highly technical nature of the issue-area governed by the IMF and the related ease of objectively determining rank, therefore, that best explains the flexibility of the IMF's hierarchy of influence.

The UN Security Council, on the other hand, deals with an issue-area of international governance that is significantly less technical insofar as no universally accepted, objective criteria exist that would allow for a ranking of members' capabilities. For this reason, upward and downward

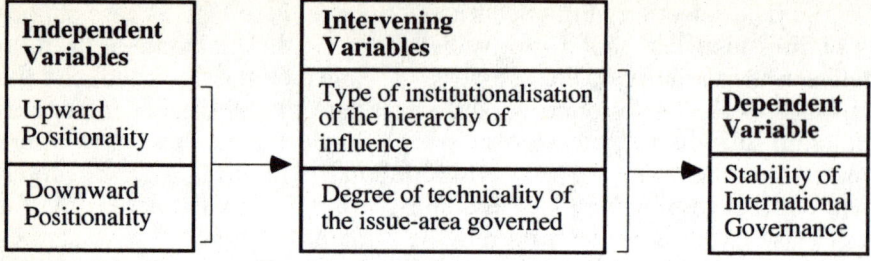

Figure 5   **The Variables for Analysis**

positionality play a much more important role in the Security Council and, since universal agreement cannot easily be reached on who is more important than whom in the global security system, it is more difficult to adapt the Security Council's hierarchy of influence.

This is a plausible alternative explanation of the variance on the dependent variable between the chosen cases. If it is valid, the theory of stability presented in chapter 3 would need to be seriously modified. In order to increase the internal validity of the research design (Yin, 1994: 35), therefore, the degree of technicality of the issue-areas governed will be treated as an additional intervening variable in the empirical analysis. The variables to be examined in the empirical analysis are presented in figure 5.

Increasing the Number of Observations

Stanley Lieberson (1992) has made it abundantly clear that there are serious dangers associated with drawing big conclusions from the examination of a small number of cases.[6] Although he is mainly concerned with the utility of Mill's methods of difference and agreement, his warnings are applicable to all research using the comparable case study method. Under normal conditions, Lieberson argues, the results of small-N studies are only generalisable if the following assumptions are made:

> A deterministic set of forces; the existence of only one cause; the absence of interaction effects; confidence that all possible causes are measured; the absence of measurement errors; and the assumption that the same "clean" pattern would occur if data were obtained for all cases in the universe of relevant cases (Lieberson, 1992: 114).

Even if we find, therefore, that our theory of stability holds with regard to the initial conditions and outcomes of the two cases we examine, we cannot be overly optimistic that it would also be supported if applied to other cases - even though, in selecting a methodology and cases, precautions have been taken to maximise the likelihood that it would be supported if applied to other cases. The generalisability of the findings of small-N research may be further improved, however, by the techniques used in examining empirical evidence. In this sense, it is true that "improving theory does not end when data collection begins" (King, Keohane & Verba, 1994: 99). At this stage, therefore, it is useful to pose the following question: How may the way in which the empirical analysis is conducted improve the generalisability of this project's findings?

King et al. (1994) suggest a number of techniques for improving the generalisability of small-N studies, thereby increasing the likelihood that "disciplined comparison of even a small number of comparable case studies... can sustain causal inference" (King, Keohane & Verba, 1994: 208). Each technique focuses on increasing the number of theoretically relevant observations that can be made in a particular study, often without having to increase the number of cases examined. The following empirical analysis will make use of one of these techniques - process tracing - in order to increase the generalisability of the results obtained from the chosen case studies.

Process tracing involves the examination of "the decision process by which various initial conditions are translated into outcomes" (George & McKeown, 1985: 35). Layne has described the procedure as "opening up the 'black box'... to identify the factors to which decisionmakers respond, how those factors influence decisions, the actual course of events, and the possible effect of other variables on the outcome" (Layne, 1994: 165). This method of empirical analysis subjects the theory on whose behalf it is employed to a much more rigorous test since it provides "more opportunities to *refute* a theory, not more opportunities to evade refutation" (King, Keohane & Verba, 1994: 228). It does so by increasing the number of theoretically relevant observations against which the specific predictions of the theory may be compared. Process tracing is a useful analytical tool, therefore, because it allows "each decision in a sequence, or each set of measurable perceptions by decisionmakers of others' actions and intentions, [to become] a new variable" (King, Keohane & Verba, 1994: 227).

Furthermore, process tracing is particularly suited to the detailed analysis of the IMF and the UN Security Council in which the writings and comments of senior state representatives constitute an important source of information. In these cases, decisionmakers "should speak, write, and otherwise behave in a manner consistent with the theory's predictions" (Van Evera, 1993: 2). Likewise, King et al. point out that the technique of process tracing:

> Often reaches the level of the individual actor. A theory that links initial conditions to outcomes will often imply a particular set of motivations or perceptions on the part of these actors. Process tracing will then involve searching for evidence... about the decisional process by which the outcome was produced. This procedure may mean interviewing actors or reading their written record as to the reasons for their action (King, Keohane & Verba, 1994: 227).

The technique of process tracing will be used as a supplemental research tool within the framework of the method of structured, focused comparison. The aim is not only to increase the generalisability of the findings but also to support causal inference.

Postulating Causality

Choosing the comparable case study method and subsequently restricting the analysis to two cases necessitates postulating a causal, as opposed to a probabilistic, relationship between the operative variables.[7] This is the case because, as Lieberson (1992: 109) has pointed out, "small-N studies cannot operate effectively under probabilistic assumptions, because then they would require much larger N's to have any meaningful results." In other words, it is untenable to argue that X increases the likelihood that Y will obtain if one only tests this hypothesis against two or three cases. The danger of selection bias and the heightened effect of chance undermine probabilistic statements made at this level. Probability cannot be tested unless a much larger number of cases is examined. At low levels of N, therefore, the researcher is obliged to argue that X *causes* Y.

The research methods that I have chosen, however, are well suited to supporting causal inference. As King Keohane and Verba (1994: 208) have pointed out, "disciplined comparison of even a small number of comparable case studies, yielding comparable observations, can sustain causal inference." The chosen method of structured, focused comparison is well equipped in this regard. Also, the technique of process tracing not only increases the generalisability of research findings but also supports causal inference by taking seriously the "fundamental rule of quantitative social science... that 'correlation is not causation'" (Ragin, 1992: 2). Rather than focusing solely on initial conditions and outcomes and on establishing correlations between them, this technique opens up the black box and focuses attention on the *process* by which initial conditions cause outcomes. It allows for a much richer analysis of events and lends itself to identifying the causal chain that links the independent to the dependent variables.

However, rather than just being an imposed burden that requires special methodological precautions, postulating causality also has two distinct advantages: First, it makes a theory more easily falsifiable. King, Keohane & Verba (1994: 100) argue that "we should design theories so that they can be shown to be wrong as easily and quickly as possible." To postulate a probabilistic relationship between the independent and dependent variables would involve the danger of stating the theory of stability in such broad terms that it could not be proved wrong even in principle. Postulating a causal relationship, on the other hand, while undoubtedly requiring greater methodological care, at least makes it easier to show that the theory is wrong. Second, the internal validity of the research design is strengthened by "establishing a causal relationship, whereby certain conditions are shown to lead to other conditions, as distinguished from spurious relationships" (Yin, 1994: 33).

Specifically, then, the theory of stability presented in the previous chapter may be shown to be wrong in two ways: First, by finding that a flexibly institutionalised hierarchy of influence did not result in the incremental adaptation of a system of international governance to shifts in the international distribution of power or, second, by finding that a rigidly institutionalised hierarchy of influence resulted in the incremental adaptation of a system of international governance to shifts in the international distribution of power.

Overview of Research Strategy

To recapitulate briefly on my overall research strategy, I have decided, in accordance with the advice of Verba and others, against conducting a single case study. In doing so, I have rejected the configurative-ideographic approach in favour of a disciplined configurative approach. Specifically, I have opted for the method of structured, focused comparison outlined by Lijphart, George and others by which a standardised set of procedures and hypotheses is applied in a systematic manner to a small number of cases. I have chosen as cases the UN Security Council and the International Monetary Fund mainly because these cases maximise the ratio between the variance of the operative variables and the variance of the background variables and, thus, allow for a theoretical replication to be conducted. Finally, in order to maximise the generalisability of the findings and to support the postulation of a causal relationship between the operative variables, I have decided to employ the technique of process tracing as a supplemental research tool in the empirical analysis.

Notes

1. Ernst Haas makes the same hierarchical/flat distinction with regard to international organisations (Haas, 1990).
2. The remaining scientific research method, the experimental method, does not constitute a viable option for testing the theory of stability for obvious reasons that apply across most areas of social science.
3. Some methodologists prefer to describe the case study approach to research, whether using single or multiple cases, not as a methodology as such but as a research strategy (Hartley, 1994) or as an art form (George, 1979).
4. Numerous different terms have been used to refer to the comparable-cases strategy. It has been referred to as "systematic comparative illustration" (Smelser, 1967), "the method of controlled comparison" (Eggan, 1954), "specification" (Holt & Turner, 1970), "most similar systems" design (Przeworski & Teune, 1970), and the methodology of "deep analogy" (Stinchombe, 1978).
5. George also identifies additional features that make this method suitable for testing the theory of stability. He points out, for example, that "investigators who favor the controlled comparison research strategy are often attracted to it precisely because it enables the development of... differentiated, policy-relevant theory" (George, 1979: 59).
6. For a discussion of the specific problems associated with generalising from single case studies, see Hartley (1994: 224-226) and Feagin, Orum & Sjoberg (1991: 13-17).
7. Lieberson (1992: 106) distinguished between deterministic and causal statements as follows: "[A deterministic statement posits] that a given factor, when present, will lead to a specified outcome. [A probabilistic statement] is more modest in its causal claim, positing that a given factor, when present, will increase the likelihood of a specified outcome. When we say, "If X_1 then Y," we are making a deterministic statement. When we say, "the presence of X_1 increases the likelihood or frequency of Y," we are making a probabilistic statement."

5 Hierarchy and Flexibility in the UN Security Council

Introduction

What is the nature of the UN Security Council's hierarchy of influence and how was it formed? Which factors originally influenced its ability to adapt to changes in the international distribution of power and how well does it adapt to such changes? These are the questions that this chapter sets out to answer. In doing so, it seeks to test the validity of hypothesis 1 - presented in chapter 3 - which states that "the most powerful states to emerge from system-wide conflict establish and institutionalise a hierarchy of influence atop which they place themselves and through which they attempt to govern the post-war international system."

The chapter is divided into four parts. The first part examines in detail the process that led to the establishment of the Security Council's hierarchy of influence and identifies the actors that exerted most influence over this process. Part two outlines the multiple dimensions of this hierarchy. Part three identifies the factors that influenced the amount of flexibility built into the Security Council's hierarchy at the outset while part four assesses the extent of this flexibility. Strong support for hypothesis 1 is found.

The Genesis of Security Council Hierarchy

During the final years of World War II, there was much speculation concerning the most likely distribution of power in the post-war international system. Schuman (1945) correctly recognised that fundamental changes had taken place in the distribution of power since World War I, pointing out that eight great powers existed in 1914 but that only three would remain in 1945 - the United States, Britain and the Soviet Union. He argued that "[t]he Three are "Super-powers."[1] All others, including the very greatest of the lesser powers, will not be secondary but negligible. They will count for nothing in the scales of power save in so far as they join forces with one or another or all of the three" (Schuman, 1945: 25). A similar outlook on post-war international relations was shared by many of Schuman's contemporaries (for example, Fox, 1944, 1946; Briggs, 1945; Lee, 1947).[2]

The United States, Britain and the Soviet Union - the Big Three - cooperated during the final years of World War II in drafting a design for a world organisation to regulate post-war international relations. In doing so, they provided for their own predominance within such an organisation. At the United Nations Conference on International Organisation (UNCIO) held in San Francisco between April 9 and June 25, 1945, the Big Three, joined by China and France, were largely successful in imposing this design on the remaining forty five delegations.

Preparations for San Francisco

With reference to the UN Charter, one enthusiastic observer at the UNCIO proclaimed that "it is to be doubted whether any international instrument, or perhaps any human document, had ever before undergone such wide popular scrutiny, such intensive expert study, and such democratic procedure of adoption" (Eagleton, 1945: 934). This assessment is seriously misleading. The Charter signed in San Francisco on June 26, 1945 was not the end result of a democratic process of collaboration between a large number of sovereign states. Rather, it was primarily the brainchild of the Big Three and, to a lesser extent, China and France. The observation that "[p]articipation in planning for the [San Francisco] Conference was as narrow as the Conference itself was broad" (Fox, 1946: 116), is at once more accurate and relevant.

Great power collusion in reorganising post-war international security began as far back as August 14, 1941 when Roosevelt and Churchill signed the Atlantic Charter - a statement of principles intended to govern the establishment of a world-wide system of security following the war. It was subsequently supported by the 26 states that signed the "Declaration by United Nations" on January 1, 1942.

On October 30 1943, Hull, Eden and Molotov agreed in Moscow on "the necessity of establishing at the earliest practicable date a general international organization, based on the principle of the sovereign equality of all peace-loving states" (Schuman, 1945: 22). This agreement was contained in the Four Nation Declaration - also known as the Moscow Declaration. Although China was an original signatory, it did not exert a significant influence on the drafting of the declaration (Fox, 1946: 116).

On July 18, 1944, the United States submitted a draft constitution for such a general international organisation for the consideration of Britain, Russia and China. This document became the basis of great power discussions on post-war reorganisation (Eagleton, 1945). Later in the same year, two sessions of negotiations were convened at Dumbarton Oaks to elaborate further on the design of a general international organisation. The first round of negotiations - August 21 through September 29 - was attended only by the Soviet Union, Britain and the United States. In the second round - September 29 through October 7 - the Soviet Union's place at the negotiating table was taken over by China. By this time, however, the most significant decisions had already been taken (Fox, 1946: 116).

Many important, practical decisions were made at Dumbarton Oaks. The general design of a post-war world organisation, based on the US proposal, was agreed upon. Also, agreement was reached on the number of states that would sit on the Security Council, both in a permanent and temporary capacity. No agreement was reached, however, on any aspect of voting in the Security Council because of a disagreement between the United States and the Soviet Union over whether members of the Security Council should be allowed to vote if party to a dispute under consideration by the Council.[3]

Agreement on this matter was eventually reached during negotiations between the Big Three held at Yalta, in the Crimea, between February 4 and 11, 1945.[4] At this meeting, Stalin and Churchill accepted a proposal by Roosevelt regarding both the voting formula to be applied to the Security Council and the procedure to be followed when a member of the Security Council was party to a dispute under consideration by the Council. Following this agreement, the Big Three consulted with China and France before the United States included the text of a draft United Nations Charter with the invitations to 49 states to attend the UNCIO in San Francisco.

The San Francisco Conference

The detailed design for a general international organisation developed by the major powers between Moscow and Yalta was first openly shared with the wider international community in San Francisco in April 1945. The decisionmaking process at the UNCIO did not, however, correspond with the image of pluralistic democracy conveyed above by Eagleton. Rather, the process of great power collusion established during the final years of the war continued to operate in San Francisco. Decisionmaking at the conference essentially took the form of a two-level process; the first level consisting of the "Big Five"[5] coming to initial agreement during their regular meetings in US Secretary of State Stettinus' penthouse atop the Fairmont Hotel on Nob Hill, and the second level consisting of them taking their proposals to the Committee rooms of the Veteran's Memorial Building in the Civic Centre and to the plenary sessions in the Opera House.

As one observer pointed out, however, "the work of the Big Five was by no means completed once they had achieved agreement among themselves. The frequently difficult task of winning the approval of "the little forty-five" involved prolonged and sometimes heated discussions in full Conference committee" (Fox, 1946: 121). Nevertheless, for all intents and purposes, the Big Three possessed a veto on all changes to the Dumbarton Oaks/Yalta proposals despite the fact that each state in attendance formally exercised equal voting power (Finkelstein, 1955). This is borne out by the fact that the strong opposition of the little forty-five to the central proposals of the great powers - permanent membership of the Security Council for the Big Five and their right of veto - was ineffectual. Both points were enshrined in the UN Charter signed into being in San Francisco.

The Nature of Security Council Hierarchy

The Dumbarton Oaks/Yalta proposals imposed by the Big Five upon the remaining delegations at the San Francisco conference created a hierarchy of influence in the issue-area of international security the upper echelons of which were occupied by the same Big Five states. This hierarchy has three dimensions, two of which provide for a hierarchy of influence *within* the Council and one of which provides for a hierarchy of influence *around* the council. The first dimension takes the form of the limited right of permanent membership of the Security Council. The second results from the disproportionate voting power enjoyed by permanent members. The third dimension of the hierarchy is created by the relative importance of the Security Council within the UN organisation; i.e., the fact that states that sit on the Council exercise more influence that those that do not.

Permanent versus Non-permanent Membership

The first dimension of the Security Council hierarchy is formed by the limited right to permanent membership of the Council. Article 23.1 states that: "The Republic of China, France, the Union of Soviet Socialist Republics, the United Kingdom of Great Britain and Northern Ireland, and the United States of America shall be permanent members of the Security Council."[6] In accordance with Article 28.1 - which provides that "[t]he Security Council shall be so organized as to be able to function continuously" and that "[e]ach member of the Security Council shall for this purpose be represented at all times at the seat of the Organization" - these five states are always represented on the Council. The main advantage of permanent membership is, simply, the ability to exert a sustained influence of the decisionmaking process of the Security Council.

Non-permanent members, on the other hand, cannot exert such a sustained influence since they are disadvantaged in three main ways with respect to their permanent member colleagues: First, Article 23.1 stipulates that non-permanent members shall be elected by the General Assembly. Since the pool of states from which, in theory, non-permanent members may be chosen (185) is very large in relation to the number of non permanent seats available (10), the chances that any one state will be elected very often to the Security Council are not high. However, Article 23.1 also specifies criteria that should limit the number of states eligible for election. It emphasises that states should be elected on the basis of their "contribution... to the maintenance of international peace and security and to the other purposes of the Organization" with due regard also being paid in this regard to the "equitable geographical distribution" of non-permanent members.

In practice, however, the General Assembly has developed its own criteria for electing states to the Security Council. It pays great attention to the principle of equitable geographic distribution but largely ignores the contribution of states to maintaining international peace and security. The selection of non-permanent members to the Security Council, therefore, is "guided by considerations of prestige and political affiliation rather than actual or potential ability to make a positive contribution to security" (Martin & Edwards, 1955: 33). As a result, the first provision of Article 23.1 concerning the election of non-permanent members to the Security Council "has been erased from the [Charter] by deliberate non-observance" (ibid.).[7]

This approach to electing non-permanent members has had the same excluding effect as intended by Article 23.1, however. In practice, larger regional powers tend to be elected more often than do smaller powers since "within each geographic group, several large Countries tend to compete for a Security Council seat much more frequently, thus elbowing out the smaller Countries" (Italian Proposal, 1996). As of January 1996, for example, 77 states have never been elected as non-permanent members of the Security Council and 46 have served only once.

Second, Article 23.2 stipulates that "[t]he non-permanent members of the Security Council shall be elected for a term of two years."

The fact that the tenure of non-permanent members is limited to such a short term disadvantages them with respect to permanent members who do not have to acclimatise themselves repeatedly to Council procedures. As a result, it is more difficult for non-permanent members to exert consistent influence on the operation of the Council throughout the entire length of their tenure.

Finally, Article 23.2 also provides that "[a] retiring [non-permanent] member shall not be eligible for immediate re-election." It is impossible, therefore, for a non-permanent member to achieve de facto permanent status through the agreement of a sufficiently large number of General Assembly members to continuously re-elect the same state to the Security Council. However, due to the fact that the Charter does not specify a compulsory period of absence from the Security Council between periods of non-permanent membership thereof, "almost permanent membership" is possible in theory if "a regional group were willing to support a particular candidate after its year of ineligibility, thus securing membership for two years out of three" (Bailey, 1988: 157).

Examples of such collusion are few, however. Only twice between 1946 and 1992 did it occur that a state succeeded in having itself re-elected immediately following one year of absence from the Security Council.[8] Despite the fact that instances in which states managed to get themselves re-elected after two years of absence from the Council are slightly more numerous,[9] almost permanent membership of the Security Council remains merely a theoretical possibility. In sum, the distinction between permanent and non-permanent membership of the Security Council confers tangible benefits upon the Big Five and hinders the remainder of the UN membership from exercising consistent influence on the Council.

Weighted Voting

The second dimension of the Security Council's hierarchy of influence is created by the Council's decisionmaking procedures in which permanent members exercise significantly more influence than do non-permanent members. Although the principle of the sovereign equality of states espoused in Article 2.1 is echoed in the first paragraph of Article 27 - "[e]ach member of the Security Council shall have one vote" - the fundamentally unequal decision-making influence of Council members is set out clearly in the subsequent paragraphs of the same article.

The relative decision-making influence of Security Council members differs depending on whether the question under consideration is classed as being procedural or non-procedural. With regard to procedural questions, Article 27.2 provides simply that: "[d]ecisions... shall be made by an affirmative vote of nine members." Procedural matters, therefore, are not subject to weighted voting but simply to qualified majority voting, each member of the Security Council having one vote, irrespective of membership status.

In deciding upon non-procedural, or substantive, matters, however, permanent members enjoy a distinct advantage. Article 27.3 stipulates that such decisions "shall be made by an affirmative vote of nine members including the concurring votes of the permanent members..." On substantive issues, therefore, permanent members of the Security Council exercise a veto. Thus, despite the fact that the first paragraph of Article 27 gives the impression that the votes of all members of the Security Council have equal weight, this is only the case for procedural matters. In all other instances, "the vote of the permanent Members is, in fact, a plural vote in the sense that a negative vote cast by one of them nullifies the effect of all affirmative votes, regardless of their number" (Bentwich & Martin, 1969: 67).

Distinguishing Between Procedural and Substantive Issues In light of the fact that permanent members may exercise their veto on substantive issues but not on procedural ones, an interesting question is: Who decides whether a particular issue before the Security Council is substantive or procedural? The answer is that permanent members decide. By holding the power to classify issues as either procedural or substantive, the veto power of permanent members is greatly increased.

The distinction between procedural and substantive decisions is not provided by the Charter but may be traced to San Francisco. Examples of procedural issues were first specified in the "Statement by the Delegations of the Four Sponsoring Governments on Voting Procedure in the Security Council" - hereafter The Statement - at the San Francisco Conference on June 7, 1945.[10] The Statement interpreted as "procedural" all issues falling under the competence of Articles 28-32; i.e., those issues regarding the alteration of rules of procedure; the determination of method of selecting the security council president; the organisation of the Council in order to be able to function continuously; the selection of times and places of its regular and special meetings; the establishment of bodies and agencies necessary for the performance of its functions and the invitation of members of the UN not represented in the council to be heard in the council.[11] "Substantive" issues, on the other hand, were interpreted implicitly as those relating to every aspect of maintaining international peace and security (Lee, 1947).

Significantly, The Statement also determined that the

classification of a particular question as procedural or non-procedural was a "procedural" issue and, as such, would have to be decided by the affirmative vote of seven [subsequently nine] members of the Security Council, including the concurring votes of the permanent members.[12] This aspect of The Statement was voted through at the San Francisco Conference on June 12, 1945. The result is that permanent members of the Security Council exercise a veto over questions of classification. In other words, they exercise a veto over the decision on whether or not they are entitled to use their veto. The procedure by which permanent members use their veto first to classify a decision as substantive and then to block it, has become known as the "double veto" procedure (Bailey, 1988: 214-223; Martin & Edwards, 1955: 79).

In an attempt to tone down the significance of their interpretation, the authors of The Statement "disingeniously" asserted that differences of opinion regarding the classification of issues were "unlikely" to arise (Bailey, 1988: 215). In fact, such differences of opinion have often arisen and, in some instances, have lead to the use of the double veto. Permanent members have re-classified numerous motions - for example, those dealing with the labelling of a conflict as a "dispute" or a "situation" and those to request the International Court of Justice for an advisory opinion (Bentwich & Martin, 1969: 68; see also p. 78) - from being procedural to substantive issues. The most memorable instance of the use of the double veto, however, occurred after the Communist *coup* in Czechoslovakia when the Soviet Union effectively prevented the Security Council from setting up a sub-committee to hear evidence on the situation by first using its veto to classify the decision to do so as substantive and by then blocking the decision to set up the sub-committee by employing its veto (Martin & Edwards, 1955: 79).[13]

Thus, despite the fact that Article 27.2 stipulates that the veto may not be used when deciding upon procedural questions, permanent members, through the use of the double veto, are able to exercise veto power over all issues with which they are particularly concerned - even over those that, by any objective standard, should be classified as being procedural.

Bypassing the Compulsory Abstention Rule The latter part of Article 27.3 provides that any state represented on the Security Council must abstain from voting when it is party to a dispute under consideration by the Council the resolution of which falls under Chapter VI and Article 52.3, both of which concern the pacific settlement of disputes (see Bentwich & Martin, 1969: 69). This provision would seem to undermine somewhat the independent veto power of the permanent members. In practice, however, the permanent members have recourse to two strategies by which to bypass it.

First, a permanent member who is alleged to be party to a dispute under consideration by the Security Council may simply deny the existence of the dispute or contest the fact that it is party to it. In this way, the rule concerning compulsory abstention will not come into operation until the Security Council has first established that there is a dispute and that the permanent member in question is party to it. In order to establish these two things, however, the Security Council must make at least one substantive decision at which point the permanent member in question may use its veto (Martin & Edwards, 1955: 88-89; Bentwich & Martin, 1969: 69-70).

Second, since the rule of abstention only applies to decisions concerning the pacific settlement of disputes and since Security Council decisions are not binding on such issues, a permanent member party to a dispute under consideration by the Council may ignore the Council's recommendations for a peaceful settlement. If, as a result, conflict escalates sufficiently in order for the situation to be classified as a breach of the peace or as an overt act of aggression, the Council would have to proceed with preventative measures or with sanctions under Chapter VII. Since all substantive decisions under Chapter VII are subject to the veto of the permanent members, however, even a permanent member party to the dispute under consideration may use its veto to block preventative measures or to prevent the imposition of sanctions (Bentwich & Martin, 1969: 70).

On a few occasions, permanent members have abstained from voting under conditions that could be associated with the provisions of Article 27.3 (Bailey, 1988: 224-231; see also Bentwich & Martin, 1969: 69-71). There is also evidence, however, of permanent members making indirect use of their veto power in order to by-pass these provisions.[14] On the whole, permanent members have demonstrated that they are not averse to using the mechanisms made available to them by their veto power in order to bypass the Charter provisions for the obligatory abstention from voting.

The Relative Importance of the Security Council

Immediately following the creation of the UN, one observer commented that "there are two chief functional organs: one, the Security Council... the other, the General Assembly... The former has potentially vast authority and power within its field; the latter depends almost entirely upon the voluntary action of member-states" (Eagleton, 1945: 939). The potential of the Security Council as the most important UN organ has been fully realised (Briggs, 1945). The third dimension of the Security Council's hierarchy of influence, therefore, is constituted by its dominant position within the UN organisation in general. Unlike the previous two dimensions, this dimension does not refer to a hierarchy of influence that is internal to the Council but rather to one within which the Security Council itself is embedded. Stated in its simplest form, the fact that the Security Council is the most important UN organ means that those states that sit on it exercise more influence that do those states that do not.

Unlike the Covenant of the League of Nations, which granted joint responsibility to the Council and Assembly for the preservation of peace and security, the Charter of the United Nations grants "primary responsibility for the maintenance of international peace and security" to the Security Council (Article 24.1). Numerous wide-ranging powers are granted to the Security Council by the Charter. Article 106, for example, confers upon the permanent members the right to initiate joint action "on behalf of the Organization,"[15] Article 24.1 states that the Security Council acts on behalf of all members of the United Nations when carrying out its duties, and Article 25 commits all members of the United Nations to "accept and carry out the decisions of the Security Council."[16]

The powers of the Security Council are further expanded by Chapter VII of the Charter which deals with "Action with Respect to Threats to the Peace, Breaches of the Peace, and Acts of Aggression." Of prime importance here is the provision of Article 39 which confers upon the Council the power to determine the existence of situations to which sanctions or enforcement measures should be applied. Article 41 empowers the Security Council to call upon the members of the United nations to apply such sanctions or measures. If the Council decides that sanctions are inadequate, "it may take such action by air, sea, or land forces as may be necessary to maintain or restore international peace and security" (Article 42).

In sum, the nature of the hierarchy of influence devised by the great powers during their negotiations at Dumbarton Oaks and Yalta and imposed upon those states participating at the San Francisco conference may be defined by reference to three dimensions: The limited right to permanent membership of the Security Council enjoyed only by those same great powers, the disproportionate voting power enjoyed by permanent members as a result of their veto privileges, and the predominant role of the Security Council within the UN organisation in general.

The Genesis of Security Council Flexibility

> It is always a dangerous thing to bar change in a constitutional document (Eagleton, 1945: 938).

When the drafters of the Dumbarton Oaks/Yalta proposals came to San Francisco they were heavily criticised by the remaining delegations for the wide-ranging and permanent powers they had bestowed upon themselves (Bentwich & Martin, 1969; Fox, 1946). As one participant at the San Francisco conference described: "So heated did the debate on this issue become that Room 223 in the Veterans Building, where the meetings of Committee III/1 were held,[17] was dubbed the "Madison Square Garden" of San Francisco" (Wilcox, 1945: 943).

Many delegations expressed strong opposition to the proposal to grant permanent seats on the Security Council to the Big Five and suggested alternative arrangements that would grant less permanent privilege to these states. One of the most interesting in this respect was the suggestion not to name the permanent members of the Security Council in Article 23.1 of the Charter but to determine from time to time the identity of the five most powerful states in the international system and to confer upon them the privileges associated with permanent membership (Bentwich & Martin, 1969: 58).

The most serious crisis of the conference, however, arose over the proposed veto-power of the permanent members (Wilcox, 1945; Lee, 1947). At the opening of the conference, a total of 17 states, including France,[18] suggested amendments to the Dumbarton Oaks proposals on voting in the Security Council. The main onslaught on the veto proposal, however, took place between May 17 and June 12 and was led by the delegations of Australia and New Zealand who, along with the other "middle powers" and the Latin-American and Arab blocs, constituted the main opposition to the Dumbarton Oaks/Yalta voting proposals (Fox, 1946).

The Big Five made it abundantly clear, however, that "it was either the Charter with the veto or no Charter at all" (Wilcox, 1945: 954).[19] Having learned from the League experiment that the participation of all major powers was imperative to the effective operation of a major international organisation, most delegations focused their attention on trying to ensure that it would be possible in the future to revise the provisions of the Charter dealing with the privileges of permanent members:

> During the Committee debates, many delegates stated that they would not oppose the veto power so emphatically if they could have some assurance that the process of amending the Charter might be liberalized and an opportunity afforded for a reëxamination of the Organization at some future date (Wilcox, 1945: 950).

The limited success that the little forty five achieved in this regard constitutes the genesis of Security Council flexibility.[20]

The lesser powers were successful in slightly amending the Charter amendment procedure laid down in Chapter XI of the Dumbarton Oaks proposals. First, they managed to reduce the likelihood that they would be forced to accept amendments to which they were opposed. The Dumbarton Oaks proposals provided that amendments to the UN Charter would come into force for all members of the organisation when they had been adopted by a vote of two-thirds of the General Assembly and ratified in accordance with their respective constitutional processes by all permanent members of the Security Council and by a majority of the other members of the Organisation. Under pressure from the little forty five, this ratification procedure was changed so that the concurring votes of "two thirds of the Members of the United Nations, including all the permanent members of the Security Council" (Article 108) would be required for an amendment to the Charter to pass. This slight modification was significant since it reduced the risk to lesser powers of being faced with the dilemma of choosing between accepting an amendment not ratified by them or withdrawing from the Organisation.[21]

Second, the little forty five were also successful in extracting concessions from the Big Five concerning the review of the UN Charter. The original proposal by the sponsoring governments provided that a decision fixing the date and place of a Charter-review conference should require a three-quarters majority of the General Assembly and the vote of any seven members of the Security Council. As a result of the opposition of the other delegations, the sponsoring governments eventually agreed to reduce the required majority in the General Assembly from three-quarters to two-thirds (Schwelb, 1954: 69). Thus amended, the proposal was enshrined in the Charter as Article 109.1.[22]

Third, although a proposal to the effect that a date for the Charter-review conference should be specified in the Charter did not receive the required two-thirds majority support, the Big Five made a further concession on this point. The United States proposed that a provision should be enshrined in the Charter to the effect that if a general review conference had not been held within ten years after the coming into force of the Charter, the proposal to call the conference would be placed on the

Agenda of the tenth session of the General Assembly. This, according to the representative of the United States, "fixed a definite time when the members of the General Assembly would have to face the question of calling a conference."[23] Furthermore, the US proposed that, on the occasion of the tenth General Assembly, the proposal to convene the general review conference would require only a simple majority of votes in the General Assembly (Schwelb, 1954: 70). The United States proposal subsequently became Article 109.3.[24] Thus, in an attempt by the Big Five to placate the disgruntled masses:

> Article 109 in its present form was adopted. While its function was supposed to be to break or to weaken the veto, its operation was subject to the veto. The protesting delegations were not unaware of this contradiction and finally agreed to the language of Article 109 either as the best possible compromise or in self-deception or in anticipation of a change of heart by the big powers by which they would be more willing to make concessions in ten years (Robinson, 1954: 317).

Although the little forty five were almost completely unsuccessful in preventing or even circumventing the privileges that the Big Five had granted themselves at Dumbarton Oaks and Yalta, they were, to a limited extent, successful in introducing some flexibility to the international organisation subsequently created. This flexibility mainly took the form of procedures for amending the Charter that were slightly more liberal than those anticipated by the great powers prior to San Francisco. Although an improvement on the Dumbarton Oaks/Yalta proposals, the extent of the flexibility introduced was not significant. The organisation created was a relatively rigid one. This fact led one participant to observe, prophetically, that:

> If by some quirk of fate, whether by internal revolution or by natural causes, one of the permanent members should lose its status as a great power, the problem before the Organization would be a difficult one. (There is also the possibility that other states may attain the status of great powers and thus merit permanent seats in the Security Council.) In such a case, if the state in question refused to accept an amendment to the Charter re-naming the permanent members, it might become necessary to dissolve the Organization and form a new one with a reorganized Security Council (Wilcox, 1945: 955).

Even at the birth of the UN, it was obvious to some that the organisation's overall rigidity would cause serious problems in the future.

The Nature of Security Council Flexibility

> Flexibility is the life blood that sustains and perpetuates constitutions (Gross, 1954: 216).

The UN Charter provides for its own amendment in Chapter XVIII which is composed of Articles 108 and 109. These articles specify the procedures to be followed in order to amend the text of the Charter. Since the composition and voting-procedure of the Security Council are regulated by Charter provisions (Articles 23-32), Articles 108 and 109 also regulate changes in the composition and voting procedure of the Security Council. In other words, these are the articles that regulate changes in the Security Council's hierarchy of influence.

Article 108 sets out the normal procedures to be followed in amending the text of the Charter. It specifies that, for amendments to be made, a two thirds majority in the General Assembly and the agreement of all permanent members of the Security Council is required.[25] Article 109, on the other hand, introduces two mechanisms - one of which is now obsolete - that are designed to facilitate the review of the Charter but undermines the effect of both mechanisms by making the ultimate decision to amend the Charter subject to the veto of the permanent members of the Security Council.

The first facilitating mechanism takes the form of a general conference for the purpose of reviewing the Charter. Article 109.1 protects both the decision to convene such a conference and the decision-making procedures to be used during such a conference from the veto power of permanent members of the Security Council. In order to convene a Charter-review conference, all that is needed is a two-thirds majority in both the General Assembly and the Security Council. This means that if the required majority is forthcoming from the General Assembly, a Charter review conference may be held even if all permanent members of the Security Council oppose it - provided, of course, that nine out of the ten non-permanent members support the convening of such a conference. Furthermore, all states participating in a Charter-review conference have one vote.[26]

The second facilitating mechanism, now obsolete, took the form of the automatic inclusion in the agenda of the tenth General Assembly, held in 1955, of a proposal to convene a Charter-review conference, the adoption of which required only a simple majority in the General Assembly and the agreement of any seven members of the Security Council.[27]

What Article 109, paragraphs 1 and 3, give in the form of

increased ease in amending the Charter, however, Article 109, paragraph 2, taketh away. Although it provides that recommendations to amend the Charter may be taken by a two thirds majority at the Charter-review conference, it subjects their ratification to the veto of the permanent members of the Security Council.[28] With regard to the ratification of amendments to the Charter, therefore, "[t]he differences between the procedures provided for in Articles 108 and 109 respectively are formal and not substantive. The requirements for the coming into force of amendments remain the same, whichever of the two procedures is chosen (Schwelb, 1958: 306).[29]

The function of Article 109, therefore, is to facilitate the initiation of the Charter amendment process. It provides relatively lenient prerequisites for the convening of a Charter-review conference and relaxed these prerequisites even more during the tenth General Assembly in 1955. Also, it provides for the principle of one-state-one-vote during such a conference. It does not, however, introduce more lenient procedures for the ratification of proposals to amend the Charter made at such a conference. Ultimate ratification remains subject to the veto of the permanent members of the Security Council.

Conclusion

During the final years of World War II and in the immediate post-war period, the United States, Britain and the Soviet Union collaborated in creating a hierarchy of influence to govern post-war international security. In the course of their negotiations in Moscow, Dumbarton Oaks and Yalta, they refined the institutional structure of this hierarchy and, along with France and China, installed themselves at its zenith. They created a hierarchically organised Security Council with the power to act on behalf of a multitude of states and assigned to themselves the right of permanent membership thereof. Furthermore, they assigned to themselves the exclusive right of veto over practically all the decisions of the Security Council.

The designers of the post-war security order were not overly concerned with the flexibility of the hierarchy of influence they created. They were more concerned with ensuring the permanence of their own positions within this hierarchy. In reducing the prerequisites for Charter amendment, however, the delegations of the lesser powers to the San Francisco conference were successful in slightly increasing the flexibility of the Security Council's hierarchy of influence. Nevertheless, this hierarchy remains extremely rigid mainly due to the ability of permanent members to protect their position therein through the use of their veto.

Notes

1. Fox (1944) first used the term "Superpower" to describe what he considered would be the most powerful states in the post-war international system.
2. An alternative view of the post-war distribution of power is presented by Louis Sohn (1944) who, in attempting to work out a system of weighted voting for a post-war General Assembly, listed the following states in decreasing order of power: The United States, India, China, the Soviet Union, Germany, the United Kingdom and France. Sohn, however, used pre-war figures for population, production and trade in order to deduce the post-war distribution of power and, in his calculations, did not consider the military capability variable. Furthermore, he attributed population size a weight equal to that of production and trade combined, on the assertion that "in a democratic world the value attached to the human factor should exceed the value given to other factors" (Sohn, 1944: 1194). The result is an analysis skewed in favour of states that were particularly powerful before the war—Germany—and that have particularly large populations—India and China.
3. The US favoured abstention in such a case, simply to prevent the spectacle of a great power sitting in judgement on its own case (Lee, 1947; Finkelstein, 1955) and the implications for the legitimacy of the organisation that such a spectacle would generate. The Soviet Union, on the other hand, was more concerned about preserving both the principle of great power unanimity and the principle of the non-coercion of superpowers, both of which would be jeopardised if the veto-power of a superpower were undermined in any way. Furthermore, "in view of suspicions, often voiced in Russia, that there were still powerful forces in the world bent upon encircling and destroying the Soviet Union, insistence upon unanimity among the Great Powers, under all circumstances, was a necessary safeguard against a powerful anti-Soviet coalition" (Lee, 1947: 37).
4. Britain and the United States had previously held a series of meetings on the island of Malta between January 30 and February 2 of the same year in order to prepare for their meeting with the Soviet Union at Yalta.
5. The decision to include China and France in the club that would lead the Security Council—despite the fact that their power was far inferior to that of the "Big Three"—was based on considerations of prestige, moral and political weight, and future potentialities in Europe and Asia respectively (Lee, 1947; Briggs, 1945). In 1945, France and China were considered "second-class members of the first-class group" (Fox, 1946: 116) and, in the years immediately following, many states continued to oppose their right of permanent membership (Finkelstein, 1955). Contrary to conventional wisdom, therefore, the composition of the first Security Council did not strictly correspond to the relative distribution of power in the immediate post-war period. Rather, it also tried to anticipate what the distribution of power would likely be in the foreseeable future.
6. Since 1946, two changes have occurred in permanent member representation on the Security Council: The Nationalist Chinese government ceded representation of the Chinese people to the Communist Chinese government in 1971 (Bailey, 1988: 150-157) and Russia took over the Soviet Union's permanent seat in 1992 (Blum, 1992).

Neither of these changes was accompanied by an amendment of Article 23.1.

7 Up until 1965, rather than following the prescriptions of Article 23.1, the pattern governing the election of non-permanent members conformed to the recommendations of the "Gentlemen's Agreement"—an oral pact made by the members of the Security Council meeting in London in 1946. Under the terms of the agreement, the permanent members undertook to support the election of the non-permanent members according to a specific regional distribution. Following the enlargement of the Security Council in 1965, the Gentlemen's Agreement was replaced by the provisions of the third operative paragraph of General Assembly Resolution 1991 (XVIII) which records the decisions of the General Assembly concerning the pattern according to which states shall be elected to the non-permanent seats of the enlarged Security Council.

8 Brazil held a non-permanent seat for 1951/52 and succeeded in being re-elected for 1954/55. Also, Turkey managed the same feat in the same years.

9 There are five such cases between 1946 and 1992: Brazil, 1963/64 and 1967/68; Colombia, 1953/54 and 1957/58; Italy, 1971/72 and 1975/76; Japan, 1971/72 and 1975/76; Panama, 1972/73 and 1976/77.

10 UNCIO, *Documents*, XI: 699-714. This statement came as a reply to 23 questions posed to the Big Five by a subcommittee of Committee III/1 at the San Francisco conference on May 22, 1945. The questions sought to clarify the situation concerning the application of the veto to situations of peaceful settlement of disputes in light of the inconsistent interpretation of the Yalta agreement by the Big Five Powers (Bentwich & Martin, 1969: 66).

11 For a list of issues that the Security Council has treated as procedural, see Bailey (1988: 199).

12 This stance experienced considerable opposition from other delegations at the San Francisco Conference. The Egyptian delegate, for instance, was of the opinion that the decision whether a point was procedural or not should be the prerogative of a commission of jurists (Lee, 1947).

13 For eight other examples of situations in which a vote was necessary in order to decide upon the classification of the preliminary question, see Bailey (1988: 216-223).

14 In 1946, for example, France denied the Syrian and Lebanese contention that the presence of British and French troops on their soil gave rise to serious disputes. Also, in 1951 France, Britain and the United States used the threat of veto to prevent Egypt from receiving an advisory opinion from the International Court of Justice as to whether the three permanent members would be required to abstain from voting on the issue of passage through the Suez Canal of ships carrying war materials to Israel. In 1976, despite the fact that the Comoros had complained of French aggression, France vetoed a Security Council resolution critical of French policy there. When Benin pointed out that France should have abstained from the vote, the president of the Council, the United States delegate, argued that it was "right and proper" for France to have taken part in the vote. When Argentine forces landed on the Falklands, Britain introduced and voted upon a proposal designed to bring hostilities to an end and to force the withdrawal of Argentine forces, despite the fact that Panama argued that Britain should not be allowed to vote on its own proposal (Bailey, 1988: 224-231).

15 The powers granted to the permanent members of the Security Council by Article 106 were meant to apply only to the immediate post-war period. However, according to the Charter, the content of Article 106 is valid "[p]ending the coming into force of such special agreements referred to in Article 43 as in the opinion of the Security Council enable it to begin the exercise of its responsibilities under Article 42..." (Article 106). Seeing as Article 43 has never been complied with, however, the provisions of Article 106, including the right of permanent members to act in concert on behalf of the entire UN membership, remain current.

16 With regard to the specific powers of the Security Council, it may call upon parties to settle their disputes by peaceful means (Article 33.2), investigate any dispute or situation which may lead to friction or give rise to a dispute (Article 34) or recommend procedures or methods of adjustment of such disputes or situations (Article 36). If parties to a dispute fail to settle it, they are obliged under Article 37.1 to refer it to the Security Council which may then recommend methods or terms of settlement (Article 37.2).

17 At the San Francisco conference, commission III dealt with the Security Council. Committee III/1 dealt with the structure and procedures thereof. For an outline of the organisation of negotiations at San Francisco, see Eagleton (1945: 935-936).

18 France, not having been involved in the drafting of the Dumbarton Oaks/Yalta proposals and having been itself drafted to the 'Superpower' group only as late as at the San Francisco Conference itself, tabled "several distinctively French" proposals for amendment of the Dumbarton Oaks/Yalta formula (Fox, 1946: 123).

19 Wilcox (1945: 954) recounts how at the San Francisco Conference, "Senator Connally [United States] dramatically tore up a copy of the charter during one of his speeches and reminded the small states that they would be guilty of that same act if they opposed the unanimity principle. 'You may, if you wish,' he said, 'go home from this Conference and say that you have defeated the veto. But what will be your answer when you are asked: 'Where is the Charter?'."

20 With regard to the Dumbarton Oaks/Yalta voting formula, the Big Five conceded ground on only a single point; that concerning the right of a permanent member to veto the discussion of a dispute or situation brought to the attention of the Security Council. The Soviet Union grudgingly agreed not to insist on this right only after the matter had been cleared with Stalin in Moscow. This point was subsequently re-iterated in The Statement which granted that "no individual member of the [Security] Council can alone prevent consideration and discussion by the Council of a dispute or situation brought to its attention under paragraph 2, Section A, Chapter VIII [Article 35]. Nor can parties to such dispute be prevented by these means from being heard by the Council (The Statement, Cl. I.3).

21 For further discussion on this particular amendment to the Dumbarton Oaks proposals, see Schwelb (1954: 69). See also "Report of the Rapporteur of Committee I/2 on Chapter XI (Amendments)," UNCIO, Documents, Vol. vii: 461 ff.

22 Article 109.1 reads: "A General Conference of the Members of the United Nations for the purpose of reviewing the present Charter may be held at a date and place to be fixed by a two-thirds vote of the members of the General Assembly and by a vote of any nine [formerly "seven"] members of the Security Council. Each Member of the United Nations shall have one vote in the conference."

23 UNCIO Documents, VII: 411.

24 Article 109.3 reads: "If such a [general review] conference has not been held before the tenth annual session of the General Assembly following the coming into force of the present Charter, the proposal to call such a conference shall be placed on the agenda of that session of the General Assembly, and the conference shall be held if so decided by a majority vote of the members of the General Assembly and by a vote of any seven members of the Security Council."

25 Article 108 reads: "Amendments to the present Charter shall come into force for all Members of the United Nations when they have been adopted by a vote of two thirds of the members of the General Assembly and ratified in accordance with their respective constitutional processes by two thirds of the Members of United Nations, including all the permanent members of the Security Council."

26 Article 109.1 reads: "A General Conference of the Members of the United Nations for the purpose of reviewing the present Charter may be held at a date and place to be fixed by a two-thirds vote of the members of the General Assembly and by a vote of any nine [originally "seven"] members of the Security Council. Each member of the United Nations shall have one vote in the conference."

27 Article 109.3 reads: "If such a conference has not been held before the tenth annual session of the General Assembly following the coming into force of the present Charter, the proposal to call such a conference shall be placed on the agenda of that session of the General Assembly, and the conference shall be held if so decided by a majority vote of the members of the General Assembly and by a vote of any seven members of the Security Council."

   Article 109.3 has never been amended nor has it been deleted from the Charter despite the fact that it refers in its entirety to the tenth General Assembly, held in 1955. The word "seven" in this Article—changed to the word "nine" in all other articles relating to voting procedure in the Security Council—as well as the entire article itself, are retained for historical purposes. For a detailed discussion of the points of legal interest concerning Article 109.3, see Schwelb (1966: 375-377).

28 Article 109.2 reads: "Any alteration of the present Charter recommended by a two-thirds vote of the conference shall take effect when ratified in accordance with their respective constitutional processes by two thirds of the Members of the United Nations including all the permanent members of the Security Council."

29 This view is widely held despite the fact that it has been questioned on occasion. For example, Robinson (1954) has questioned whether the ratification procedure provided in Article 109.2 applies to amendments proposed by the General Review Conference under Article 109.3. He bases his argument on the order of the respective articles in the Charter and asserts that there would be much less ambiguity on this question were the order of the aforementioned paragraphs to have been reversed. For further examples of alternative interpretations of the ratification procedure for amendments of the Charter, see Finkelstein (1955).

6 The 1965 Reform of the UN Security Council

Introduction

On August 31, 1965, the UN Security Council underwent its first and only reform. The number of non-permanent members of the Council was increased from six to ten. As a result, non-permanent members as a group gained two new powers - the ability to pass procedural resolutions without the assistance of permanent members and the ability to force permanent members opposed to substantive resolutions to cast at least one veto in order to defeat them.

The impulse for the 1965 reform did, however, not stem from the desire to alter the Security Council's hierarchy of influence. No state openly expressed its aspiration for a permanent seat or the opinion that a permanent member should be demoted. Instead, the impulse for reform stemmed both from a desire to increase the legitimacy of the Security Council in light of the large increase in UN membership that occurred after 1955 and the coming into force of the provisions of Article 109.3 concerning the convening of a Charter-review conference. Furthermore, as this chapter will show, the reform also did not result in the alteration of the Security Council's hierarchy of influence.

For this reason, the 1965 reform of the Security Council has little theoretical significance for the present study. Nevertheless, it is an interesting case study that nicely compliments the examination of the current reform debate to be presented in chapter 7. First, it clearly indicates the considerable obstacles that stand in the way of initiating the Charter-amendment process in the United Nations. Second, it provides a useful insight into the decision-making procedures associated with amending the Charter. Finally, it highlights the pivotal role that permanent members of the Security Council play not only in the ratification of Charter amendments but also in the initiation of the reform process. The following brief account of the background, process, and content of the 1965 reform is also included in the interest of completeness and for the information of readers interested in the process of Security Council reform in general.

The Prelude to Reform

Charter amendment was an ever-present theme during the early years of the UN's existence. Between the first session of the General Assembly in 1946 and its tenth session in 1956, proposals to amend the Charter - Article 108 - and to hold a general conference to review the Charter - Article 109 - were repeatedly, but unsuccessfully, submitted to the General Assembly (Schwelb, 1965).

After 1955, a serious debate developed concerning the need to increase the membership of the principal UN organs - the Security Council included. This debate was generated by two simultaneous but distinct impulses; one geographic and one constitutional. The geographic impulse for reform was generated by the admission to the United Nations of over twenty new members between 1955 and 1957. The constitutional impulse, on the other hand, stemmed from the Charter provision which included in the Agenda of the tenth General Assembly a proposal to convene a Charter-review conference. The reform campaigns that accompanied these impulses were also guided by the principles of separate Charter Articles - the former campaign taking place under Article 108 and the latter under Article 109. Although the impulses and guiding principles were different, these two reform campaigns were mutually reinforcing and eventually resulted in the first reform of the membership of the Security Council.

The Geographic Impulse for Reform; Article 108

In the early years of the United Nations, deliberations in the Security Council were characterised by intense antagonism between East and West, a significant amount of which centred upon the admission of new members to the UN organisation. Because of the desire of each Superpower bloc to prevent the admission of states allied or associated with the other, no state joined the UN between September 1950 and December 1955.[1] On 14 December, 1955, however, the members of the Security Council agreed upon a "package deal" by which a total of sixteen countries - six Western European, four Communist, and six Afro-Asian - were granted membership together. By 1957, a further six countries had joined. The majority of new members admitted during this time were from South America and Africa.

As a result of the initial dramatic increase in membership in 1955, seventeen Latin American states and Spain proposed to the tenth General Assembly to include in the agenda of the eleventh General Assembly a proposal to increase the membership of the UN's major organs.[2] These states sought to update the membership of these organs in order to make them representative of the UN's enlarged membership and to make their decision-making processes accessible to new members (Schwelb, 1958).

In the course of the eleventh General Assembly in 1956, nineteen Latin American States and Spain introduced draft resolution A/3446 - "The Twenty Power Proposal" - which called for amendments to Articles 23 and 27; i.e., to those articles that provide for the composition and voting procedure of the Security Council, respectively. Specifically, it proposed increasing the number of non-permanent members from six to eight and, without addressing "the grave and thorny question of the veto,"[3] proposed increasing the number of affirmative votes needed to take decisions from seven to eight.

The discussion of the Twenty Power Proposal in the General Assembly revealed that "there was no opposition in principle to an increase in the membership of the Security Council and that there was general agreement about the desirability of such increase [sic.], although some delegations considered the proposed addition of two members as insufficient" (Schwelb, 1958: 316). However, despite its seemingly widespread support, acceptance of the Twenty Power Proposal was seriously hindered by the Soviet Union and its allies who made their support of the proposal conditional on two points: First, that eastern Europe would be guaranteed representation on an enlarged Council and, second, that the question of Chinese representation on the Council would be resolved before the Charter was amended.

The Soviet Union and its allies had long complained that Eastern Europe had not been given the representation on the Security Council to which it was entitled under the principle of equitable geographical distribution set out in Article 23.1 and under the terms of the "Gentlemen's Agreement" (Schwelb, 1958) reached by the members of the Security Council meeting in London in 1946.[4] Soviet dissatisfaction with the distribution of non-permanent seats stemmed from the fact that, from 1950 onward, the Eastern European seat on the Security Council had been allocated on purely geographical rather than political grounds, leaving the Soviet Union without allies on the Council. Yugoslavia, Turkey, Greece and even Asian countries such as the Philippines and Japan had been elected to the Security Council to fill this seat (Hiscocks, 1973: 71). The Soviet Union's need for dependable allies on the Council was heightened by the fact that the United States could normally depend on the support of at least seven of the eleven members of the Council (ibid.).

The Soviet Union also made its support of the Twenty Power

Proposal dependent on the admission to the United Nations, and to the Security Council in particular, of the representatives of the Chinese Communist Government and the expulsion of those of the Chinese Nationalist Government. It began to lodge complaints about the representation of China in the autumn of 1949 when the United States refused to recognise the Chinese Communist Government and to admit its representatives to the UN. The Soviet Union was so vehement in its objection to this state of affairs that its representative walked out of the Security Council on 13 January 1950 and did not return to take part in the Council's deliberations for over five weeks (Hiscocks, 1973: 68-70).

The sponsors of the draft resolution could do little to fulfil the Soviet Union's demand regarding China. With regard to its demand regarding Eastern European representation on the Council, however, nineteen of the original twenty sponsors tabled an amendment to the draft resolution that would reserve one seat on the Security Council for an Eastern European State.[5] This proposed amendment aroused vehement opposition, however, from Asian and African delegations who argued that the distribution of the non-permanent seats on an enlarged Security Council would discriminate against Asia and Africa.[6] This opposition made it highly unlikely that the resolution would be adopted by the two-thirds majority required by Article 108.

Instead, sixteen Asian and African states proposed an alternative draft resolution that reiterated the desirability of increasing the membership of the Security Council and proposed the appointment of a fifteen-member committee to study the question in detail.[7] In the end, however, neither the Latin American/Spanish nor the African/Asian draft resolutions were put to a vote. Subsequently, in February 1957, the President of the General Assembly was advised by UN members to postpone the question of enlarging the membership of the UN's main organs until the twelfth General Assembly in 1957. There was no objection to the postponement.

The twelfth General Assembly decided to further postpone the question until its thirteenth session in 1958.[8] Central to this decision was the widespread recognition that the Soviet Union would not support the amendment of the Charter before the question of Chinese representation had been resolved. Most states reasoned that it would be pointless to push for a General Assembly resolution on Charter amendment when it was almost certain to be vetoed by the Soviet Union.[9]

The thirteenth General Assembly in 1958 postponed the question of Charter amendment to the fourteenth session.[10] Likewise, the fourteenth General Assembly in 1959 postponed it to its fifteenth session[11] despite the fact that a great majority of UN members favoured an increase in the number of non-permanent members of the Security Council (Schwelb, 1960: 242). However, the resolution passed by the fourteenth General Assembly specified that:

> If progress is not made during the fifteenth session of the General Assembly towards the achievement of an increase in the membership of the Security Council and of the Economic and Social Council, the Assembly should set up at that session a committee to study the possibilities of arriving at an agreement which will facilitate the amendment of the Charter to achieve the increase in membership referred to above (G.A. Res. 1404 (XIV)).

At the fifteenth General Assembly, a special political committee again grappled with the question of enlargement of the Security Council and of the ECOSOC, this time against the background of an "involved political situation and... acrimonious debate" (Schwelb, 1965: 837). Although the issue was for the first time put to a vote in the political committee, no results were achieved. After many attempts at amending the draft resolution under consideration, the committee ultimately found itself with no recommendations to make to the General Assembly. After four postponements, much involved debate and the frustrated and acrimonious atmosphere of the fifteenth General Assembly, the proposal to amend the Charter under Article 108 in order, among other things, to increase the membership of the Security Council finally ran out of steam. No other serious attempt was made to increase the membership of the Council under Article 108 until the eighteenth General Assembly in 1963.

The Constitutional Impulse for Reform; Article 109

In accordance with the provision of Article 109.3, a proposal to convene a Charter-review conference was included, ipso jure, in the Agenda of the tenth General Assembly. After considering the point in six plenary meetings, the General Assembly passed a resolution at the end of November, 1955,[12] underlining the need to review the Charter but postponing such a review until appropriate "auspicious international circumstances" should present themselves. Furthermore, the resolution established a committee - consisting of all UN members - that, in consultation with the Secretary General, was given the task of deciding upon a time and a place for a Charter-review conference and of reporting back to the twelfth General Assembly.

This resolution represented a compromise between three sets of countries: First, the United States and others saw the convening of a Charter-review conference as a matter of obligation. Second, Britain, Canada, New Zealand and others believed that a review of the Charter should only take place under "auspicious international circumstances." They preferred a more cautious approach, fearing that a failed attempt to amend the Charter could exacerbate differences of opinion among the permanent members of the Security Council. Third, the Scandinavian countries, Yugoslavia, India and others believed that differences of opinion among the permanent members on the issue of a Charter-review conference were so great that no decision to convene one should be taken at the tenth General Assembly (Schwelb, 1958). The Soviet Union, for one, had made it abundantly clear that it would not support any recommendations to review the Charter made at such a conference. In its opinion, the Charter was "fully satisfactory as an instrument reflecting the vital interests and aspirations of the peoples and did not require any alterations" (Schwelb, 1958: 309).

The Assembly's resolution was submitted to the Security Council which passed its own resolution on December 16 in which it expressed its "concurrence in the Assembly's decision..."[13] In voting on this resolution, the Security Council followed the special procedure set out in Article 109.3 which is immune to veto power. The resolution was adopted by nine votes in favour, one against (the Soviet Union) and one abstention (France). For the first time, the dissenting vote of a permanent member was not enough to prevent a decision being taken by the Security Council.

The Charter-review committee created by the General Assembly resolution - the "Committee on arrangements for a Conference for the purpose of reviewing the Charter" (hereafter the Committee on Arrangements) - was threatened by boycott by the Soviet Union, who had voted against its creation both in the General Assembly and in the Security Council. The Soviet Union did eventually take part in the deliberations of the Committee on Arrangements but abstained from voting on its recommendations (Schwelb, 1958).

When the committee convened to report to the twelfth General Assembly in 1957, there was general agreement that the "auspicious international circumstances" referred to in the original resolution had not materialised. The Committee recommended to the General Assembly that it be kept in operation and be allowed to report once again not later than at the fourteenth General Assembly in 1959. The recommendation of the committee was accepted by the Assembly.[14]

When the Committee on Arrangements convened again to report to the fourteenth General Assembly in September 1959, it repeated the recommendations it had previously made and asked to be given the opportunity to report again to the sixteenth General Assembly in 1961. The majority of the members of the Committee, while recognising the merits of reviewing the Charter in light of the political, economic and social changes that had occurred since 1945, did not think that the time was ripe for such a review (Schwelb, 1960). The General Assembly again accepted the committee's proposal.[15] At the routine committee sessions held in 1961 and 1962, no serious attempts were made to decide on a date for convening a Charter-review conference.

A major breakthrough was achieved, however, at the Assembly's eighteenth session in 1963. Before examining the reasons for this breakthrough, however, it is necessary to outline briefly the nature of the opposition to Charter amendment that existed up until 1963.

Soviet Opposition to Charter Amendment

Up until now, attempts to amend the Charter under Articles 108 and 109 have been examined separately in the interests of analytic clarity. In order to understand the general failure to initiate the Charter reform procedure under both of these Articles, however, it will be necessary from now on to consider both reform processes together.

The General Assembly's reluctance to initiate procedures that could have led to Charter amendment can be explained by the Soviet bloc's open opposition to amending the Charter. The Soviet Union and its allies indicated their opposition to Charter amendment when the Committee on Arrangement was first established at the tenth General Assembly. They even opposed the convening of a Charter-review conference, the recommendations of which would have been subject, in any case, to the Soviet veto. Nevertheless, the resolution which established the Committee on Arrangements, was adopted by a two-thirds majority of the then sixty members of the General Assembly. Furthermore, the Security Council concurred with the Assembly's decision against the dissenting vote of the Soviet Union.

At the eleventh General Assembly's in 1956 - the first to deal seriously with Charter amendment under Article 108 - the Soviet Union clearly indicated the main reason for its opposition to Charter amendment; namely, the absence from the UN of the government of the People's Republic of China. According the Soviet UN ambassador:

> It would be a flagrant and unthinkable violation of the Purposes and Principles of the Charter to engage in any discussion of the question [of

amending the Charter] so long as 600 million Chinese people were not represented in the United Nations and the lawful representative of the Chinese people was denied the right to his seat in the Organization. [...] ...the Soviet Union would never ratify amendments to the Charter which were adopted without the participation of the People's Republic of China.[16]

The reaction of the general UN membership to the Soviet opposition to Charter amendment took two forms. First, many states believed that it was pointless to pursue a General Assembly resolution in support of increasing the membership of the principal UN organs if the Soviet Union had promised to veto such a resolution. Second, many states thought it a bad idea to force the Security Council into a situation in which one of the two most powerful permanent members would be forced to cast a veto on the delicate question of Chinese representation in the United Nations. Although the former belief centres on the futility of supporting a resolution that is bound to fail and the latter focuses on the importance of keeping Security Council tension at a minimum, both were based on the credibility of Soviet opposition to Charter amendment.[17]

The Reversal of the Soviet Position

Soviet and eastern-European opposition to Charter amendment held firm from 1955 to 1962 after which it began to wain under severe pressure from the general UN membership. At the Assembly's eighteenth session in 1963, a survey of UN members conducted by the Committee on Arrangements revealed that a large majority of UN members supported an increase in membership of both the Security Council and the Economic and Social Council.[18] Furthermore, in an independent move, a large number of Asian and African delegations proposed the inclusion in the agenda of the General Assembly an item concerning the "Question of equitable representation on the Security Council and the Economic and Social Council" (Schwelb, 1965: 840).[19] The fact that the Soviet Union continued to categorically oppose Charter amendment against the general will of the General Assembly significantly increased the acrimony of the eighteenth Assembly.

The African states were the first to call the Soviet bluff in the eighteenth General Assembly by openly questioning the seriousness of the Soviet intention to veto any proposal to amend the Charter in order to increase the membership of principal UN organs. The representative of Guinea implied that the government of the Chinese People's Republic considered its representation on the Security Council and the amendment of the Charter to be separate, unconnected issues[20] while the representative of Albania questioned the validity of the Soviet Union's use of the Chinese case as a justification of its own position.[21] The representative of Albania further accused the Soviet delegation of misquoting Chinese sources in order to mislead the Assembly, thereby making it seem as if the Communist Chinese government held a stance that, in fact, it did not hold (Schwelb, 1965: 843).[22] Since Albania acted as a spokesperson for mainland China in the United Nations in the years preceding 1963, the weight of this intervention was very significant.

As a result of this direct attack on the Soviet position, attention in the last days of the Assembly turned away from the intransigence of the Soviet position and towards the actual content of the Charter amendments to be adopted. As a consequence of the collusion of Latin American, African and Asian states, a resolution was tabled to increase the membership of the Economic and Social Council from eighteen to twenty-seven and the membership of the Security Council from eleven to fifteen. These proposed increases were greater than those envisaged in earlier draft proposals - the numbers usually discussed were twenty-four and thirteen respectively. The fact they were agreed upon so quickly by so many states put the representatives of the western powers in a difficult position: Some representatives had been authorised to support an amendment of the Charter, but only in order to facilitate more modest membership increases. All representatives were faced with very limited time at the end of the eighteenth General Assembly in order to consider the new proposals.

The resolution concerning the increase in membership of the Security Council was ultimately adopted by the General Assembly by 97 votes to 11 with 4 abstentions, the large majority being attributable to the support of the sponsoring states - the Latin-American, African and Asian blocs.[23] Shortly after the adoption of the resolution by the General Assembly, the Soviet delegation issued a lengthy statement in which it agreed to support the proposed amendments to the Charter if the government of the People's Republic of China expressed support for the amendments.[24] The Soviet Union explained further that, had the government of the Chinese People's Republic made it clear during the earlier debates that it did not oppose Charter amendment in order to increase the membership of the principal UN organs, the Soviet delegation would have voted in favour of Charter amendment all along (Schwelb, 1965).

The Soviet statement marked the beginning of a policy u-turn on the question of Charter amendment. From being the only vehement opponent to any Charter amendment - as well as the reason why many other states opposed passing an amendment resolution - the Soviet Union became the new champion of Charter amendment. By the end of 1964, the Supreme Soviet of the USSR had ratified the Charter amendments as required under Article 108 and, on December 18, called upon the other Great Powers to follow its example. On February 10, 1965, the Soviet Union deposited its instrument of ratification; it was the first of the permanent members to do so. The United States was the last of the permanent members to deposit its instrument of ratification and, since more than two-thirds of the members of the United Nations had submitted their instruments of ratification before the United States, the date of the latter's deposit is also the date on which the amendments to the Charter came into force - August 31, 1965, one day before the deadline specified in the original General Assembly resolution.[25]

Content of the 1965 Reform

The 1965 reform of the membership of the Security Council and the Economic and Social Council necessitated the first ever textual amendment of the San Francisco Charter.[26] In increasing the number of non-permanent members from six to ten, the reform had a slight effect on the balance of decision-making power within the Security Council.

Before the reform, non-permanent members of the Security Council could not pass even procedural resolutions without the assistance of at least one permanent member - seven votes were required to pass such a resolution and there were only six non-permanent members. When it came to passing substantive resolutions, non-permanent members were doubly disadvantaged: Permanent members could individually block substantive resolutions by casting a veto or could collectively block them by agreeing to abstain from voting.[27] Non-permanent members, therefore, could not force a permanent member opposed to a substantive resolution to cast its veto if all other permanent members agreed to abstain from voting. Abstention, as well as the veto, was a powerful tool for permanent members.

After the reform, the number of votes required to pass a procedural resolution was increased from seven to nine. Since the number of non-permanent members was increased from six to ten, non-permanent members gained the ability to pass procedural resolutions without the assistance of permanent members. Furthermore, they gained the ability to force permanent members opposed to substantive resolutions to cast at least one veto in order to defeat them. It became no longer technically feasible for permanent members opposed to a substantive resolution to collectively abstain from voting. In such a case, non-permanent members could pass substantive resolution on their own. In sum, the 1965 reform of the Security Council gave non-permanent members the ability to pass procedural resolutions on their own and undermined the utility of abstention as an option for permanent members.

The procedure to be followed when electing non-permanent members was not changed by the reform. However, the Gentlemen's Agreement which had governed the geographical distribution of non-permanent members between 1946 and 1964 was replaced by the third operative paragraph of the reform resolution. The term of office of non-permanent members was also not changed by the reform. However, the transitional provision of the San Francisco text that "[i]n the first election of the non-permanent members however, three shall be chosen for a term of one year" (Article 23.2),[28] was replaced with another transitional provision to the effect that "[i]n the first election of the non-permanent members after the increase of the membership of the Security Council from eleven to fifteen, two of the four additional members shall be chosen for a term of one year" (Article 23.2).

Conclusion

The impulse behind the 1965 reform of the Security Council did not stem from a desire to alter the hierarchy of influence in the Security Council. No state aspired to permanent membership nor demanded that a permanent member be demoted. Rather, the impulse for reform stemmed from two mutually reinforcing factors - the large increase in UN membership after 1955 and the coming into force of the provisions of Article 109.3 concerning the convening of a Charter-amendment conference.

Nor did the 1965 reform result in the alteration of the Security Council's hierarchy of influence. The additional powers gained by non-permanent members were technical, not practical. Although they gained the ability to pass procedural resolutions without the assistance of permanent members, their ability to do so remained subject to the decision whether to classify decisions as procedural or substantive - a decision that is subject to the veto of permanent members. Although they gained the ability to force a permanent member to cast a veto, in practice they always had this power since it never occurred that all permanent members reached agreement to abstain from voting on a substantive resolution.

Nevertheless, the reform process tentatively initiated on

November 21, 1955 and brought to a conclusion on August 31, 1965 clearly illustrates the significant difficulties associated with amending the UN Charter, even when a majority of member-states support reform. Above all, it underlines the significant influence that permanent members exert on the reform process, not only during the ratification stage, when permanent members may use their veto, but also during the initial stages, when the veto does not directly apply.

Notes

1 Article 4.2 grants the permanent members of the Security Council a veto over the decision to admit new states. It reads: "The admission of any... state to membership in the United Nations will be effected by a decision of the General Assembly upon the recommendation of the Security Council."

2 The Security Council, the Economic and Social Council, and the International Court of Justice.

3 UN Doc. A/PV.620, paragraph 100 (Schwelb, 1958: 315).

4 Under the terms of the Gentlemen's Agreement, the permanent members undertook to support the election by the General Assembly of the non-permanent members of the Council according to the following regional distribution: Latin America, 2 seats; British Commonwealth, 1 seat; Middle East, 1 seat; Western Europe, 1 seat and Eastern Europe, 1 seat.

5 The proposed allocation was as follows: "Latin-America, two seats; Asia and Africa, two seats; the Commonwealth of Nations, one seat; Western and Southern Europe, two seats; Eastern Europe, one seat" (A/L.217/Rev.1).

6 The representative of India, for example, expressed the hope that "no country from his part of the world would cast its vote in favour of a draft resolution which would lower the dignity and self-respect of their peoples" (Schwelb, 1958: 317).

7 A/3468/Rev.1

8 GA Res. 1190(XII) of December 12, 1957.

9 See UN Doc. A/SPC/SR.74 in which the representative of India expressed the view that "there was no point in dealing with the items [to increase the membership of the Security Council and of ECOSOC] until it was fairly certain that the permanent members of the Security Council would agree to the proposals." See also Schwelb (1960: 248-249) for a discussion of the legal role of the permanent members of the Security Council in the General Assembly phase of the Charter amendment procedure.

10 GA Res. 1299 (XIII) of December 10, 1958.

11 GA Res. 1404 (XIV) of November 25, 1959.

12 GA Res. 992 (X) of November 21, 1955.

13 UN Doc. S/3504.

14 GA Res. 1136 (XII) of October 14, 1957.

15 GA Res. 1381 (XIV) of November 20, 1959.

16 UN Doc. A/SPC/SR.197, paragraphs 14 and 17.

17 Neither of these reasons for opposing the initiation of procedures to amend the Charter are based in law, however, since "the privileged role of the permanent members of the Security Council comes into play only in the ratification phase of the amending process" (Schwelb, 1960: 248). However, the reluctance to initiate such procedures is understandable seeing as "the requirement of ratification of an amendment by all the permanent members of the Security council does, in fact, cast its shadow upon the initial and deliberative stages of the process" (ibid.). It was argued in vain, especially by the representative of Nationalist China, that it was "putting the cart before the horse to say that the consent of all the permanent Members of the Security Council had to be obtained before the General Assembly could adopt an amendment to the Charter" (Schwelb, 1965: 836; see also UN Doc. A/SPC/SR.137, par. 31 (1959)).

18 Report of the Committee on Arrangements, UN General Assembly, 18th Session, Official Records, Annexes, Agenda Item No. 21 (A/5487).

19 See also Letter of September 16, 1963 (UN Doc. A/5520, 1963).

20 UN Doc. A/SPC/SR.423, par. 47 (1963).

21 UN Doc. A/SPC/SR.428, paragraphs 21 et seq. (1963).

22 The Albanian representative went on to quote a report published by the Chinese news agency Hsinhua, which accused the Soviet representative of having misrepresented the Chinese position for its own motives and of having spread the erroneous impression that the Communist Chinese government did not support the push for Charter amendment of the African and Asian blocs (Schwelb, 1965: 843).

23 GA Res. 1991 (XVIII) A, of December 17, 1963.

24 The statement was dated December 21, 1963, and was transmitted to the Secretary General along with a letter dated December 23, 1963, UN Doc. A/5686 (1963).

25 For an examination of the implications of the late ratification of a resolution, see Schwelb (1965: 849).

26 According to US Secretary of State Rusk, "this is enough by itself to endow the event with considerable significance" (Hearings on United Nations Charter Amendments Before the Senate Committee on Foreign Relations, 89th Cong., 1st Session: 9. From Schwelb, 1965: 835).

27 A strict interpretation of Article 27.3—which calls for "the concurring votes of the permanent members"—would require that all permanent members cast a positive vote in order for a substantive resolution to be adopted. In practice, however, this Article has been interpreted much more loosely. The representative of the Soviet Union set the precedent in this matter when, in a vote on a substantive resolution in April 1946, he abstained from voting, explaining that his decision was motivated by his dislike for the resolution. He added, however, that a further motivation for his action lay in the fact that he did not want to prevent the resolution being passed by casting a negative vote. Although the Soviet representative stated that he did not want his action to be taken as a precedent, it has subsequently been treated as such (Hiscocks, 1973: 89).

28 "This transitional provision has, of course, been of only historic interest since 1947. It was, to use the terminology of the International Law Commission, 'terminated through the operation of its own provision'" (Schwelb, 1965: 846-847).

7 Positionality, Tension and Instability in the UN Security Council

> If ... the Security Council emerges as defender or apologist for the status-quo, it will become the agent of the disorder it strives to avoid (Fromuth, 1993: 365-66).

Introduction

UN member states are currently engaged in a debate on Security Council reform that, in contrast to the debate of the early 1960s, goes far beyond the question of simply increasing the Council's non-permanent membership. At stake in the current debate is the question of permanent membership and whether, and to whom, it should be extended. For this reason, the current Security Council reform debate is of great theoretical significance for this study. Although the debate is far from over, an examination of how the UN organisation deals with contemporary calls for fundamental reform of the Security Council serves to answer an important question: How well does the Security Council adapt to shifts in the relative power of UN members? In other words, how stable an institution of international governance is the UN Security Council?

In order to answer these questions, this chapter will apply the remaining hypotheses presented in chapter 3 to the current debate on Security Council reform. To this end, the chapter is divided into four parts. Parts one and two identify the presence of upward and downward positionality, respectively, in the context of the reform debate. Part three examines the extent of the tension generated by the interplay of these opposing positional tendencies. Finally, part four identifies the mechanisms that have been employed by the UN organisation in order to diffuse this tension and appraises their effectiveness.

Upward Positionality

Since the beginning of the 1990s, the Security Council has been the focus of especially strong upward positional forces. There are three main reasons for this, the first two of which concern the increased dissatisfaction of developing countries with the structure and membership of the Security Council and the last of which concerns the desire of Japan and Germany to play a bigger role in the Council's decision-making.

Dissatisfaction in the Developing World

First, between 1963 and 1998, UN membership has increased by almost 70 percent. Since most of these new members come from the developing world, this increase in membership has skewed even more the geographical distribution of representation on the Security Council in favour of western developed states. It has also made it more difficult for individual developing states to be elected to serve as non-permanent members of the Security Council. Finally, it has caused a relative decrease in the representation of the developed world in the UN in general and has, accordingly, led the developing world to demand stronger representation on the Security Council.

Second, the end of the Cold War has significantly contributed to the dissatisfaction of developing countries with the structure and membership of the Security Council. During the Cold War, developing countries did not have to worry that the Security Council could be used as an instrument against them by powerful industrialised states acting in concert. Cold war rivalries within the Council and their ramifications in certain regions of the Third World precluded this from happening. Since the end of the Cold War, however, rivalries within the Security Council have become less intense. The result has been a striking reduction in the use of the veto and a significant increase in decision-making capacity.

These developments have heightened the fear among developing countries that control of the Security Council has fallen into the hands of powerful northern states (Russet, O' Neill & Sutterlin, 1996; Wagner, 1993; Luck & Gati, 1992). A strong foundation for this fear was provided by the 1991 Gulf War during which "the West demonstrated its overwhelming military superiority over a 'Third World' country... and was able to do it with full legitimacy afforded by the UN Charter" (Ciechanski, 1994: 414). In order to wrest control of the Security Council from the relatively unified influence of the industrialised world and so protect itself from similar future occurrences, the developing world demands that the Council be reformed so as to make it more representative and legitimate.[1]

Dissatisfaction in Japan and Germany

Finally, differential growth in capabilities among states has generated a great deal of upward positionality in the UN. Since 1945, and even since 1965, the concentration of capabilities in individual states has tended to decline as capabilities have disseminated among a larger number of states. True, the most powerful states in the international system at the time of the Security Council's previous reform in 1965 remain, for the most part, the most powerful states but their power has declined relative to the power of other states in the system.

The permanent members of the Security Council constitute a good example of the effects of differential growth. The US is arguably still a hegemon in international affairs although the extent of its hegemony is considerably less than it was at the closing of the Second World War. This is due, inevitably, to the fact that its growth in capabilities has not outstripped that of the newly industrialised countries and the countries it defeated in that war. The United Kingdom and France suffered significant reductions in their international reach and influence as a result of the de-colonisation process. The Russian Federation now occupies the permanent seat once held by the bigger and more powerful Soviet Union. China is arguably the only permanent member to have maintained or improved upon its relative standing in international affairs since the founding of the United Nations.

On the other hand, certain other states have significantly improved their relative standing in international relations since 1945. The two most important states in this respect are Japan and Germany. Both countries have moved from defeat and devastation to build, respectively, the second- and third-largest economies in the world. Furthermore, Germany, through re-unification, has significantly added to its population and territory. As a result of the increase in their relative capabilities, both countries have clearly indicated that they aspire to permanent representation on the Security Council.

A Coalition of Dissatisfactions

The upward positionality generated by the developing world on the one hand and by Japan and Germany on the other would seem, at first glance, to be essentially incompatible. Developing countries in general do not wish to see increased representation for developed northern states on the Security Council and are seriously opposed to further European representation therein. Nevertheless, these two sources of dissatisfaction with the status-quo have combined to create a strong concerted push for reform with the dual aims, generally speaking, of permanent representation for Japan and Germany *and* greater representation for the developing south. This unlikely coalition of interests has formed due to the fact that, on the one hand, Japan and Germany need the support of the developing world if they are to succeed in becoming permanent members of the Security Council and, on the other, that developing countries need Japan and Germany to continue their campaigns in order that the debate on Security Council reform maintains its current momentum.

Why Japan and Germany Need the Developing World Japan and Germany have found it necessary, on the one hand, to court the developing world since without the support of a sizeable number of developing countries, neither has a chance of generating the two-thirds majority support necessary under Article 108 to amend the Charter in order to allow them to become permanent members of the Security Council. As a result, both Japan and Germany have incorporated within their respective campaigns for permanent membership the imperative of improving the representation of developing countries on the Council.

Japan initially envisaged that any reform that would grant it permanent membership should also allocate extra non-permanent seats to developing countries on the basis of geographical distribution (A/48/264: 54). Despite hinting on occasion that some permanent seats should also be made available to developing countries (JEI Report, 25.03.1994; Jiji Press, 09.06.1994), Japan preferred to advocate only an increase in non-permanent seats for developing countries. As Foreign Minister Koji Kakizawa put it in June of 1994, Japan and Germany were the only likely candidates for permanent membership since Brazil, Egypt, India and Nigeria, who had also been named as candidates, had failed to win majority support among UN members (Kyodo News Service, 15.06.1994).

Under concerted pressure from Brazil, Chile and Equador, however, Japan stepped up its support for developing country representation on the Security Council. First, the Japanese Foreign Ministry suggested a rotating seating system for the non-permanent membership which would provide easier access to a larger number of developing countries (Jiji Press, 05.09.1994). Subsequently, however, Japan expressed its outright support for extra permanent seats for developing countries. In February 1995, Japanese UN Ambassador, Hisashi Owada, explained that "it is the considered view of Japan that this new permanent membership could also include such qualified countries as may be selected by agreement from Asia, Africa and Latin America based on judgement of their capacity and willingness to assume global responsibilities" (Lau, 10.02.1995; see also Owada, 13.11.1995). The present Japanese position, therefore, does not reject the possibility that developing countries could also be added to the Security Council as permanent members (Interviews, New York).

Germany occupies a similar position on this issue. It sees its campaign for permanent membership in the context of a broader reform of the Security Council that would result in greater representation for the developing regions of the world. Foreign Minister Kinkel argued in 1993 that "we will only be able to maintain and strengthen the credibility of the Council... if, in deliberating on its reform, we also take into our consideration the growing importance of the Third World" (Agence France Presse, 27.09.1993) and has stated more recently that "wir setzen uns dafür ein, daß die Reform des Sicherheitsrats auch zu einer besseren Vertretung Asiens, Afrikas, Lateinamerikas und der Karibik führt" (Kinkel, 25.10.1995).

Like Japan, Germany supports granting permanent seats to an unspecified number of countries from the developing world. Its preferred reform solution is the so-called "two-plus" formula by which the permanent membership of the Security Council would be expanded to include Germany and Japan (two) and some other unspecified countries from Africa, Latin America, and Asia (plus) (Graf zu Rantzau, 13.10.1994). The so-called "quick fix" solution - granting permanent membership only to Germany and Japan - is not considered feasible by Germany since it estimates that such a reform proposal would never achieve the required majority in the General Assembly (Interviews, New York).

Why the Developing World Needs Japan and Germany The developing world needs Japan and Germany, on the other hand, because without their active involvement in the debate on Security Council reform, no progress on the matter is likely to be made and the debate is likely to lose its current momentum. A glance at the recent history of reform debate within the UN suffices to support this contention. The topic of Security Council reform re-emerged during the 34th General Assembly in 1980 but "lingered hopelessly for several years in General Assembly commissions" (Ciechanski, 1994: 414). In marked contrast, the beginning of the current, relatively dynamic, debate on Security Council reform coincided with indications by Japan and Germany in the early 1990s that both would pursue permanent membership.

Notwithstanding the provision of Article 108 that amendments to the Charter need the support of two-thirds of the UN membership, developing world dissatisfaction on its own is slow to move the UN organisation to reform. This has been made clear in the examination of the 1965 reform of the Security Council undertaken in chapter 6. Because any amendment proposal must also be ratified by all the permanent members of the Security Council, the UN general membership recognises the futility of tabling reform proposals that they know will not be supported by the P-5. In the current reform debate, however, the permanent members are more supportive of initiating reform for the purpose of securing the financial engagement of Japan and Germany than they are of reforming the Council for the sole purpose of increasing its legitimacy. Japan and Germany were the catalysts for, and continue to be the main engine of, the current reform process. Without their engagement, the debate would either never have reached its current stage or would have taken significantly longer to do so.

Who needs Whom Most? In pooling its dissatisfactions with the structure and membership of the Security Council with those of Germany and Japan, the developing world has had seriously to compromise its preferences. In effect, it has had to support the increased representation on the Security Council of industrialised countries of the North as well as the addition of yet another European permanent member - preferences that are anathema to developing countries under normal conditions. In supporting the increased representation of developing regions on the Security Council, on the other hand, Japan and Germany have not had to compromise as much. Even advocating permanent seats for developing countries does not greatly impinge upon the declared aims of either country.

This demonstrates that the upward positional forces exerted by Japan and Germany constitute the main engine driving the reform debate and that the dissatisfaction of the developing world, while being important in its own right, is not essential to the continuation of the reform process. A few hypothetical examples serve to illustrate this point: If Japan and Germany were to declare that they no longer aspired to permanent seats on the Security Council, the current reform process would most likely grind to a halt since dissatisfaction of developing countries, no matter how great, is not a sufficient condition for the maintenance of the reform debate at its present level. If, on the other hand, the developing world were suddenly to decide that it was satisfied with its representation on the Security Council, the reform process would most likely continue since the aspirations of Japan and Germany carry sufficient weight to maintain the reform debate. While neither of these things is likely to happen, the hypothetical examples illustrate that the developing world needs Japan and Germany more than Japan and Germany need the developing world.

The German and Japanese Campaigns for Permanent Membership

The permanent membership campaigns conducted by Japan and Germany have been aimed at winning support from both the general UN membership and the five permanent members of the Security Council. Different, and not altogether compatible, strategies have been used in each case. To win the support of the general UN membership, on the one hand, both countries have been careful to communicate their desire for permanent representation on the Security Council in ways that avoid the perception that they are conducting independent, aggressive campaigns. This strategy has involved relying on the solicitation of other states and on playing down the military responsibility normally associated with permanent membership.

To win the support of the permanent members of the Security Council, on the other hand, Japan and Germany have taken steps towards bolstering their international military responsibility. By doing so, they have attempted to deflect the complaints of some permanent members that constitutional barriers against foreign troop deployments in place in both countries would make them privileged permanent members of the Security Council insofar as they would enjoy strong decision-making influence without playing a corresponding role in international military affairs.

Communicating Intent and Generating Support Japan's campaign for permanent membership began relatively recently and in heavily muted tones. One of the first clear indications that Japan was seriously considering permanent membership came at a dinner for US president Bush held in Tokyo on January 8, 1992. Japanese Prime Minister Miyazawa stated then that "the days are gone when the question of world peace and stability could be left in the hands of the superpowers. The building of a new international order is calling on each country benefiting from such order to make a contribution befitting its national strength and characteristics" (Mc Carthy, 10.01.1992).[2] Later in the same month, at the first ever UN Security Council summit meeting in New York, Miyazawa called for an overhaul of "the functions, composition, and other aspects [of the UN] ...so as to make it more reflective of the realities of the new era" (Kyodo News Service, 09.10.1992). To push the point even further home, a spokesman for Miyazawa stated that Japan was paying more to the UN than Britain and France combined and that there should be "no taxation without representation" (Doyle & Brown, 01.02.1992). In September of the same year, Japanese foreign minister, Michio Watanabe, focused Japanese dissatisfaction on the composition of the Security Council by calling for an expansion of its membership.

By mid 1993 the Japanese desire for permanent representation on the Security Council was becoming more coherent. In a position paper submitted to Boutros-Ghali in July, Miyazawa argued that those states most involved in the implementation of Security Council's resolutions should be more actively involved in the decision-making process. He supported Japan's adoption as a member, stating that Japan was "prepared to do all it can to discharge its responsibilities on the Security Council" (A/48/264: 54; Sieg, 27.09.1993). However, the position paper did not state outright that Japan was seeking permanent membership of the Council although it is not difficult to deduce such an aspiration from the wording of the document.[3]

Japan's progression towards clarity on permanent membership was interrupted, however, when Miyazawa's government was replaced in August 1993 by a seven-party coalition led by Morihiro Hosokawa; despite the fact that Japan's new prime minister said he would continue the former government's foreign policy (Daily Yomiuri, 26.08.1993). In his first address to the 48th General Assembly, Hosokawa argued that the functions of the Security Council needed to be strengthened and that "it is important that those countries having both the will and the adequate capacity to contribute to world prosperity and stability be actively engaged in that effort" (Agence France Presse, 27.09.1993). However, not only did he not argue for a permanent seat for Japan but, in a television interview following his address, stated that "I don't think that Japan should go out of its way to make a campaign to become a member" (Sieg, 27.09.1993). His statement caused some concern in the Japanese foreign ministry. Shunju Yanai, director general of the Foreign Ministry's Foreign Policy Bureau, worried that "such modesty is understood only in Japan" and that it is "indisputable" that other states will interpret Hosokawa's statement as a lack of interest (Isaka, 29.11.1993).

Japan moved quickly to avert speculation that it was diverging from its aim of openly asserting its candidacy for a permanent seat on the Security Council. Chief Cabinet Secretary Takemura told a press conference that the Japanese policy on permanent membership had not changed from that outlined in the position paper submitted by Miyazawa to Boutros-Ghali (Jiji Press, 17.03.1994). Furthermore, in an address to a meeting of the Open Ended Working Group on Security Council reform (OEWG) in New York on March 16, 1994, Japanese ambassador to the UN, Yoshio Hatano, reiterated that "countries that have in recent decades emerged as major political and economic powers should be added to the council's permanent membership" and that Japan was prepared "to do all it can to discharge its responsibilities on the Security Council" (Lau, 18.03.1994).

Japan's position became more consistent when Hosokawa's governing coalition was itself replaced in June 1994 although some ambiguity remained as to the extent of Japan's interest in permanent membership. Time and again, Japanese officials expressed Japan's aspiration to permanent membership in various sub-bodies of the UN and in the Japanese Diet (Isaka, 13.06.1994; Reuters, 15.06.1994) and, finally, on September 13, Japan's cabinet authorised its foreign minister, Yohei Kono, to officially express Japan's desire for a permanent seat on the Security Council before the 49th General Assembly. By this time, over 40 countries had already backed Japan's campaign. In August, the Philippines and Malaysia had added their support, strengthening Japan's claim that it would represent other Asian states if granted permanent membership (Economist, 17.09.1994).[4]

And so, in a speech to the 49th General Assembly on September 27, 1994, Kono made it official, or so he hoped. He stated that "it is... necessary to restructure and strengthen the Security Council, while ensuring its efficiency, so that it reflects world realities" and that "Japan is prepared, with the endorsement of many countries, to discharge its responsibilities as a permanent member of the Security Council" (Kono, 27.09.1994).

Even after such a seemingly straightforward statement, however, confusion remained as to Japan's intentions, at least within the Japanese administration. Following Kono's speech, Chief Cabinet Secretary Igarashi stressed that Kono's remarks should not be construed as meaning that Japan was intent on seeking a permanent seat. Nevertheless, Kono's speech was widely interpreted as constituting Japan's official bid for permanent membership and was so described in an in-house report distributed among UN leaders, including the Secretary General, Boutros-Ghali (Masui, 26.10.1994).

Japan has taken an extremely cautious approach to expressing its upward positionality. The coherence of its position on permanent membership as it developed was not helped by the fact that the various parties within the coalitions that have ruled Japan since 1993 have had different ideas on how actively Japan should pursue permanent membership. Furthermore, it has been Japan's policy to wait for the support and solicitation of other states rather than to actively pursue permanent membership itself in an independent campaign. As one official put it, this is simply good tactics since Japan will, in any case, need the support of two thirds of the UN membership to achieve its aim (Interviews, New York). However, now that Japan has made it absolutely clear that it wants a permanent seat and can thereby rely on the support of between 80 and 85 UN member states, the Japanese strategy is becoming more and more active (ibid.).

The German campaign for permanent membership of the Security Council has been as subdued and subtle as the Japanese but has been significantly more consistent. However, like the Japanese, it has gained increased momentum and support over a number of years. It began some time after Chancellor Kohl stated during his traditional New Year's press conference in January 1992 that Germany would not be seeking to become a permanent member of the Security Council. That was the last such statement to be made by a high German official.

In September of the same year, German Foreign Minister, Klaus Kinkel, took the first tentative step towards informing the world that Germany was interested in becoming a permanent member of the Security Council. He informed the 47th General Assembly that debate on Security Council reform was already underway and added that "Germany will not take the initiative in this respect... [but] if a change in the council's membership is actually considered we, too, shall seek a permanent seat" (Pick, 25.09.1992; Kinkel, 1992).

In a position paper submitted to Boutros-Ghali in June 1993, Germany argued that the changed international situation and increasing UN membership necessitated a reconsideration of the composition of the Security Council. Germany acknowledged the fact that a number of states had expressed the opinion that Germany should be a candidate for permanent membership. The report asserted that: "The Federal Government is... prepared to assume the responsibilities which permanent membership of the Security Council entails" (A/48/264: 44).

Germany's position on achieving permanent membership of the Security Council has never been in doubt since it began its campaign in 1992. Like Japan, up to now Germany has been careful to lead a measured, conservative campaign and to rely to a large degree on the support and solicitation of other states. More recently, however, Germany's confidence in the broad base of its support has lead it to push more actively and independently for its own permanent membership in particular and for the broader reform of the Security Council in general (Interviews, New York).

Bolstering International Military Responsibility Both Japan and Germany have long been sensitive to the argument forwarded by some permanent members that permanent membership of the Security Council has as a prerequisite a high degree of international military responsibility that includes the ability to participate in UN peacekeeping activities. Much confusion continues to surround this contention, however. Stark disagreement existed, for example, between the Secretary General, Boutros Ghali, on the one hand and most of the permanent members of the Security Council on the other over whether participation in peacekeeping operations is a prerequisite for permanent membership. Although Boutros Ghali did, on one occasion, encourage Japan to amend its constitution so that it might participate more fully in peace enforcement operations (Mc Carthy, 19.02.1993), his position leaned clearly in the opposite direction. Boutros Ghali expressed the opinion on numerous occasions that participation of Japanese or German troops in UN peacekeeping operations is not a prerequisite for their permanent membership of the Security Council (Independent, 26.05.1994; Mc Carthy, 14.09.1994; Storch, 12.07.1994) and argued that "if a member state for constitutional reasons or for political reasons is not interested in military operations, there is no obligation" (Kyodo, 05.09.1994).

Certain permanent members of the Security Council, on the other hand, support the view that every permanent member must accept a significant share of international military responsibility, an integral part of which is participation in UN peacekeeping operations. French president Mitterrand stressed the military responsibilities that permanent membership of the Security Council entails (Agence Europe, 05.10.1994) and French Foreign Minister, Alain Juppé, argued that any aspirant to a permanent seat on the Security Council would have to at least have the possibility of participating in military operations (Le Monde, 26.09.1994). France's official position is that any increase in the permanent membership of the Security Council should take account of the "participation and willingness [of prospective permanent members] to participate in peace-keeping operations and the interest evinced by them in discharging global responsibilities in the field of international peace and security" (A/48/264: 41).

Russia supports the tacit understanding that permanent members of the Security Council take on a greater share of international military responsibility (Interviews, New York) while the preferred British phrase has long been "you have to have global responsibilities to be one of the Permanent Five" (Walker, 11.06.1993). Former British Foreign Secretary Hurd stressed that Germany and Japan would be natural choices for permanent membership of the Security Council provided that they were "fully able to take part in peace-keeping" (Savill, 09.07.1993). His successor argued that "permanent members of the Security Council must be both willing and able to make a significant contribution through the

UN to international security" and to accept "the wider responsibilities to contribute to security and peacekeeping" (Rifkind, 26.09.1995). The US position is that "permanent membership entails assuming an active role in global peace and security activities" (A/48/264: 92).

Both Japan and Germany agree with Boutros Ghali that no formal link exists between permanent membership of the Security Council and peacekeeping responsibility but concur with the opinion of the current permanent membership that a moral link does exist between the two (Interviews, New York). For this reason, both have taken steps to facilitate their participation in UN peacekeeping operations in order to increase their capacity to accept greater international military responsibility.

Japan's constitution, drafted by the Allied Forces following the end of the Second World War, imposes severe restrictions on the foreign deployment of Japanese troops. Despite the fact that Article 9 prohibits Japan from having an army, navy or air-force as well as "war potentials," *Self Defence Forces* were established in 1954 to protect Japan against outside aggression. The ruling Liberal Democratic Party of the time argued that Article 9, while denying Japan the right of belligerency, granted it the right to respond to aggression in self-defence. It added, however, that "the constitution did not allow Japan to exercise this right in the context of collective self-defense" (Susumu, 1996), i.e., by deploying its troops abroad in support of international efforts to safeguard peace and security.

Mindful of the view recently expressed by some permanent members, however, that permanent membership of the Security Council implies a heightened degree of international military responsibility, Japan responded to this possible obstacle to achieving its goal of permanent membership by taking steps towards increasing its profile in international affairs. Japan's first attempt to loosen constraints on foreign troop deployments failed when an attempt to pass a bill allowing Japanese self-defence forces to participate in UN peacekeeping operations was blocked in December 1991 by politicians who feared that other Asian countries would criticise Japan for embarking upon a militaristic course (Mc Carthy, 10.01.1992). Undeterred by this development, however, the Japanese government sought the approval of foreign nations in its bid for permanent membership by contributing in a non-military fashion to UN peacekeeping operations in Cambodia and by providing humanitarian aid to the former Yugoslavia and Somalia (BBC, 16.12.1992).

In June 1993, after almost two years of acrimonious debate, the Japanese Diet passed an International Peace Cooperation Law (IPCL) which allows Japanese troops to take part in UN peacekeeping operations subject to five essential conditions; (1) that a cease-fire agreement is already in place, (2) that the parties to the conflict have given their consent to the deployment of peacekeeping troops and to the participation of Japanese troops, (3) that the peacekeeping force maintains impartiality, (4) that the use of weapons is limited to the minimum necessary to protect the lives of Japanese armed forces and (5) that the Japanese government may withdraw its contingent should any of the other conditions cease to apply (Susumu, 1996).

At present, Japanese troops deployed abroad may not participate in operations that may involve the use of force for purposes other than self-defence. They are limited to providing logistical support to other UN units and to participating in civilian peacekeeping activities. Under the IPCL, Japan has sent Japanese electoral observers to Angola, Cambodia and El Salvador; it has deployed military observers, civilian police and a 600-strong construction unit in Cambodia, and has also sent staff officers and a movement control unit to Mozambique. Most recently, it has deployed self-defence forces to the United Nations Disengagement Observer Force (UNDOF) operating in the Golan Heights.

While these are important peacekeeping contributions, they do not significantly add to Japan's share of international military responsibility. Minister for Foreign Affairs Kono made it clear that, even with a fully operational IPCL, Japan will be unable to participate in peace-enforcement operations as envisioned by Boutros-Ghali (Kono, 24.04.1995). According to Mr. Kono, Japan is willing to fulfil its responsibilities as a permanent member "in accordance with its basic philosophy regarding international contributions, including the non-resort to the use of force prohibited by its constitution" (Kono, 26.09.1995).

However, Japan's inability to participate in military-style peace-enforcement operations does not deter it from continuing with its campaign for permanent membership since it argues that the resources needed to contribute to international peace and security in the modern world differ from those needed in the past. According to Japan, nowadays such a contribution depends more and more on economic and non-military factors (A/48/264: 54; Katzenstein, 1996). Its strong financial support of UN peacekeeping bears this out. Japan proposed the United Nations Peacekeeping Reserve Fund, established in January 1993, which tries to ensure that start-up funds are readily available for launching peacekeeping operations. Japan also serves as vice-chair for the Special Committee on Peacekeeping Operations which is the principal UN forum concerned with reviewing all aspects of peacekeeping operations. Furthermore, Japan alone funds over 14% of the total cost of UN peacekeeping operations.

Like Japan, Germany has also taken steps towards improving its international military responsibility. Unlike Japan, however, it has largely succeeded in doing so. In order to reinforce the fact that its campaign for permanent membership had begun, German Foreign Minister Kinkel told the 47th General Assembly in September 1992 that Germany was determined to change its constitution to allow its troops to participate in UN peacekeeping and peacemaking operations in order to end "any discrepancy between our verbal commitment to peace and human rights and our active involvement in their defence" (Pick, 25.09.1992). It was not Kinkel's active petitioning, however, but domestic dissatisfaction with the use of German troops in Bosnia and Somalia that eventually lead to the loosening of the constitutional restrictions. Neither was it necessary to amend the Grundgesetz. A more liberal interpretation of its provisions by the German Federal Constitutional Court (FCC) sufficed to give the German government more freedom in deploying its armed forces abroad.

The process that led to the lifting of some restrictions on the out of area deployment of German troops began early in 1994 when the SPD fraction of the German Bundestag submitted a case to the FCC disputing the constitutionality of two actual and one proposed deployment of German troops - a unit of the Bundesmarine to the Adriatic, the participation of German soldiers in integrated NATO units flying AWACS reconnaissance missions over Bosnia, and the April 1993 decision of the Government to send German soldiers to Somalia. The SPD fraction, along with the FDP fraction which added its voice to disputing the constitutionality of the AWACS deployments, argued that these were out of area deployments of German troops and, therefore, required an amendment to the Grundgesetz (Europa Archiv, 1994: D427).

After considering the arguments, the FCC ruled on July 12, 1994, that the Grundgesetz allows for the out of area deployment of German armed forces participating in joint military operations under the auspices of NATO or the WEU for the purpose of implementing resolutions of the UN Security Council. It also ruled that participation of German troops in UN peacekeeping and peace-enforcement operations is compatible with the Grundgesetz. However, the FCC's ruling also makes it the responsibility of the German government to obtain, before each such deployment, the agreement, in principle, of the Bundestag. If the agreement of the Bundestag is forthcoming, all decisions regarding the modalities of the deployment - the number of troops, the duration of the deployment, co-ordination with other organisations, etc. - are the responsibility of the government. However, the FCC ruling also allows the German government, in cases of particular emergency, to deploy its troops first and seek parliamentary support later (PIB, 08.1994; PIB,

07.1994).

In effect, therefore, the German government is now in a position to deploy its troops world-wide provided they participate in UN-sponsored multilateral operations and that, under normal circumstances, prior support from the Bundestag is forthcoming.[5] As a consequence of its new-found freedom in the area of foreign troop deployment, Germany has declared itself ready to provide "stand-by forces" to the UN for use in peacekeeping operations. These will be established, according to Generalleutnant Manfred Eisele of the UN department for peacekeeping operations, after the restructuring of the Bundeswehr is completed; probably early in the next century (Moniac, 20.11.1995).

At present, Germany is deploying soldiers, military observers, civilian police, or medical personnel to UN operations in Iraq, Bosnia, Georgia, Angola, Kuwait and Liberia. Of these, 4,000 soldiers and 150 state and federal police officers are deployed in the former Yugoslavia. Thus, Germany has been largely successful in increasing its international military responsibility. Unlike Japan, its troops may now carry out multilateral military operations in support of Security Council resolutions.

Both Germany and Japan, therefore, have attempted to increase their international military responsibility in order to strengthen their respective cases for permanent membership of the Security Council. In this respect, Germany has met with more success than has Japan. Nevertheless, the actions of both countries clearly indicate that each aspires to a greater share in the governance of the international system. The current climate in the UN, therefore, is characterised by the strong upward positionality of Japan and Germany and, to a lesser extent, by the upward positionality of developing countries who wish to see their increased representation in the UN organisation translated into greater decision-making influence.

Downward Positionality

The same factors that have lead to the upward positionality of Japan, Germany and the developing world, have also lead the current permanent members of the Security Council to display strong downward positionality; i.e., to behave so as to protect their privileged position in the UN's hierarchy of influence.

Even before Japan and Germany made public their intention to campaign for permanent seats, the permanent members were careful not to encourage debate on the question of altering the membership of the Security Council. For example, in December 1991 Britain, as chair of the

Security Council, smoothed the way for the Russian Federation to take over the Soviet Union's permanent seat despite the fact that the process by which this was achieved is suspect under international law (Blum, 1992; Daley, 1992).[6] Britain, France and the US feared that indecisiveness in appointing the Soviet Union's successor would lead to a deeper questioning by UN member states of the validity of Council membership and, therefore, preferred a quick, if legally dubious, solution to a more protracted, politically sensitive one. The inheritance by Russia of the Soviet Union's permanent seat did not meet with much opposition from the UN membership at large, suggesting that the permanent members were successful in expediting the process and, thus, minimising debate on it.

Initial Opposition to Reforming the Security Council

When Germany and Japan made official their intentions to push for permanent membership, the reaction of most of the permanent members was negative. Certain among them offered various reasons as to why the addition of extra permanent members to the Security Council was not to be desired. France focused on the detrimental effects that enlargement would have on the effectiveness of Security Council decisionmaking (Walker, 11.06.1993). A French report on Security Council reform also stressed that "France is of the view that the prime dictate of effectiveness should be maintained" and stressed the importance in this respect of maintaining the small size of the council (A/48/264: 41; Inter Press, 03.08.1993).

Britain's initial position was no different. When queried on the subject of Security Council reform in the House of Commons in February 1992, British Prime Minister, John Major, insisted that "Security Council reform is neither necessary nor desirable" (Oakley, 04.02.1992). Also, in a UN report Britain expressed its satisfaction with the way the Council was operating and warned against any initiative that might interfere with its effectiveness (A/48/264: 90-91). "If it ain't broke, don't fix it" suggested British Foreign Secretary Hurd (Inter Press, 03.08.1993) who also went on record as being "cautious" about letting Germany gain a permanent seat on the Security Council (Independent, 05.07.1993). Likewise, while attending a G7 summit meeting in Tokyo in July 1993, Mr. Major expressed cautious opposition to Japanese permanent membership of the Council (Savill, 09.07.1993).

Both France and the UK also played the nuclear card in support of their opposition to permanent membership for Japan and Germany. French UN Ambassador Merimee referred to the "unwritten rules" surrounding the nuclear status of all current permanent members. Likewise, referring disapprovingly to the idea of adding Japan and Germany as permanent members, a British official argued in June 1993 that "the nuclear status lurks understood in the background" (Walker, 11.06.1993).

The strength of this initial response by France and Britain may be attributed to the fact that their positions as permanent members are most threatened by the aspirations of Japan and Germany. Of the five permanent members, France and the UK are the most insecure about their status on the Security Council. In 1993, for example, British Chancellor of the Exchequer, Norman Lamont, reportedly admitted in private that Britain's permanent seat on the Security Council was too costly and that the government should seriously consider giving it up (Savill, 25.11.1993). In July of the same year the Commons Select Committee on Defence warned the Treasury that cutting deeper into Britain's defence budget would seriously undermine Britain's ability to hold onto its permanent seat.

Furthermore, developments within the UN indicate that Britain and France no longer exercise as much influence there as they once did. In November 1993, Britain lost its seat on the UN Advisory Committee on Administrative and Budgetary Questions (ACABQ), one of the most significant bodies in the United Nations the recommendations of which play an important role in determining the Secretary General's regular and peacekeeping budgets. The Committee also examines the budgets of all UN agencies. In November 1995, the UK failed in its attempt to regain its seat while France also lost its seat. Significantly, the other permanent members of the Security Council are represented on the committee as are Japan and Germany.

Perhaps another setback to Britain's attempt to persuade the world and its own citizens that it deserves its place on the Security Council is the loss of its long-serving ambassador to the UN, Sir David Hannay, who retired in July 1995. He was the longest-serving ambassador on the Security Council and was widely credited with being a significant force in putting down suggestions that Britain should be removed from the Council's permanent membership. As one diplomat pointed out; "He didn't just nail down the seat, he welded it in place" (Leopold, 27.07.1995).

Despite these developments, however, its is highly unlikely that either France or the UK will renounce the privileges of permanent membership. Certainly, they cannot be forced to do so and both have given every indication that they intend to hold on to their permanent seats. British Foreign Secretary Hurd stressed that "the British and French position [as permanent members of the Security Council] is safeguarded and no one is suggesting that it should be altered" (Savill, 09.07.1993).

The initial US response to the German and Japanese permanent membership campaigns, on the other hand, was quite different to that of France and Britain. The United States has been a consistent supporter of adding Germany and Japan to the permanent membership of the Security Council. As early as January 1992, US President Bush expressed support for the idea that Japan be granted a permanent seat on the Security Council (Mc Carthy, 10.01.1992). During his presidential campaign in 1992, Bill Clinton also expressed his support for making both Japan and Germany permanent members. The Clinton administration has since maintained this position. In June, 1993, U.S. Ambassador to the UN, Madeleine Albright, made it official that adding Germany and Japan to the Security Council had become an integral part of US proposals to reform the UN (A/48/264: 91-92). "It was time the Security Council reflected the world of the 1990s and not that of 1945," she explained (Walker, 11.06.1993) adding that US support for expanding permanent membership to include Japan and Germany was based on the US conviction that both countries had gained economic and political significance and were able to contribute to the promotion of international peace and order (Masui, 26.10.1994).

US support for the addition of Japan and Germany as permanent members of the Security Council does not correspond with the behaviour to be expected from a downwardly positional state. Instead of jealously guarding its privileged position in the upper echelons of the UN's hierarchy of influence - a strategy that both Britain and France initially followed - the US has actively supported the granting of additional shares in the governance of the international system to Japan and Germany. How can this deviant behaviour be explained? One explanation might be that, because the US is still the most powerful state in the international system, it feels less threatened by the aspirations of Japan and Germany than do, for example, Britain and France who fear that their influence in the UN organisation may be eclipsed if Germany and Japan are granted permanent membership. Another explanation might be that US support of Japanese and German permanent membership is a manifestation of the desire of a declining hegemon to underwrite its global activity by granting additional decision-making powers to the like-minded, rich countries.

Subsequent Acquiescence to the Necessity of Limited Reform

Britain and France hoped that their strict initial opposition to reforming the Security Council would quell interest in the topic. As soon as it became apparent, however, that a major debate on Council reform was developing within the United Nations, both realised that their opposition to reform would soon become untenable in the face of strong support for reform among the general UN membership. Faced with this dilemma, both modified their official positions and declared themselves open, in principle, to the idea of extending the membership of the Council to reflect both the increase in membership of the UN and the changes that had taken place in international relations since 1945. France and the UK began publicly to support Japan and Germany as future permanent members of the Security Council. Both reasoned that, if reform was inevitable, it would be best to add those countries with whom positive relations already existed (Interviews, New York).

The "shift in emphasis" of the British position was particularly marked. During the course of the same July 1993 G7 summit meeting at which Major had expressed his cautious opposition to Japanese permanent membership, Foreign Secretary Hurd stated that Britain now accepted the need for Security Council reform and that, if agreement on the matter were reached, Japan and Germany would be the "natural beneficiaries" of permanent seats. This statement marked the beginning of a new British policy on Security Council reform that has since remained steadfast.[7] As if to underline the drastic change in British policy since the early 1990s, John Major, speaking before the 50th anniversary commemorative session of the General Assembly on October 23, 1995, asked "should the Security Council be reformed?" and answered "I believe it should. The subject has been on the agenda for too long. It raises difficult questions; but the issues are clear, and decisions are needed" (Major, 23.10.1995). In the words of one British UN official, the UK has become an "enthusiastic convert" to the idea of Security Council reform (Interviews, New York).

Change in the official French position on Security Council reform was just as striking. On the eve of his visit to Tokyo on March 29, 1994, French Foreign Minster, Alain Juppé, expressed support for the idea of extending permanent membership, with full responsibilities, to Germany and Japan stating that France considered it a "necessity" to enlarge the Council and that "il est donc naturel de donner un siège à L'Allemagne et au Japon" (Le Monde, 29.03.1994). Addressing the 49th General Assembly, Mr. Juppé was the only foreign minister to refer specifically to Japan and Germany in the context of Security Council reform.

Despite the fundamental change in its position, however, France is of the opinion that neither Germany nor Japan are yet ready to assume the responsibilities of permanent membership. It is not satisfied with the level of international military responsibility that either has assumed thus far. According to one senior French UN official, further change - most probably constitutional - is necessary in both countries if international military responsibility is to be brought to a level commensurate with the responsibilities associated with permanent membership (Interviews, New York). France's current support for the permanent membership of Japan and Germany is, therefore, based on the priority that each has placed on increasing military responsibility and on the steps that each has already taken towards achieving this goal. France's support, however, is conditional on the achievement of this goal.

China and the Russian Federation did not actively oppose the idea of German and Japanese permanent membership from the outset but preferred instead simply to urge great caution and reserve when dealing with such an important question. China agrees that there is a need to expand the membership of the Security Council "in an appropriate manner when the time is ripe" (A/48/264: 18) and is concerned that any reform should not have an adverse impact on the effectiveness of the Council. It foresees a long, careful process of reform the end result of which will be reached by "broad consensus and universal acceptance of the Member States" (A/48/264: 19; Xinhua, 01.07.1993; Jianxiong, 08.10.1993). China's cautious position on Security Council reform is also influenced by its "unofficial" opposition to Japanese permanent membership.

Likewise, the Russian Federation has approached the question of reforming the Security Council with a great deal of caution. It recognises that changes in the international system over the past fifty years have led to the need to reform the United Nations system as a whole and that "expansion of the Security Council should be considered in a wider context of the general task of adapting the United Nations to realities of today" (Fedotov, 15.11.1995; A/48/264). Russia's support is tempered with reservations, however. It has argued that any reform of the Security Council should strengthen its new-found effectiveness and has gone as far as to argue that the UN "cannot afford to engage in an overhaul of machinery which not only is not broken but is in fact in good working order" (A/48/264: 82). It has also suggested various ways in which the operation of the Security Council might be improved without having to resort to expanding its membership (A/48/264: 83).

In sum, despite the fact that all permanent members have acquiesced to the necessity of limited reform of the Security Council, their motivations for doing so and the general reserved nature of their support clearly indicate characteristics of downward positionality. All recognise that the reform debate has achieved a critical momentum within the UN and that opposing the general will of the UN membership by refusing to countenance reform is not a viable course of action. Their support of Security Council reform is motivated more by a desire to make the most out of a difficult situation by salvaging as many of their privileges as possible intact than by a belief that reforming the Security Council is a virtuous goal in its own right. Permanent members have not, on the whole, been willing collaborators in the reform process. Rather, they have been reluctant participants in a process driven by the ambitions of rising states.

Tension

The interplay of the upward positionality of Japan and Germany, on the one hand, and the downward positionality of the permanent members of the Security Council, on the other, has generated a significant amount of tension in the United Nations organisation. This tension manifests itself, in increasing order of importance, in the different levels of urgency with which various states view reform of the Security Council, in the acrimonious debate on the future of the veto, and in the major disagreements over how many permanent and non-permanent seats should be added to the Council and who should fill them.

The Urgency of Reform

Tension is generated by the interplay of the different degrees of urgency that states attach to the need for reform. Some states consider reform to be essential, some to be necessary and others merely consider it hypothetically desirable. The urgency attached by states to achieving reform tends to correlate with whether they are attempting to improve their position in the institutional hierarchy or to maintain their position therein. On the one hand, states displaying upward positionality - Japan and Germany, for example - tend to attach great urgency to achieving reform. The German Permanent Representative, for example, told the 49th General Assembly that "the general exchange of views [on reforming the Security Council] has run its course and in-depth discussion of concrete reform proposals must begin" (Graf zu Rantzau, 13.10.1994). Likewise, his successor, Tono Eitel, called for "substantial achievements" to be made on the subject of reforming the Security Council during the 50th General Assembly, warning that "we must make good use of the momentum created. It will not last forever" (Eitel, 13.11.1995). Likewise, Japan sought to begin the reform process by 1995 (A/48/264) and, when that deadline passed, pushed to resolve the question of Security Council reform by September 1996 (Kono, 26.09.1995; Owada, 13.11.1995; Kyodo, 12.06.1995).

On the other hand, states displaying downward positionality - permanent members of the Security Council - tend to approach the subject of reform in a more casual manner and tend also to foresee the process of reform taking a longer time to complete. China, for example, foresees a long process of reform characterised by prudence and caution and by aim of achieving unanimous agreement. Chinese Foreign Minister, Qian Qichen, told the 48th General Assembly that the reform process should not be rushed and that the result should be generally accepted by all (Jianxiong, 08.10.1993). Also, Chinese Deputy UN Permanent Representative, Wang Xuexian, argued that Security Council reform "remains arduous and a serious, practical and patient approach is required to continue extensive exchange of views and seek common ground step by step" (Xinhua, 13.10.1994).

Likewise, the Russian Federation has stressed that it will co-operate in the reform debate so long as "any steps taken in this field are gradual and decided on by consensus, after general agreement has been reached in the Council and universally acceptable criteria have been worked out" (A/48/264: 83). Andrei Kozyrev, as Russian Foreign Minister, stressed the importance of not rushing the reform process (Gornostayev, 02.11.1994) and the Russian Deputy UN Permanent Representative stressed that "improvement of the Security Council's methods and procedures must be staged and well-balanced, without haste and rash decisions" and that "any practical steps should be weighed, thought of and taken on the basis of consensus" (Fedotov, 15.11.1995).

Britain would seem to be worried both about taking too much, and too little, time to decide upon the exact configuration of Security Council reform. A 1993 British report on the matter warned that "it is crucial that neither a protracted debate on enlargement, nor precipitate action, should be allowed to diminish the Council's effectiveness" (A/48/264: 90-91; Inter Press, 03.08.1993). However, Foreign Secretary Hurd admitted in an address to the Royal Institute for International Affairs in January 1993, that "this is a huge debate and it will go on for a long time... An outcome will be very hard and slow to reach" (Doyle, 28.01.1993).

Once more, the US constitutes somewhat of an exception in this regard. As a permanent member of the Security Council, it has an obvious interest in maintaining its privileged position in the institutional hierarchy. Nevertheless, it is most concerned that reform of the Security Council be carried out quickly. The Assistant Secretary for International Organisations, for example, advised that "the [Security] Council should not proceed too far into its second half-century without updating its membership" (Ward, 10.02.1995) and the US did not rule out that some major agreement on reform is possible before the end of 1996 (Interviews, New York).

The Veto

A significant amount of tension is also generated by the controversy surrounding the question of how best to deal with the veto in the context of Security Council reform. Generally speaking, four opposing positions dominate the debate according to which the right of veto should be (1) phased out altogether, (2) limited in scope, (3) retained by the existing permanent members but not extended to any new permanent members, or (4) extended to new permanent members.

The first proposal, that the veto should be abolished altogether (C.G.G., 1995; Hoffmann, 1994; Sellen, 1992), is a non-starter since all permanent members have indicated that they are not willing to relinquish their right of veto. From the point of view of the P-5, the function of the veto has not changed since 1945. It still fulfils the task of preventing concerted action being taken against a permanent member of the Security Council. The threat of veto - or the "hidden veto" - is also a powerful negotiation tool. It can deter states from bringing certain issues to the negotiation table in the first place - an example is the Soviet Union's promise to veto reform proposals in the early 1960s - or, once negotiation has commenced, it can be used to force important concessions. Following the end of the Cold War, increased use of the hidden veto has provided permanent members with the added advantage of being able to exercise veto power without having to be exposed to the indignation of the international community. Without the acquiescence of the permanent members in the matter of abolishing the veto, therefore, it remains essentially unassailable for the simple reason that each permanent member has a veto over the question of abolishing the veto. As one Russian UN official put it, until the P-5 agree to contemplate phasing out the veto, it is not at all productive to discuss that option (Interviews, New York).

Proposals to limit the scope of the veto by restricting the range of issues to which it applies have also been made (I.W.G., 1995; I.P.A. & Stanley Foundation, 1994). It has been suggested, for example, that the range of matters treated as procedural, to which the veto does not apply, be expanded so as more closely to comply with the spirit of the Charter. One concrete expression of this proposal could be the non-application of the veto to the election of the Secretary General or to the admission of new members. Another popular proposal is that the veto not be applied to action under Chapter VI (Pacific Settlement of Disputes) but restricted to action under Chapter VII (enforcement action).

There are several problems associated with this proposal that seriously impinge upon its chances of success. First, although only four vetoes have been cast since 1988, recent evidence suggests that permanent members are not willing to accept restrictions on their use of the veto. Russia, for example, cast one of these three vetoes on a minor budgetary matter "mainly to demonstrate that it was still willing to use its privilege and thus reinforce the credibility of its threat" (Russet, O'Neill & Sutterlin, 1996: 70).[8] Likewise, the election of a successor to Boutros-Ghali demonstrated that permanent members still consider the veto a vital weapon in their decision-making armoury.

Second, any restriction on the use of the veto would have to be voluntarily accepted by all of the permanent members. Since compliance with the restriction would be at the discretion of each permanent member, it is unlikely that veto use would be restricted for longer than was convenient for a given permanent member. Finally, voluntarily restricting the use of the veto would involve relinquishing the application of the hidden veto in negotiations that fall outside of the scope of Chapter VII, seriously curtailing the negotiating leverage of the permanent members. It is unlikely that the permanent members will agree to restrict their own influence.

The proposal that veto power be retained by existing permanent members but not extended to new permanent members is, understandably, vehemently opposed by Japan and Germany. Japan is acutely aware of the negotiation leverage associated with the right of veto and is against the creation, as part of an overall strategy to reform the Security Council, of a new class of permanent membership without veto powers (Interviews, New York).[9]

Likewise, Germany's Chancellor Kohl has clearly stated that his country would not accept a permanent seat on the Security Council if it did not come with all usual rights, including the right of veto (Kyodo, 09.07.1993). The Acting German Permanent Representative has explained that, "the right to veto is per se not an objective for us. But our bottom line is clear: If Germany... shall become permanent member of the Security Council this has to be on an equal footing with the other permanent members, without discrimination, i.e. with the same rights and the same obligations" (Henze, 17.05.1994). If Germany were to achieve permanent membership of the Security Council without veto rights, so the argument goes, the German government would find it extremely difficult to explain to its citizens why Germany was being treated differently than, for example, France or the UK (Interviews, New York; Kühne & Baumann, 1995; Kühne, 1994).[10]

The proposal that the right of veto be extended to any new

permanent members of the Security Council is supported, therefore, by Japan and Germany. A number of permanent members have also expressed support for this option. French Foreign Minister, Alain Juppé, underlined that "Les nouveaux membres permanents devront jouir des droits et assumer les responsabilités de leur charge" (Le Monde, 29.03.1994). British Foreign Minister, Douglas Hurd, also stressed that "any extension of the permanent membership should be on a normal basis, that it to say, new permanent members should have the same rights as existing permanent members" (Daily Yomiuri, 30.09.1994). Russia has also expressed its support for extending veto rights to new permanent members (Kühne & Baumann, 1995).

It would seem at first glance that by supporting the extension of veto-rights to new permanent members, these permanent members are collaborating in the dilution of their own influence. It is not difficult to understand, however, why they are following this course of action. Extending veto-privileges to states that achieve permanent membership of the Security Council is, in fact, in the best interests of the current permanent members. If they were to refuse to do so, the veto would lose most of the scant legitimacy it has left since it would essentially become a relic of the past, attributable only to the historical fact of having been an original permanent member (Ciechanski, 1994).

The majority of UN member states, however, oppose the idea of extending the right of veto and a significant number of them support its outright abolition. The main line of contention separates the present permanent members along with Japan and Germany, on the one hand, from most of the rest of the UN membership, on the other. The current debate on the veto is reminiscent of the one that took place during the San Francisco conference. In 1945, the majority of the 51 original UN members also opposed the idea of veto power in the Security Council. It was the price they had to pay, however, to ensure that all of the most powerful states would participate fully in the new organisation. Today, the UN membership in general is powerless to deprive the permanent members of their veto rights against their will. It remains to be seen whether extending veto powers to Germany and Japan will be the price it has to pay to ensure that both play larger roles in world affairs.

Adding Permanent and Non-permanent Seats

Most tension is generated by the question of how to expand the membership of the Security Council. On this issue, broad agreement exists on several general points but deep-seated disagreement plagues specific reform proposals. For example, there is broad agreement among

UN member states that the number of seats on the Security Council should be increased. A sizeable number of UN member states, including most of the permanent members, also agree that Japan and Germany should have permanent representation, albeit on certain conditions. Furthermore, there is widespread agreement that any reform should improve upon the present representation on the Council of the regions of Asia, Africa and Latin America. This is as far as agreement stretches, however. On the subject of how many permanent and non-permanent seats should be added, and on who should fill them, broad disagreement reigns.

The issue of how the Security Council should be reformed is a highly complex one. A report issued by the Secretary General in 1993 (A/48/264) demonstrated that there are almost as many opinions on the details of reform as there are members of the UN. Despite the fact that efforts have been made to simplify and systematise the array of preferences on reform (Kühne & Baumann, 1995; Ciechanski, 1994; A/49/965), the task of highlighting common threads of preference that link significant numbers of states remains a difficult one. Nevertheless, some degree of generalisation is possible.

The majority of tension in the reform debate is generated by differences of opinion over how best to reconcile two broad areas of agreement - that Germany and Japan should become permanent members and that developing countries should be better represented. This is the problem at the heart of the reform debate. Developing countries, while generally supporting the permanent membership campaigns of Japan and Germany, have long argued that permanent membership of the Security Council should not be limited to industrialised countries of the north. A brief overview of the reform preferences of the permanent members, however, serves to illustrate that this is a major point of contention.

It was France's position in 1993 that: "Any enlargement there may be that admits new permanent members should not diminish the ability of other States in the different regions to secure representation in the Council as non-permanent members" (A/48/264: 41). Since then, France has maintained its support for improved non-permanent representation of the developing world. French Foreign Minister Juppé argued that the presence of strong third-world countries would lend balance to the Council (Le Monde, 10.05.1994) and regularly re-affirmed his support for a significantly stronger developing world presence on the Security Council (Daily Yomiuri, 30.09.1994; Le Monde, 30.09.1994).

French support does not extend, however, to advocating permanent seats for individual developing countries. France recognises both the difficulty of achieving agreement on which countries should represent the regions of Asia, Africa and Latin-America and that the addition of further permanent members, outside of Japan and Germany, would seriously impinge upon the effectiveness of the Council; something that France would like to avoid at all costs. France is, however, open to the idea of a rotating permanent representation for each of the three developing regions. It is encouraged by the progress that has been made on this issue in Latin America where Brazil has, more or less, accepted that it is not going to win permanent representation on the Security Council by itself. Further progress could, according to a French Official, be made in Latin America by experimenting with a rotating seating arrangement and by making Latin America a test case of creative solutions for regional permanent representation on the Council (Interviews, New York).

With regard to improving the representation of the developing world, Britain is less generous. In a position paper submitted to Boutros-Ghali in 1993, it argued that present arrangements in the Security Council already allow for the equitable representation of the various regions of the world (A/48/264: 90). While the UK envisions the addition of a number of non-permanent seats in order to ensure that "broad geographical balance in an enlarged Council... [is] maintained," it is concerned that any reform should be limited in scope so as to ensure that the Council's effectiveness is not adversely affected (Rifkind, 26.09.1995).

Of all the proposals on reforming the Security Council, the US ranks the "quick-fix" solution number one - adding only Germany and Japan as permanent members (Interviews, New York). As it has become more obvious, however, that this solution is not feasible in the face of strong opposition from developing countries, the US has come round to supporting increased representation for the developing world as an integral part of any realistic reform proposal. US UN Ambassador, Madeleine Albright, admitted that granting permanent seats to Japan and Germany would only risk making the Security Council even more "industrialised-centric" and expressed understanding for the demands for representation made by other regions of the world (Albright, 03.02.1995). Also, Secretary of State, Warren Christopher, while arguing that Japan and Germany should be added as permanent members, stressed that "we should ensure that all the world's regions are fairly represented" (Christopher, 25.09.1995). However, the US position stops well short of advocating permanent seats for developing countries.

China and Russia, on the other hand, are more sympathetic than the other three permanent members to calls that developing countries be permanently represented on the Security Council. Significantly, however, neither has openly supported such a course of action. China is concerned that any reform of the Security Council should, in the words of Chinese Foreign Minster, Qian Qichen, "take full account of the concerns and interests of the developing countries" and that "any enlargement of the council's membership must fully conform to the principle of equitable geographical distribution to ensure a broader representation" (Daily Yomiuri, 30.09.1994). More recently, he re-iterated that "any increase in the number of members of the Security Council of the United Nations - permanent or non-permanent - should reflect an equitable and fair geographical distribution" (Agence France, 10.03.1995; see also Romanov, 10.03.1995). This sentiment has been echoed by numerous influential Chinese politicians and diplomats (Xinhua, 13.10.1994) including Chinese president, Jiang Zemin, who argued that, when reforming the Security Council, account should be taken of the balance between various regions and particularly the balance between developing and developed countries (Xinhua, 11.11.1994; BBC, 14.11.1994). China has not, however, publicly advocated the permanent representation on the Security Council of developing countries.

The Russian Federation, likewise, is torn between its desire to limit the influence of the west and to increase the number of its potential allies on the Security Council, on the one hand, and its desire to maintain the Council's new-found effectiveness, on the other. In 1994, for example, it was reported that, in order to counterbalance the West, the Russian Federation was unofficially lobbying for permanent seats on the Security Council for Brazil and India (Gornostayev, 02.12.1994). At the same time, however, Foreign Minister Kozyrev worried that if the Council were improperly reformed it could turn into "a mini-General Assembly" and lose its effectiveness (ibid.).

Russia now stresses the importance of preserving "the current status of the Permanent Members of the Security Council in the organic inter-connection of their rights and responsibilities" (Fedotov, 15.11.1995). With regard to improving the representation of the developing world, Russia prefers less radical solutions. Russian UN Ambassador, Yuri Fedotov, suggested that renewed attention be paid to the criteria set out in Article 23.1 of the Charter, regarding selection of non-permanent members and that the present ban on immediate re-election of non-permanent members to the Security Council be lifted (ibid.).

The P-5 are, therefore, generally supportive - with the possible exceptions of China and Russia - of the idea of adding Japan and Germany as permanent members but are not supportive - with the possible exception of China - of the idea of adding developing countries as permanent members of the Security Council. From the point of view of those permanent members that are both rich and industrialised - the US, Britain and France - there is good reason for this since:

> Germany and Japan vote regularly with other rich industrial states in the General Assembly, and in the Security Council when they happen to hold nonpermanent seats. So long as their alignment in international politics holds relatively constant..., their acquisition of permanent (and veto-wielding) membership would not fundamentally alter the balance of political forces on the council. Anything they might wish to veto would probably be opposed by the United Kingdom, France, and/or the United States anyway. However, giving such membership to members of the Nonaligned Movement (for example, India, Nigeria, or to a lesser degree Brazil) would greatly complicate efforts to pass resolutions [since] ...a new nonaligned permanent member would be likely to have substantive views quite different from those of the developed northern countries... (Russet, O'Neill & Sutterlin, 1996: 71).

For China and Russia, on the other hand, the temptation does exist to loosen the grip of rich western states on the Security Council by supporting the permanent representation of developing countries although neither country has openly supported such a course of action. For China, having developing countries permanently represented on the Council would provide it with allies who could support it in its ideological struggle with the West. China's approach to date, however, suggests that it prefers no reform at all even to reform that might include the permanent representation of developing countries. Its vague and general statements, its conviction that debate on reform will carry on for a very long time, and, most important, its insistence that agreement on reform must be arrived at by consensus - a most unlikely development - all point to its overwhelming preference for the status-quo.

Russia, likewise, has good reason to prefer the status-quo. Russia's permanent seat on the Security Council represents a relic of the former Superpower status of the Soviet Union. It elevates Russia to a formal position of international influence that belies its de facto capabilities thus ensuring that, despite its relative decline, it retains a strong voice in world affairs. Were Russia to risk, in the words of Kozyrev, turning the Security Council "into a mini General Assembly" by supporting the permanent representation of developing countries, it would be a conspirator in the sabotage of the one institution that provides it with disproportionate influence in international politics. Such a course of action would be tantamount to political suicide.

The interplay of upward and downward positionality, therefore, has generated tension in three main areas - in the debate over how urgently the Security Council needs to be reformed, in the debate over the future of the veto, and in the debate over the number of permanent and non-permanent seats that should be added to the Council. To different extents in each of these debates, the preferences of upwardly and downwardly positional states stand in opposition to one another.

Diffusing the Tension

How has the UN organisation fared in diffusing this tension? The UN does not possess a formal review mechanism that periodically assesses the need for reforming the UN's hierarchy of influence in light of significant shifts in the distribution of power among states. However, the UN organisation has made use of a separate mechanism - its power to appoint working groups - in order to tackle the problem of diffusing tension and reaching agreement on reform. Despite significant short-comings in the procedural and decision-making rules governing the operation of the UN working-group established to examine the issue of Security Council reform, it has succeeded in making an important contribution to advancing the reform debate.

The Open-Ended Working Group (OEWG)

Although the question of expanding the membership of the Security Council has been raised intermittently since the Council underwent its last, and only, reform in 1965, it was only given official institutional recognition on December 11, 1992, when the 47th General Assembly unanimously adopted resolution 47/62, introduced by Japan, India, and other states, on the "question of equitable representation on and increase in the membership of the Security Council." The resolution called on Secretary General Boutros-Ghali to work out a proposal for reform based on the preferences of UN member states and called on him to present his findings to the General Assembly in the autumn of 1993.

    In accordance with the resolution, Boutros-Ghali submitted a report (A/48/264) to the 48th General Assembly containing the reform preferences of about one third of UN member states. During the same session, the General Assembly approved by consensus resolution 48/26 which established an "Open-ended Working Group on the Question of Equitable Representation on and Increase in the Membership of the Security Council" (OEWG), consisting of all UN member states, to consider all aspects of Security Council reform.

    The OEWG met on 22 occasions during the 48th General

Assembly but submitted only a two-page progress report at the end of the session. Needless to say, little progress had been made. The report stated, in essence, that "there was a convergence of views that the membership of the Security Council should be enlarged" but that "there was also agreement that the scope and nature of such enlargement require further discussion" (A/48/47: 2). The failure of the OEWG to make any substantive progress on the question of reforming the Security Council during the 48th General Assembly dimmed Japan and Germany's hopes of being included in the Council's permanent membership during the UN's 50th anniversary in 1995.[11]

During the course of the 49th General Assembly, the co-chairmen of the OEWG - Wilhelm Breitenstein of Finland and Nitya Pibulsonggram of Thailand - produced, on their own initiative, a "compendium of observations" on Security Council reform (A/49/965). The document was an improvement on the Secretary General's earlier report (A/48/264) - which simply listed given state preferences - insofar as it attempted systematically to assess state preferences and to underline areas of broad agreement among groups of states. The document's main contribution was in breaking the general problem of Security Council reform into a set of specific sub-problems. Its aim was to advance the reform debate to a new level by dispensing with the general exchange of views that characterised the OEWG's first two sessions in order to "move on to the next phase of the work, i.e., a process of actual negotiations" (A/49/965: 16).

In its second report to the General Assembly, however, the OEWG as a whole displayed significantly less confidence and ambition than had its co-chairmen. It distanced itself from the co-chairmen's report complaining that it had not taken into account all opinions on reforming the Security Council, stressing that the co-chairmen's compendium "[had] no legal status, that it [did] not constitute the position of the Open-ended Working Group, nor [did] it prejudice the position of any delegation" (A/49/47: 4). The report concluded in a similar vein as the previous one by stating that "important differences continue to exist on key issues before the Open-ended Working Group, and, therefore, further in-depth consideration of these issues is still required" (ibid.: 5).

The Impact of the OEWG

Despite the fact that the OEWG's reports to date have not pointed to any immediate resolution of the question of Security Council reform, the Working Group has been relatively successful in advancing the reform debate, albeit slowly. There are three main reasons for this success. First, the OEWG has facilitated the dissemination of detailed information among UN member states regarding the reform preferences of all states.

Second, as a direct result of creating an information-rich environment, the OEWG has succeeded in breaking the overarching problem of Security Council reform into a small number of more easily digestible sub-problems. Good examples of these are given in the Co-Chairmen's Report wherein they list the various issues to be addressed in resolving the question of equitable representation on and increase in membership of the Security Council[12] and provide specific questions to be addressed by each member while engaging in the debate on reform (A/49/965: 19).

It is interesting to note, however, that many OEWG members consider these sub-problems to be tightly inter-linked, the resolution of each being dependent on the resolution of all others.[13] In the terminology of organisational learning, therefore, the problem of reforming the Security Council constitutes a non-decomposable or, at least, a nearly non-decomposable set (Haas, 1990) - a general problem area within which sub-problems may be identified but not easily dealt with in isolation from all of the other sub-problems in the set. Since any reform solution will, by necessity, be a "package-deal," a great amount of negotiation, compromise and side-payments will be necessary. The OEWG provides an ideal forum for such interactions.

Finally, the OEWG has begun to learn, despite its relatively short existence, to adapt its operational procedures in order to improve its own effectiveness. The extent of this learning to date has been small but augurs well for the future effectiveness of the Working Group. As a result of disappointment with progress towards initiating actual negotiations on reform, the OEWG has adopted a number of innovations intended to increase the productivity of its deliberations. During the 49th General Assembly, it divided its discussions into two "clusters;" one dealing with equitable representation on and increase in the membership of the Security Council and the other dealing with all other matters related to the Security Council. This allowed the OEWG to decouple reform-related issues from issues not directly related to the reform of Security Council membership and to advance with the former independently of the latter.

A second innovation has been the increased use of informal consultations between smaller groups of OEWG members. As well as conducting 11 formal meetings during the 49th session of the General Assembly, the OEWG met for informal consultations on an additional 21 occasions. Because these consultations normally involved the participation of a smaller number of states, they operated more like subcommittees than like a plenary session of the General Assembly.

Restricting the size of meetings improved the group's decision-making capacity since, as one observer pointed out, "when the entire group [met], it [made] no progress (Bauer, 1995).

Having taken into consideration these positive influences of the OEWG, however, it would be a mistake to overvalue its contribution to diffusing tension in the UN organisation. Although it has succeeded in advancing the reform debate in the ways outlined above, the OEWG has failed thus far to initiate an actual reform process. This is mainly due to the nature of the OEWG itself. It is simply an instrument of the UN member states established to bring the question of Security Council reform to the forefront of UN debate. Whether and how the debate is resolved depends entirely on the actions of its members, all 185 of them. The OEWG does not itself possess any special procedural mechanisms or decision-making rules that might speed agreement on reform. Furthermore, the negative reaction of the OEWG to the initiative displayed by its co-chairmen does not augur well for the future effectiveness of the working group.

Conclusion

Since the beginning of the current debate on Security Council reform in the early 1990s, the UN organisation has witnessed an intense interplay of positionality forces. On the one hand, rising states have displayed upward positionality by attempting to improve upon their position in the UN's hierarchy of influence. On the other hand, those states whose positions are most threatened by the aspirations of rising states have displayed downward positionality by resisting demotion therein. As a result of the interplay of these opposing positionality forces, tension has been generated. The UN organisation has responded by establishing a working-group to facilitate agreement on Security Council reform and thereby to diffuse tension in the organisation. Despite having made important progress in advancing the reform debate, however, this working-group has not succeeded in significantly reducing this tension.

According to the definition of stability presented in chapter 3, therefore, the UN Security Council is an unstable system of international governance. It is ill-equipped with effective mechanisms for diffusing the tension generated by the interplay of upward and downward positionality. In other words, it has difficulty adapting its hierarchy of influence in line with shifts in the distribution of power among states.

The reasons for this may be found in the Security Council's institutional structure. The rules governing the structure and procedure of the Security Council tend to bolster downward positionality and undermine upward positionality. Since only permanent members possess the right of veto, it is impossible to dislodge them from their privileged position in the UN's hierarchy of influence without their consent. In this way, downward positionality is strengthened by the institutional design of the Security Council. On the other hand, rising states that aspire to greater influence within the organisation - rather than being automatically entitled to it as a direct consequence of a relative increase in their capabilities - must gain the support of two-thirds of the UN membership, including all permanent members of the Security Council, in order rise in the UN's hierarchy of influence. In this way, upward positionality is undermined by the institutional design of the UN.

The Security Council can only be made more stable by reversing this state of affairs; i.e., by undermining downward positionality and by supporting - or at least not inhibiting - upward positionality. Providing for the latter without also ensuring the former is not enough, however. In other words, simply facilitating the achievement of permanent membership by rising states will not make the Security Council more stable unless the possibility also exists to demote current permanent members. Even if the OEWG succeeds, therefore, in reaching agreement on reform that adds a number of permanent members to the Security Council, it will not contribute to the overall stability of the Council since it is impossible to demote any of the current permanent members. This may not present much of a problem the first time that permanent members are added to the Security Council. In the longer run, however, continually adding permanent members without also demoting others will seriously undermine the Council's effectiveness.

In order to improve the stability of the Security Council, therefore, it is just as important to undermine downward positionality as it is to support upward positionality. If this could be achieved, the ability of the Security Council to adapt its hierarchy of influence in line with shifts in the relative power of UN members would be greatly facilitated and, thus, its stability greatly improved. Here lies the main problem, however. Undermining downward positionality in the Security Council will remain extremely difficult for as long as permanent members have the power to maintain their position through the use of their veto. Since it does not seem that this state of affairs will change in the foreseeable future, the prospects for improving the stability of the Security Council are not good.

Notes

1. It is important to point out that, despite the impression that this very general analysis may give, developing countries do not hold identical views on how the Security Council should be reformed. On the contrary, there is a rich debate among developing countries as to how the membership of the Security Council should be recast. This is, nevertheless, a debate about the details, not the necessity, of reform. For a survey of the different reform preferences of developing countries, see Kühne & Baumann (1995).

2. The fact that, at the same dinner, President Bush collapsed on live Japanese television added extra resonance to Miyazawa's remarks and provoked some snide headlines in the Japanese press such as the Sankei Daily which announced; "Bush Shock Resounds—Symbolic of an Ailing America" (Mc Carthy, 10.01.1992).

3. It suggests, for example, that in expanding the membership of the Security Council, a certain number of permanent and non-permanent seats should be added and that "special consideration should be given to the question of equitable geographical distribution in relation to non-permanent members." It suggests further that "as regards the permanent membership, consideration should be given to whether the weight that the Member State in question carries is global in political, economic and other terms" (A/48/264: 54).

4. Japan's promise to the effect that, if elected as a permanent member of the Security Council, it would act as a representative of Asian states and also of small states (Reuters, 15.06.1994; Economist, 17.09.1994) may have been a ploy to win support for its permenent membership campaign. More recently, a senior official of the Japanese Permanent Mission to the UN stressed that if Japan were to become a permanent member, it would have global concerns and would not be interested in restricting itself to being a representative of a wider Asia (Interviews, New York). In any case, Indonesia, for one, does not believe that Japan could, even if it wanted to, fulfil the task of being the representative of Asia on the Security Council since it is not a developing country and, therefore, could not adequately represent the interests of the region (Wisnumurti, 30.01.1996).

5. Up to now, the Bundestag has given every indication that it will support the participation of German armed forces in multilateral military operations. Following the ruling of the FCC, it voted overwhelmingly to sustain the deployments the constitutionality of which had been brought into question. In November 1995 the cabinet decided to contribute around 4,000 troops to the Bosnian peacekeeping mission and on December 7, the Bundestag supported this decision with a majority of 81 percent.

6. This is not the first occasion, however, on which the representation of a permanent member has been altered. In 1971, the communist government of mainland China took over the Chinese permanent seat from the nationalist Chinese government in Taiwan (see Bailey, 1988).

7. However, some resistance to the idea of expanding the permanent membership of the Council remained in the British camp. Martin Morland, British permanent representative to the UN in Geneva until late 1993, mourned that "there has been a brief golden interlude after the Cold War when the clouds parted and the Security Council was able to exercise real power, but when the Germans and Japanese join I can see the clouds drawing in once again" (Sheridan, 01.11.1993).

8   Russia cast this veto in May of 1993 killing a resolution aimed at restructuring UN peacekeeping in Cyprus. Moscow opposed joining with other UN members in paying its share (less than $2 million) to support a smaller peacekeeping force that would have taken over from a larger force financed by Britain. See J. Bone, "Russia Vetoes Plan to Cut UN Cyprus Force," *The Times* (May 12, 1993): 11.

9   "Japan is not enthusiastic about proposals to establish a new category of membership of the Security Council, be it in the form of semi-permanent membership or otherwise" (Japanese Ministry of Foreign Affairs document [http://www.nttls.co.jp/infomofa/unj/reform.html]).

10 Nevertheless, Germany supports any attempt to phase out the veto. Beginning from the assumption that the current permanent members will not voluntarily relinquish their veto privileges under present conditions, the German strategy, according to an official, is to gnaw away at the veto from the inside, having first itself achieved permanent membership and veto rights (Interviews, New York).

11 Following the submission of the OEWG's report, Boutros Ghali asked "will we be able to have this reform for the 50th anniversary in 1995?" and answered "Two years ago I was hoping. Now, I'm less sure" (Kyodo, 05.09.1994).

12 The report breaks the problem of Security Council reform into the following sub-problem areas: Principles of membership expansion, optimal size of an expanded Security Council, criteria for new permanent members, extension of veto to new permanent members, removal of re-election ban, and new categories of membership.

13 In reporting on the various sub-problems facing OEWG members, the Co-Chairmen frequently make observations of the kind that suggest strong issue-linkage; i.e., "Some delegations suggested that this question depends on other aspects of a proposed package agreement" (A/49/965: 8); and "the question of the extension of the veto could only be decided after an agreement had been reached on whether or not there would be new permanent members and on who would occupy these seats" etc. (A/49/965: 11).

8 Hierarchy and Flexibility in the International Monetary Fund

Introduction

This chapter asks the same questions of the International Monetary Fund (IMF) as chapter 5 asked of the UN Security Council: What is the nature of the IMF's hierarchy of influence and how was it formed? Which factors originally influenced its ability to adapt to changes in the international distribution of power and how well does it adapt to such changes? Again, in answering these questions, this chapter seeks to test the validity of hypothesis 1 - presented in chapter 3 - which states that "the most powerful states to emerge from system-wide conflict establish and institutionalise a hierarchy of influence atop which they place themselves and through which they attempt to govern the post-war international system."

The structure of this chapter is also identical to that of chapter 5. It is divided into four parts. The first part examines in detail the process that led to the establishment of the IMF's hierarchy of influence and identifies the actors that exerted most influence over this process. Part two outlines the multiple dimensions of the IMF hierarchy. Part three identifies the factors that influenced the amount of flexibility built into the IMF's hierarchy of influence at the outset while part four assesses the extent of this flexibility. As in chapter 5, strong support for hypothesis 1 is found.

The Genesis of the IMF Hierarchy

Two factors are of particular importance in explaining the emergence of the hierarchical governance structure of the IMF; the leading role played by British and US experts in designing the post-war economic system and the political imperatives imposed by these two states on the organisation being designed.

First Steps in Post-War Economic Organisation

The "supreme act of faith" involved in the creation of the International Monetary Fund can only be explained, according to the official IMF history, "by the coincidence of the hour and the men" (Horsefield, 1969: 3). What is particularly noteworthy, however, is the earliness of the hour during which plans for the organisation began to be conceived and the expertise and relative independence of the men who conceived them.

Perhaps an even more profound act of faith underpinned the insistence of the United States and, especially, the United Kingdom to begin planning for a post-war economic order well before it was at all clear that such an order would be of their making. In 1940, when the Axis powers had firmly established political and economic control over most of Europe, Walther Funk, German Minister for Economic Affairs and President of the Reichsbank, publicised his own plan for the reconstruction of the German and European economy following the war. At that time, with the US not yet militarily involved in the war in Europe and the UK focusing most of its attention on avoiding invasion from the continent, it must have seemed to many that Funk's so-called "New Order" had a better chance of prevailing than did any plan being incubated in either the US or Britain.

But it was precisely Funk's speculative economic planning that spurred the main architect of the post-war economic order, John Meynard Keynes, to seriously consider the task at hand (Van Dormael, 1978). Soon after the release of the Funk plan, the UK Ministry of Information entrusted Keynes with the task of discrediting German economic propaganda over the radio-waves. From this beginning emerged Keynes' plan for the establishment of an International Clearing Union.

Across the Atlantic, planning for a post-war economic order was also proceeding apace. The US administration was convinced that economic cooperation, even more than political cooperation, was vital to a peaceful post-war era. It was determined to reject isolationism and economic nationalism and to construct a multilateral system (Gardner, 1980). The US Treasury also had vision and expertise on its side in the form of Harry Dexter White, who would eventually produce a key plan for the establishment of an International Stabilisation Fund.

Whereas the impetus for British thinking of post-war economic organisation stemmed mainly from the need to curb German propaganda, the lessons of the inter-war period served to consolidate the US conviction that timely economic planning was necessary. As Van Dormael (1978: 3) succinctly points out in his analysis of the creation of the Bretton Woods system, after World War I there had been no economic cooperation. On the contrary, reparations were extracted from the vanquished while burdensome war-debts exacerbated tension among the victors. In the early 1920s inflation played havoc with the German economy. Efforts to ameliorate the situation, in the form of the Dawes and Young plans, "provided temporary but artificial relief." The crash of 1929 introduced a shift towards isolationism, economic self-sufficiency and impoverishment. As a result, "the 'have-nots' resorted to armed aggression on the plea of economic self-defence" and another world war erupted.

The US administration in particular was determined that a similar chain of events should not be allowed to unfold following the cessation of hostilities against the Axis powers and was convinced that this goal could only be achieved by establishing and maintaining liberal international trade practices. Britain, for its part, was more concerned with the policies that it might be forced to pursue following the war. Keynes had warned early in 1941 that, were the UK to be beset by grave post-war economic conditions, it might be forced to instigate protectionist policies and to discriminate against US goods. At the Atlantic Conference in August 1941, Roosevelt and Churchill made a first attempt to reach a compromise on these potentially divergent outlooks and to define common post-war economic objectives. During the negotiations, the US effectively used its lend-lease agreement with Britain as a leverage tool to move the British government away from the idea of protectionist economics. In parts four and five of the resulting Atlantic Charter, provision was made, admittedly in vague terms, for equal access to trade and raw materials and for international collaboration for economic advancement following the war.

US efforts to convince Britain to refrain from resorting to protectionist tactics after the war achieved further success with the signing of the Mutual Aid Agreement in February 1942, once more with the help of leverage gained from the lend-lease arrangement. The Mutual Aid Agreement set out the principles governing the provision of lend-lease supplies to Britain. In return for a US promise of a generous lend-lease settlement, Britain agreed to the wording of the Mutual Aid Agreement's article seven which elucidated a binding international commitment to multilateralism on the part of the United States and Britain. According to Gardner (1980), the long-fought-over agreement over article seven effectively ended arguments about the objectives of post-war economic policy - the policy would be liberal and multilateral - and heralded in the real planning stage of post-war economic reconstruction.

Two independently devised, yet surprisingly similar, plans formed the foundation upon which Anglo-American discussion of post-war economics took place. The plans, one British and one American, were products of the individual expertise and vision of two former academic economists - John Meynard Keynes and Harry Dexter White. It is significant that their economic expertise, more than considerations of a purely political nature, was the driving force in the design of the post-war economic order. Although, as I shall demonstrate later, political considerations did play an important role in determining various aspects of the IMF - such as its size, voting arrangements etc. - the principles according to which the Fund was originally conceptualised were overwhelmingly those of economics.

The Keynes and White Plans traversed the Atlantic numerous times and, between 1942 and 1943, were closely examined by officials at the US and British treasuries and underwent numerous re-draftings. In May and June of 1943, the US held consultations on the White Plan with numerous countries in Washington, following which it consulted once more with Britain alone. Around this time, alternative plans for the organisation of the post-war economic system also emerged; the French plan, the Canadian plan and the Federal Reserve Board Plan although none of them, save, perhaps, for a few innovations of the Canadian plan (Horsefield, 1969), had any significant impact on the design of the IMF. Even when other countries were allowed to participate in the planning of the post-war economic order, the leading role played by the US and Britain remained evident.

The culmination of the Anglo-American exchange of views on the White and Keynes Plans came when officials from the US and Britain meeting in Washington in late 1943 produced the first draft of what would become the "Joint Statement by Experts on the Establishment of an International Monetary Fund." Following this agreement, which set the ground-rules for the negotiations to follow, the US invited 44 governments to attend a formal conference at Bretton Woods for the purpose of formulating concrete proposals for the establishment of post-war economic institutions and, before the conference began, consulted with 16 countries in Atlantic City.

It is not necessary here to provide a description of the Keynes and White plans nor to describe in any more detail the series of events that led from the drafting of the plans to the Bretton Woods conference. Much has already been written on these subjects both in the official history of the IMF (Horsefield, 1969) and in other impressive historical works (Gardner, 1980; Van Dormael, 1978; Dam, 1982). The purpose of this introduction to the pre-history of the IMF is to emphasise three things: The preponderant role played by the United States and Britain in planning for the post-war economic order (De Vries, 1986), the strong US commitment to establishing a liberal post-war economic order and its ability to impose that commitment on Britain and, finally, the important role played by technical expertise in conceptualising an institution for that purpose.

The Hierarchy Takes Shape

Just as the United States and Britain played a dominant role in initiating post-war economic planning, their experts also determined that the institution responsible for post-war economic regulation would be hierarchical in structure and would grant different levels of influence to different members depending upon some measure of their economic capabilities. In their respective plans for post-war economic institutions, both Keynes and White foresaw a system of weighted influence whereby the extent of a country's participation in the institution would largely determine it share of decision-making power.

In the April 1943 version of his plan, Keynes wrote that: "Each member State shall have assigned to it a *quota*, which shall determine the measure of its responsibility in the management of the Union... Quotas, according to Keynes, should be "fixed by reference to the sum of each country's exports and imports..." but should be flexible enough to allow for special adjustments "where this formula would be, for any reason, inappropriate" (Horsefield, 1969a: 22). In this latter statement, Keynes wished to allow for political input into the determination of quotas in cases when a quota generated by objective means was unacceptable to the member in question.

White, in the July 1943 version of his plan, proposed a novel compromise between the principle of sovereign equality and the principle of weighted decision-making that, nevertheless, strongly favoured the latter principle. He argued that "the distribution of *basic votes* shall be closely related to the quotas of member countries, although not in precise proportion to the quotas." He suggested that "[a]n appropriate distribution of basic voting power would seem to be the following: Each country shall have 100 votes, plus 1 vote for the equivalent of each 100,000 unitas ($1 million) of its quota" (Horsefield, 1969a: 93).

From the outset, therefore, "both Keynes and White accepted the principle of weighted voting power, and there is no record of any objection to it in the discussions before or during the Bretton Woods Conference" (Gold, 1981: 26). All participants at the conference, in fact, "entertained few thoughts about abstract principles of sovereign equality" (Zamora, 1980: 576). While this did constitute a significant departure from conventional representational patterns in other international organisations where the principle of the sovereign equality of states still largely supported the one-state-one-vote standard, the decision to organise the IMF according to a hierarchy of influence did not represent a complete break with tradition. It followed on the heels of the precedent set by an increasing number of technical organisations and unions that, beginning with the Central Commission for the Navigation of the Rhine in 1804, had used weighted voting in their decision-making processes.

An immediate concern with 'value for money' also played an important role in determining that the Fund would be hierarchically organised since "it was... inconceivable that the countries which were going to put up much the largest part of [the] money should not take it for granted that... the size of their monetary contributions would also be recognized in determining their power to mould the decisions" (Fisher, 1968: 335). Furthermore, the technical nature of the proposed Fund and the related hope that its activities would remain above politics may also have accounted in some part for the willingness of participants to accept the principle of weighted voting. US Treasury Secretary Henry Morgenthau Jr. was determined to maintain the technical integrity and political independence of the organisation being created; "these are to be financial institutions run by financial people, financial experts, and the needs in a financial way of a country are to be taken care of wholly independent of the political connection" (quoted in Gardner, 1980: 11).

Political Determinants of the Hierarchy

As it turned out, however, political considerations played a much more prominent role in determining the shape of the Fund's hierarchy of influence than Morgenthau had originally hoped. The "formula" suggested by White to determine objectively the level of members' quotas - and thereby their relative decision-making power within the organisation - became the channel through which political influence came to be applied to the formation of the IMF's hierarchy of influence.

As early as 1943, Professor Raymond Mikesell of the US Treasury had come up with a formula for calculating quotas by first of all establishing a US subscription the size of which would be acceptable to Congress and, from that point, deriving the quotas of other important members on the basis of a hierarchy and a relative distribution of influence that had already been determined by the United States government. As Susan Strange argues:

> United States officials had decided that to avoid congressional opposition, they could raise their own Fund subscription most painlessly by assigning to the Fund the surplus of over $2.8 billion that had accrued

to the U.S. Treasury (as guardian of Fort Knox) when the dollar had been devalued against gold in 1934. They had then, in effect, calculated a formula that gave the United States a quota of about this size, and - in relation to the other countries - a dominant voice in the conduct of the organization (Strange, 1973: 264).

White had made it clear to Mikesell that the formula to be devised should allocate to the US a quota of about $2.5 billion, about half that to Britain and appropriate quotas to the USSR and China that would guarantee them the third and fourth spots on the hierarchy respectively (Horsefield, 1969). In order to achieve this outcome, Mikesell found it necessary to introduce into the formula data on national income and use it in conjunction with the, more appropriate, data on international trade and exchange reserves.[1] Doing so provided two major advantages to the United States. First, since national income figures for the US were considerably higher than those in the rest of the world, it helped the US to justify its preponderant position in the hierarchy of the proposed Fund. Second, since considerable uncertainty shrouded the national income figures of many countries, a certain degree of flexibility was created that proved advantageous in adjusting certain quotas in order to make them conform with political realities.

Despite Mikesell's best efforts, however, his formula could not calculate politically acceptable quotas for all of the countries involved in the negotiations leading up to the Bretton Woods Conference. This was made clear by the negative reactions of various states to a list distributed by the US Treasury before the conference showing what the quotas of participating countries would be according to the formula. As a result, in May 1944 the US and Britain decided to discard the idea of devising a single formula altogether. Instead, the two focused their attention on reaching agreement on the size of the US quota, the size of the British quota and the overall size of the proposed Fund, i.e., the size of the aggregate quota. This strategy caused one French delegate to the Bretton Woods conference to complain that "quotas were established more or less arbitrarily by the United States in a series of deals" (quoted in Horsefield, 1969: 97).

In determining the quotas of lesser members, however, the Mikesell formula did play a limited role. The formula generated quotas that served as starting-points for negotiation with individual prospective members; negotiation that depended as much on political considerations as it did on economic ones. Looking back on the Bretton Woods negotiations three years after, White recollected that:

At Bretton Woods the results given by the formula were discussed among various delegations and were given to the members of the Quota Committee as a reference point for their work. The Committee undertook negotiations and reached agreement with all but a few delegations, but generally not at the amount set in the formula. [...] Thus in the final result it was recognized by all concerned that the formula was only one of the factors entering into consideration and could in no sense be called definitive. The only significant figures were those which had been negotiated and accepted by the participating nations (quoted in Horsefield, 1969: 97-98).

Good examples of the role of the formula in bargaining over quotas are provided by the attempts to agree upon a quota for the Soviet Union and China that took place in 1944. The USSR was wholly dissatisfied with its proposed quota, calculated under the Mikesell formula, of $763 million. White assured the Soviet delegation attending a series of meetings with the US Interdepartmental Committee, however, that they could count on receiving 10% of the total votes of the proposed organisation. At the Bretton Woods Conference a year later, the US delegation supported an increase in the Soviet subscription to $1.2 billion "almost entirely in recognition of its political and potential economic importance" (Altman, 1956: 138).

Similarly, during the course of consultations prior to Bretton Woods, China had been promised fourth place in the Fund's hierarchy of influence by the United States. As a result, its calculated quota of $350 million - under a US calculation of July 1944 - had to be substantially increased - to $550 million - in order for it to occupy this position. In both the Soviet and Chinese cases, therefore, figures generated by the Mikesell formula bore little relation to the final quota-level granted to each country. Because these figures failed to grant Russia and China the amount of influence within the IMF that they had been promised, new figures were generated out of political necessity.

Formulas continued to be taken lightly following the Bretton Woods conference. When the Executive Board began reviewing some members' requests to have their quotas increased immediately after the Fund had commenced operations, they rejected member's arguments for higher quotas made on the basis of Mikesell formula calculations stating that this formula had "no official standing" (De Vries, Horsefield et al., 1969: 354). Likewise, in dismissing staff proposals in the period prior to the second quintennial review of quotas that relative increases should be granted to members both with mushrooming international trade and with quotas grossly out of line with those calculated by the Mikesell formula,

Executive Directors concurred with the Managing Director that "quotas could not be fixed on statistical grounds alone" (ibid. : 356) warning that the ranking of countries agreed upon at Bretton woods on the basis of economic and political considerations should not be altered solely on the basis of economic criteria (Horsefield, 1969: 451).

The measurement of objective economic indicators, therefore, played an extremely limited part in establishing the Fund's original hierarchy of influence. Although a formula was devised for this purpose, its variables were manipulated so as to generate a pre-ordained hierarchy that was based on political expediency. What is more, during the Bretton Woods conference this formula was used only as a starting-point for negotiating the size of individual member's quotas. The negotiations that led to the final determination of the quotas incorporated political as well as economic considerations. For the vast majority of the 45 original IMF members, the quota assigned to them at Bretton Woods differed, sometimes significantly, from the figure generated by the Mikesell formula: "Eight quotas were more than 20 percent higher and nine more than 20 percent lower than indicated by the calculations. The actual range of variance was from 67 percent higher than formula to 75 percent lower, a rather wide spread" (Lister, 1984: 53).

The hierarchy of influence created at Bretton Woods was more a product of political wrangling than of economic objectivity. The fact that agreement was reached at all was due largely to the nature of quotas themselves. As Susan Strange (1973) has pointed out, because quota-levels not only determine decision-making influence within the Fund but also the size of each member's subscription to the Fund, a quarter of which had to be paid in gold, agreement on quota sizes was easier to reach than would have been the case if quotas had only determined a member's right to draw on the fund and to exercise influence within it. Nevertheless, even after the close of the Bretton Woods conference, many countries remained dissatisfied with the quota that had been assigned to them.

The Nature of the IMF Hierarchy

The quotas assigned at Bretton Woods created a hierarchy of influence within the IMF headed by the two states that, between them, had determined the shape of the institution. With the passing of time, the complexity of the Fund's hierarchy has become apparent. It is determined not only by the differential distribution of voting power among members but also by the composition of the Fund's three decision-making bodies, the majorities required in order to pass different categories of decisions, and the use of voting - or, more accurately, the lack of it - in the Fund's decision-making process.

Voting Power

In accordance to the Articles of Agreement signed at Bretton Woods, the influence of states within the IMF is determined by their quota size. Quota size, in turn, determines how much each states contributes to the Fund. Thus, the more states contribute to the IMF's fund of currencies and gold, the more influence it has in deciding how these funds will be used. Each member is allocated 250 basic votes and one additional vote for every part of its quota equivalent to SDR 100,000 (originally $100,000). The basic vote allocation, first suggested in the White Plan, was intended to increase the influence of the smallest members and to prevent the domination of the Fund by one or two members (Gold, 1981). It also represented a compromise between the dominant doctrine of sovereign equality and the idea of weighted influence (Gold, 1974a) that had become more popular in technical international organisations since the early nineteenth century.

With time, however, the intended effect of basic votes has lessened due to the fact that the ratio of basic votes to quota votes has tended to decrease for all members due to general increases in quota-levels over the years. The result has been that voting power in the Fund is now more directly determined by quota-size than it was when the Fund commenced operations. Even then, however, the basic vote allocation, while increasing the influence of the smallest members, did not significantly effect relative voting power in the Fund.

Decision-Making Bodies

The differential influence of Fund members is reflected in the Fund's three main decision-making bodies - the Board of Governors, the Executive Board and the Interim Committee. The Board of Governors is the highest decision-making body and is composed of one Governor per member. The Governors, being usually ministers of finance or economics or governors of central banks, meet only once a year. At its inaugural meeting in Savannah, Georgia in March 1946, the Board of Governors delegated all of the powers that it is permitted to delegate by the Articles of Agreement to the Executive Board, in effect giving the latter the power to govern the day-to-day activities of the Fund (Gold, 1972). As a result of subsequent amendments to the Articles, further powers have been reserved for the Board of Governors that concern sensitive, sometimes political, issues that impinge upon the Fund membership as a whole.

Whereas the Board of Governors retains jurisdiction over all vital aspects of IMF decision-making - the admission and expulsion of members, the revision of quotas, the interpretation of the Articles of Agreement, etc. - the Executive Board is most involved with the everyday operation of the Fund and with preparing resolutions for the consideration of the Board of Governors. It is in permanent session and is composed of 24 - up from 12 in 1946 - Executive Directors either appointed or elected by member states every two years. Those members in possession of the five largest quotas are entitled to appoint their own Executive Director. Usually, these five countries will also account for the two currencies most used by the Fund during the course of the previous two years of transactions. If this is not the case, however, those two countries whose currencies have been most used are each also entitled to appoint an Executive Director. Remaining members form electoral colleges in order to elect representatives to the remaining Executive Director posts. Elected Executive Directors cast, as a block, all the votes of the members that elected them.

The most influential members of the IMF, therefore, also find it easiest to protect their own interests since they exercise permanent influence on the Executive Board and need not worry about representing the interests of other states. Less influential members, on the other hand, must entrust the promotion of their interests to a, more often than not, foreign representative who may not necessarily hold the same opinions on all matters as they do. From the perspective of interest representation, therefore, the holders of the five largest quotas enjoy a distinct advantage. Furthermore, Executive Director-appointing states exercise relatively more influence on the Executive Board than they do on the Board of Governors due to the fact that, on the Executive Board, other members are forced to vote in groups (Dreyer & Schotter, 1980).

A similar situation exists on the Interim Committee, which has the same number of delegates representing the same voting constituencies as the Executive Board. The Interim Committee is a relatively new addition to the Fund's decision-making apparatus. It was established in 1974 pending the completion of the second amendment of the Articles of Agreement which foresaw the establishment of a permanent Council of Governors. It is an "interim" committee insofar as it will remain in operation only until such a permanent council is established. The Interim Committee is composed of Finance Ministers or Central Bank Governors and meets more often than the Board of Governors. It acts as a kind of clearing-house for politically contentious issues that cannot be resolved in the Executive Board. It has come to constitute a very effective part of the Fund's decision-making machinery and, as will be demonstrated, has played an important role in facilitating shifts in the relative influence of Fund members.

Majorities

As a natural compliment to weighted voting, majority decision-making is practised in all bodies of the IMF. However, different majorities are required for different categories of decision, more important decisions requiring higher majorities. The use of high or "special" majorities in the IMF has increased significantly since its foundation and reflects, in the words of Lister (1984: 80), "a kind of balancing of risks and opportunities for the international community." In other words, as a price for the delegation by governments to the IMF of ever more important tasks, some governments have demanded closer control over the work of the Fund in the form of higher voting majorities for important decisions.

During the negotiations leading up to the Bretton Woods Conference, the United States insisted that special majorities be required for all decisions of importance in order to allow it to exercise a veto over decisions it opposed. By the time of the conference, however, Britain had managed to persuade the US that special majorities should be required for as few decisions as possible (Gold, 1981). At Bretton Woods, only seven categories of decision were subject to special majorities and two were subject to special participation. This represented a very small fraction of the decision-making powers entrusted to the fund (Lister, 1984).

Since Bretton Woods, however, the role of special majorities has increased dramatically, largely due to the insistence by the United States that it retain a veto over the Fund's most important categories of decision. During the early years of the IMF, the US exercised strong influence over the changing pattern of special majorities, subjecting more and more important decisions to an effective US veto (Kahler, 1990). Also, as a result of amendments to the Articles of Agreement, the number of decision-categories subject to special majorities has increased significantly (see Gold, 1977, 1978) due both to increased concern among states with the extent of new powers adopted by the Fund and to a general softening of negative attitudes towards special majorities (Lister, 1984). Finally, when the US share of total voting-power in the IMF fell below 20 percent for the first time in 1963, the number of decision-categories subject to an 85 percent special majority increased, thus ensuring a continued US veto over these decisions, many of which had previously been subject to an 80 percent majority.

Decision-Making Procedures

Although influence within the IMF is determined by share of total voting-power which, in turn, is determined by quota-level, actual voting occurs only rarely on the Executive Board, the decision-making body that governs the Fund's day-to-day activities. It is interesting to note that, in designing the Fund, Keynes foresaw that voting would rarely happen and that, if it did, it would foreshadow the demise of the institution (Gold, 1981, see also Besteliu, 1977). Subsequently, during the Executive Board's first meeting in 1946, a rule was adopted declaring that "the Chairman will ordinarily ascertain the sense of the meeting in lieu of a formal vote" although the rule also stipulated that any director would be entitled to call for a vote (Horsefield, 1969a: 290).

The fact that voting rarely takes place does not mean, however, that relative voting power is irrelevant to decision-making on the Executive Board. In May 1947, a decision was also taken that "in ascertaining the sense of the meeting the Chairman must take account of voting power" (Gold, 1969: 516). Thus, despite the fact that voting itself does not normally take place, the relative voting power of Executive Directors does play a central role in determining the outcome of decisions (Horsefield, 1969; Zamora, 1980).

Nevertheless, it is probably true that "the avoidance of formal voting has tended to moderate the effect of discrepancies in voting strength" (Gold, 1969: 516) - at least to some limited degree - since it is true that the outcomes of some decisions of the Executive Board have not conformed with the outcomes that would have been predicted by reference to the distribution of voting power among Directors (Kahler, 1990). This apparent dilution of the influence of pure voting power may be at least partly explained by reference to the nature of the post of Executive Director. Executive Directors are neither purely employees of the IMF nor purely delegates of their home countries. Rather, the post occupies a relatively neutral space somewhere between the two (Hexner, 1964). Thus, notwithstanding the fact that Executive Directors are differentially subject to instructions from their governments, they share a sense of common identity created by their partial allegiance to the organisation for which they work.

This common bond has generated a high level of collegial respect among Directors which has tended to heighten each Director's consideration of the problems faced by other Directors (Lister, 1984; Gold, 1972). As a result, when taking decisions on the Executive Board, Directors tend to attach "more importance to arguments used in support of a certain position than to the possible voting power of the member state supporting it" (Besteliu, 1977: 526). This high level of mutual respect has created a web of reciprocal obligations within which Directors are encouraged to accept decisions that are not in their immediate interest in return for an understanding that their sacrifice will be considered when future decisions are being made.

This also partially explains why Directors are loath to resort to formal voting since doing so could result in a decision being imposed upon other Directors against their will. Thus, even when a majority of voting power on the Executive Board supports the adoption of a decision but this majority is wielded by a numerical minority of members, the Board usually prefers to postpone the decision until broader agreement can be achieved (Gold, 1972; Hexner, 1964).

In general, therefore, the IMF hierarchy rests on the distribution of quotas among members. The higher a member's quota, the more influence it exerts on the Fund's decision-making process. Two factors serve to slightly increase the influence of smaller members: the allocation of an equal number of basic votes to all and the fact that voting takes place only rarely in the Executive Board. On the other hand, two factors also serve to increase the influence of the largest members above and beyond the influence afforded them by their quota allocation: The fact that on the Executive Board the five largest members are permitted exclusively to represent themselves while all others are forced to organise themselves into groups, and the fact that the largest member of the IMF - the United States - possesses a veto over the most important decisions taken by the Fund.

The Genesis of IMF Flexibility

Consistent with the apolitical convictions with which the Anglo-American designers of the IMF approached the task of creating an institution to regulate the post-war international economy, it was never in doubt that the hierarchy of influence created within the Fund would be flexible; i.e., capable of being recast to fit the realities of the shifting distribution of international economic power (Gold, 1974a). In the April 1943 version of his Clearing Union proposals, Keynes suggested that "quotas should be revised annually in accordance with the running average of each country's actual volume of trade in the three preceding years" (Horsefield, 1969a: 22). Likewise, White in his Stabilisation Fund proposal argued that: "Quotas shall be adjusted on the basis of the most recent data 3 years after the establishment of the Fund, and at intervals of 5 years thereafter, in accordance with the agreed upon formula" and further provided that: "In the period between adjustment of quotas, the Fund may increase the quota of a country, where it is clearly inequitable" (Horsefield, 1969a: 87).

Both Keynes and White took for granted that a successful institution would have to remain sensitive to changes in the relative economic capabilities of its members. They proposed achieving such flexibility by regularly reviewing members' quotas on the basis of largely objective economic criteria and thus updating the Fund's hierarchy of influence on a regular basis. As has already been demonstrated with regard to the genesis and nature of the Fund's hierarchy, however, the initial apolitical idealism of the Fund's founding fathers disintegrated in the face of the political manoeuvrings that eventually determined the shape of that hierarchy. The situation is no different in the case of the Fund's flexibility. Initial hopes that adjustment of the Fund's hierarchy would take place solely with reference to the economic performance of its members as determined by objective criteria have given way to an adjustment mechanism that is driven as much by political as by economic considerations.

The Nature of IMF Flexibility

The ability of the IMF to adapt its hierarchy of influence in line with shifts in the relative capabilities of its members is provided by two elements, one of which promotes flexibility by dint of its inclusion in the Articles of Agreement and the other of which promotes flexibility precisely because it is not enshrined therein. The first of these elements is the provision contained in the Articles of Agreement that quota reviews shall be conducted at regular intervals in order to allow the changing economic performance of members to be reflected in the Fund's hierarchy of influence. The second element is the freedom allowed Fund members in determining the criteria to be used in measuring economic performance.

The Quota Review Mechanism

The first element of IMF flexibility - the provision for the periodic review of quotas contained in Article III, Section 2 (a) - enshrines the principle of flexible hierarchies in the Fund's constitution. It stipulates that:

> The board of Governors shall at intervals of not more than five years conduct a general review, and if it deems it appropriate propose an adjustment, of the quotas of the members. It may also, if it thinks fit,

consider at any other time the adjustment of any particular quota at the request of the member concerned (Article III, Section 2 (a)).[2]

Since its inception, the IMF has undertaken eleven general reviews of its quotas, not including individual increases undertaken under the latter part of Article 3.2 (a), of which there have been many more. As a result of these eleven general reviews, members' quotas have been increased on seven occasions, no increases having been proposed in the course of the first, second and third quintennial reviews and the tenth general review.[3]

On all seven occasions on which members' quotas have been increased as a result of a general review, increases have been composed of two elements - equiproportional increases and special increases. Equiproportional increases raise members' quotas by an equal percentage of their existing quotas and, therefore, do not alter the position of members in the hierarchy of influence. Special increases, on the other hand, are granted to a small number of select members in recognition of their above-average economic performance. They have the effect of altering the relative voting power of members and sometimes of modifying the institution's hierarchy of influence by promoting one member above another in the institutional pecking-order. Special quota increases constitute the main means by which the IMF adjusts its institutional hierarchy of influence in line with changes in the de facto distribution of economic power in the international system.

Dynamic Formulas

No mention is made in the Articles, however, of the criteria to be used in carrying out a general review of quotas. No formula for the calculation of new members' quotas or for the determination of quota increases for existing members is contained in the Articles. This silence is the second element of IMF flexibility. Because no formula is stipulated, members are free to determine collectively the most appropriate formula for the purpose of evaluating the closeness of fit between the relative influence of members within the IMF, on the one hand, and their economic influence outside of it, on the other. Because no formula is pre-ordained, formulas devised by the membership - or, more accurately, the IMF staff - may be updated regularly to fit the needs of the moment, be they determined by political or economic considerations, or both. When the use of one particular formula begins to generate hierarchies that are obviously at odds with the de facto hierarchy of economic influence, members may agree to modify the formula in order to generate more realistic hierarchies. A brief survey of the history of IMF quota formulas illustrates how this adjustment mechanism has worked.

The formula devised by Prof. Mikesell of the US Treasury in 1943 was used as a starting-point for determining the quotas of the Fund's original members. In order to keep the quotas of the first wave of new members comparable to those of the original members, it was also used to calculate the initial quotas of the 27 countries that joined the Fund between 1946 and 1958 (Gold, 1974). The Mikesell formula relied solely on pre-war data, however, and, as time went on, became more and more unsuitable for the determination of quotas. Nevertheless, it continued to be generally applied during the first two decades of the Fund's existence. Its application was not always even, however. As Lister (1984: 53) has pointed out, "the quota system had to be stretched this way and that, sometimes even circumvented... The old formula was used when it could be used and set aside when its use produced embarrassing results."

There were many temptations during the early years to update the Mikesell formula all of which were resisted because of the dependence of the US quota on the strong national income variable of that formula. Since the early Fund relied for its liquidity on the supply of US dollars, other members had little incentive to pursue a course of action that might have reduced US interest in the Fund (Lister, 1984).

Instead, attention was focused increasing the quotas of the Fund's smallest members in order to better enable them to meet their balance-of-payments borrowing needs. A "small quota policy" was introduced in 1955 under which a minimum quota of $7.5 million was established and sympathetic consideration was given by Executive Directors to requests by small members to double their quotas (up to $20 million). A subsequent 50 percent general increase in quotas undertaken in 1959 raised this minimum quota to $11.25 million. The small quota policy, in doubling many of the small quotas already in existence and in establishing relatively high quotas for new small members, completely disregarded the Mikesell formula. As the Fund's official history points out, the minimum quota of $11.25 million "was greatly in excess of the figure reached by applying the Bretton Woods formula to data for a large number of the newly established African countries which joined the Fund in 1963" (De Vries, Horsefield et al., 1969: 360-61).

As well as bypassing the Mikesell formula in setting and increasing the quotas of small members, the Executive Board also began in the mid 1950s to bypass the formula when determining the extent of special increases for the Fund's most dynamic members. In determining the extent of the special increases granted to Canada, Germany and Japan during the general quota increase of 1954, for example, the Executive

Board preferred to rely on post-war trade data and not on pre-war data as stipulated by the Mikesell formula (Lister, 1984, De Vries, 1985). Although no specialised formula was devised for this purpose, the Directors realised that the Mikesell formula had become obsolete for the purpose of calculating special increases and that, if some parity was to be maintained between the institutional and de facto economic influence of Fund members, an alternative means of measurement had to be employed. As early as the mid-1950s, therefore, the Fund had already begun to modify its quota formula in order to ensure the relevance of its institutional hierarchy.

Following the introduction of the small quotas policy, the Mikesell formula had already become relatively obsolete in establishing even a general starting-point for negotiations on the size of new members' quotas. After 1960, the Mikesell formula was downgraded even more in this regard by the introduction of an alternative method of setting the initial quotas of new members. The Executive Board introduced a new guideline called "comparability with other members" whereby, instead of calculating a new member's quota by reference to a formula, a tabular comparison was made between the prospective member's exports, imports, national income and estimated population, on the one hand, and those of similarly endowed existing members, on the other, in order to reach an approximation of what the new member's quota should be. This approximation was then used as a point of departure for negotiations.

Since, by the early 1960s, the Mikesell formula was no longer being used either to determine the extent of increases in large or small members' quotas or to set the quotas of new members, it was clear that it had become outdated and was in need of modification. As a result, in 1962 the IMF staff was asked to undertake research into possible ways of modifying the original Mikesell formula in order rectify the situation. As had been the case with the development of the original formula, efforts to modify it were guided by a number of pre-ordained considerations; this time (1) that the new "calculated quotas" of smaller members - i.e., the quotas generated for them by the new formula - should be substantially increased, (2) that the existing hierarchy of decision-making influence among developed countries should be kept largely intact, and (3) that the aggregate calculated quota should be close to the actual size of the Fund's resources (Lister, 1984; De Vries, 1985).

Finding it impossible to fulfil all of these requirements within the framework of a single formula, the staff came up instead with five new formulas, all of which were modelled, to a greater or lesser degree, on the Mikesell formula and which, between them, met all of the above prerequisites. The first of the five new formulas - known as the "reduced

Bretton Woods formula" - bore the closest resemblance to the Mikesell formula and fulfilled the task of maintaining the hierarchy of quotas among developed countries. It retained the same variables as the Mikesell formula but reduced the weight assigned to each by 50 percent, thus also generating an aggregate quota that more closely reflected the extent of the Fund's resources (Treasurer's Department, 1995: 23).

The remaining four formulas were intended to generate larger quotas for developing countries. They did so by increasing the weights attached to the import, export and export variability indicators, by reducing the weight attached to national income, and by eliminating the variable for reserves (Lister, 1984). Furthermore, two of these four formulas eliminated the non-linear element of the Mikesell formula created by a multiplicative ratio of exports to national income. By manipulating the variables in this way, it became possible to "calculate" significantly larger quotas for developing countries.

In mid-1963, the staff's proposals were coolly received by the Executive Directors who, unwilling to reduce the flexibility of quota determination, reluctantly and somewhat condescendingly agreed to treat the proposals as "a valuable point of reference in the consideration which would be given to quota increases when asked for by members" (Horsefield, 1969: 538). They were adamant, however, in not treating the modified formulas as "explicit guidelines for decisions on such requests" (ibid.). The reasoning behind their less than enthusiastic reception of the modified formulas seems to have been that, since the original formula simply established a point of departure from which negotiations could begin, there was little need to adopt new formulas that would simply establish new points of departure when negotiations would lead to the same end-point anyway. This reaction underlines the acceptance by Executive Directors that politics were just as important in determining quota-levels as were economics. As the Canadian Executive Director put it at the time; "men were masters of formulae, not formulae of men" (Horsefield, 1969: 538).

Nevertheless, the new formulas devised by the Fund staff did play an important role in the determination of quotas until 1980 (Treasurer's Department, 1995) due to the fact that they provided for immense flexibility in quota calculation. The number of available formulas was essentially doubled since calculations made with the five new formulas were made with two different sets of data - one using figures for national income, reserves, exports, imports, and the variability of exports - Set I data - and another, incorporating a wider definition of international trade, that substituted figures for current receipts, current payments, and the variability of current receipts for exports, imports, and the variability of exports - Set II data (Treasurer's Department, 1995). Under this new system, a "quota range" was calculated within which the quota of a member might fall (De Vries, 1985). If a specific calculated quota was needed, the higher of two figures was used: (1) the average of the two calculations made using the revised Mikesell formula and (2) the figure generated by a complicated procedure using the remaining four new formulas and data for both imports and exports and current receipts and payments (Lister, 1984: 59).

Using this system, the Fund was not only able to justify higher quotas both for developing countries and for industrial countries with unusually high rates of economic growth, it was also able to retain a great deal of flexibility in calculating other quotas. In 1965, the new system began to be employed in calculating the quotas of new members. Once more, however, the results generated by it were treated as guidelines only, although, under the new system, calculated quotas did tend to remain closer to actual quotas than had been the case under the original formula. On numerous occasions, however, quotas were granted to new members that departed significantly from their calculated quotas. Also, during the course of various general quota increases over the years, some industrial members declined quota increases that were due to them under the new formulas. In sum, although the new system did close the gap between calculated and actual quotas, it continued to be used as a means to a specific end. In cases where it was not capable of generating the desired result, it was simply bypassed.

At the end of the 1970s, the Fund turned its attention once more to the way in which members' quotas were being calculated. Concerned that a gap was again opening up between members' institutional and de facto influence in the international economic system, it proposed in its Annual Report of 1979 that a review should be undertaken to examine "the quota shares of members in relation to their positions in the world economy with a view to adjusting their shares better to reflect members' relative economic positions..." (IMF Annual Report, 1979: 62). Under the subsequent eighth general review of quotas, further modifications were made to the formulas used to calculate quotas.

Since the ten-formula system had operated "really well" for more than fifteen years (Lister, 1984: 65), only relatively minor changes needed to be made in order to bring calculated quotas closer to the actual quotas of Fund members. The new system reduced the number of formulas from ten to five by relying solely on broader indicators of international trade - payments and receipts as opposed to imports and exports. A reserve variable, already present in the reduced Bretton Woods formula, was introduced into the four other equations as well. The weight attached to the variability of receipts was reduced by 20 percent in all formulas except the reduced Bretton Woods formula. Also, the formulas were improved by updating some of the variables: National income was replaced by GDP and a wider definition of reserves - including SDRs and ECUs - took the place of year-end gold and foreign exchange reserves. The new calculated quota used for each member in the course of the eighth general review was the higher of two figures; the reduced Bretton Woods calculation or the average of the lowest two calculations using the remaining four formulas.

Following the review, the Executive Board preempted the need for similar future modifications in quota formulas in order to minimise discrepancies between actual and calculated quotas. It decided that "the changes that have been made do not preclude further appropriate changes in connection with future reviews" (IMF Survey, March 7, 1983: 67). As well as foreshadowing future reviews of quota formulas, this decision also allows for a closer link between negotiations about the composition of formulas and negotiations about quota increases; sets of negotiations that have, until now, remained largely isolated from one another.

By stipulating in its Articles of Agreement that quotas must regularly be reviewed but by omitting to specify the criteria to be used in undertaking these reviews, the IMF has provided for a great deal of flexibility in its hierarchy of influence which has allowed the Fund to repeatedly update its hierarchy in line with actual relative power relationships in the international economic system.

Strange is correct to point out, however, that whereas decision-making in the IMF "has always been quick to reflect any changes in the specific environment" of the Fund - i.e., the international monetary and financial system - the Fund's specific environment "is itself in very large part the product of much more widely felt developments in the broad political and economic environment" (Strange, 1973: 295). This fact is evidenced by the brief review of the history of formula adjustments given above. On both occasions when the Fund chose to amend the way in which it calculated quotas, it did so not with the intention of subsequently adjusting members' quotas in line with new formulas, but to come up with new formulas that would generate calculated quotas that approximated those already held by members. In other words, the purpose of formula reviews has not been to adjust the Fund's hierarchy of influence in order to make it conform with the hierarchy generated by the formulas, but vice-versa - to adjust the hierarchy generated by the formulas in order to make it conform with the existing hierarchy of influence.

This fact underlines the limited role that formulas have actually played in determining the hierarchy of influence in the IMF, even though the express purpose of formulas is to allow the Fund "objectively" to set its members' quota levels. Quota formulas are, in actuality, a kind of "front" used by the Fund in order to lend its hierarchy of influence a certain air of objectivity and impartiality. In fact, the Fund's hierarchy of influence is determined just as much, if not more, by its general politico/economic environment than it is by its specific monetary/financial environment; i.e., more by decisions made by the Fund's most important governments as a result of their reactions to developments in the international political economy than by balance-of-payments fluctuations experienced by its members. Changes made, or threatened to be made, in the Fund's hierarchy of influence as a result of political and economic developments have been given a veneer of objectivity, post hoc, by adjusting formulas in order to make them generate the desired results. Just as when the original Mikesell formula was being devised, formulas in the IMF continue to play second fiddle to political and economic realities and are largely determined by them.

Conclusion

During the final years of World War II and in the immediate post-war period, the United States and Britain collaborated in creating a hierarchy of influence to govern the post war international economy. Under the guidance of John Meynard Keynes and Harry Dexter White, they elaborated an intricate set of rules and procedures that were to determine the relative decision-making influence of each member of the International Monetary Fund. The formula by which this influence was distributed, however, was determined as much by political as by economic considerations. Furthermore, the position of states in the upper echelons of the original IMF hierarchy of influence was determined not by an even application of the formula devised for this purpose, but by a set of promises made by the United States in the final years of the war. The principal designers of the IMF - the United States and Britain - occupied the top positions in the Fund's original hierarchy of influence.

Keynes and White were greatly concerned with providing for the flexibility of the Fund's hierarchy of influence. They realised that the differential growth in economic capabilities among states would make it necessary to regularly update the distribution of decision-making influence within the Fund. To achieve the desired flexibility, they included within the Articles of Agreement a provision to completely review the Fund's hierarchy of influence every five years and provided for the review of individual members' quotas whenever necessary. By not specifying the criteria to be used when conducting quota reviews, the designers of the IMF, knowingly or not, further increased the Fund's stability.

First, the stipulation in the Fund's Articles of Agreement that quota reviews be regularly undertaken lowers the threshold which tension in the organisation must reach before discussion of hierarchy reform can take place. The amendment of Article III, Section 2 (a) - under the first amendment of the Articles of Agreement adopted in 1969 - to allow for the conduct of quota reviews at intervals less than five years, lowers this threshold even further by allowing persistent dissatisfaction with the Fund's hierarchy to be reflected in more frequent quota reviews.

Second, the fact that the Articles of Agreement do not stipulate the criteria to be used in undertaking quota reviews provides Fund members with the freedom to incorporate political as well as economic considerations into the determination of the Fund's hierarchy. Fund members, with the aid of the Fund staff, have achieved this by developing a series of flexible quota formulas that have proved as sensitive to the economic realities of the Fund's specific environment as they have to the political realities of its general environment. The formulas, on the one hand, and the Fund's hierarchy, on the other, have accommodated one another in equal measure. During the earlier period of the Fund's history, formulas tended to be adjusted in order to fit the realities of the Fund's hierarchy. More recently, however, it has been the Fund's hierarchy that has more often been adjusted in order to fit the realities of the formulas. The formulas and the hierarchy have always been mutually constitutive, however, and are likely to become even more so as debate about the composition of formulas becomes a more integral part of debate about the adjustment of hierarchies.

Finally, because the identity of Executive Directors - the individuals responsible for the day-to-day governance of the Fund - is defined by the perception that their role falls somewhere between that of a representative of the country or countries that appointed them, on the one hand, and that of an employee of the IMF, on the other, they have succeeded in developing a strong bond of collegiality and mutual respect that has had important implications for decision-making on the Executive Board: Directors are loath to resort to voting, an aversion that tends to moderate the effect of the unequal distribution of decision-making influence on the Board. Since consensus is preferred, states that possess lower quotas tend to enjoy a disproportionately high influence in the decision-making process. This contributes to the flexibility of the Fund's hierarchy by instilling in members a sense of common cause that is tempered both by the realities of unequal economic influence and by the realisation that, for the common cause to prevail, hierarchies must remain relevant.

Notes

1. The Mikesell formula was as follows:
   90% of the total of:
   2% of national income, 1940
   plus   5% of gold and dollar balances on July 1, 1943
   plus   10% of maximum variation of exports, 1934-38
   plus   10% of average imports, 1934-38
   increased for each country in the same ratio as average exports, 1934-38, bore to national income (Horsefield, 1969: 95).
2. The wording of this article was changed by the first amendment of the Articles of Agreement, adopted in 1969, in order to allow for general quota reviews to be conducted at intervals of less than five years. The original article stipulated that reviews take place every five years. The amendment was made to placate developing members who were dissatisfied with the extent of the sixth general review of quotas.
3. Reviews of quotas changed from being called "quintennial" to "general" as a result of the first amendment of the Articles of Agreement, adopted in 1969, which, among other things, allowed quota reviews to be held at intervals of less than five years if necessary.

9 Positionality, Tension and Stability in the International Monetary Fund

> The stated objective of Bretton Woods was 'the expansion and balanced growth of international trade'. The principal method used to achieve this end was the restoration of orderly exchanges between member countries: 'stability without rigidity and elasticity without looseness'. This, it was hoped, would prevent another worldwide depression (Van Dormael, 1978: ix).

Introduction

The institutional design of the International Monetary Fund (IMF) constitutes an innovation in international organisation. It was devised not by politicians but mainly by expert economists intent on avoiding the economic malaise that characterised the inter-war years. It was created at a time when the concept of the sovereign equality of states held sway in all but the most technical of international organisations and yet there was never a doubt during its formation that states would be unequally represented within it. Furthermore, since its foundation in 1945, the IMF has been largely successful in adapting its hierarchy of influence in line with the changing realities of international economic power created by the differential economic growth of its members.

It would be a mistake, however, to attribute this stability to the nature of the Fund's activities. In other words, it would be wrong to argue that the IMF is able regularly to update its hierarchy of influence because it deals with financial and monetary matters that are objective and immanently quantifiable and that, therefore, it is spared the political confrontation that hinders other international institutions from responding to the differential growth of their members. Nothing, in fact, could be further from the truth. Chapter 8 has demonstrated the strong influence that political considerations played both in the formation of the Fund's original hierarchy of influence and in the development of its methods of adaptation. This chapter will further show that a long history of political tension generated by the interplay of upward and downward positionality lies behind the Fund's technical façade.

If the Fund's stability is not mainly the result of its largely technical activities, what, then, accounts for its flexibility in the face of the positional forces that cripple many other organisations? This chapter attempts to provide an answer to this question. In doing so, it applies the remaining hypotheses presented in chapter 3 to an examination of the adaptability of the Fund's hierarchy of influence between 1946 and 1995.

Upward and Downward Positionality in the IMF 1946-1995

The examination of the genesis and nature of both the Fund's hierarchy and its hierarchical flexibility undertaken in chapter 8 suggested one main theme: The IMF is as subject to internal political wrangling as is any international organisation dealing with more political issues. Nevertheless, through the review of quotas and quota formulas it has managed regularly to adapt its institutional hierarchy to changes in the distribution of economic and political power while at the same time retaining an air, however thin at times, of impartiality and objectivity. It is this feat that distinguishes the IMF from most other international organisations.

The purpose of this chapter is to examine in detail the obstacles that the Fund has had to overcome in order keep its hierarchy relevant. It examines the tension generated by the interplay of upward and downward positional forces at each of the Fund's most significant quota reviews. It demonstrates that, consistent with the analysis thus far, hierarchy adjustments in the IMF are by no means automatic - i.e., ruled by pre-existing formulas and procedures - but are subject to political quarrels and manoeuvres sparked by the desire of some states to improve upon their position in the Fund's hierarchy and the desire of others to retain their position therein.

The interplay of upward and downward positional forces in the IMF may best be analysed by examining the fluctuating relative influence of Fund members over the course of its history. In order to simplify matters and focus attention on only the most significant developments in this regard, the following analysis will involve only the Fund's most influential members; i.e., those, that, by dint of the large size of their quota or the popularity of their currencies, have had the right to appoint a Director to the Fund's Executive Board.

Since quotas have been reviewed at least every five years since the establishment of the IMF and since, as a result of these reviews, numerous shifts have taken place both in the relative influence of Fund members and in their standing in the hierarchy of influence, the analysis of positionality in the IMF may draw on a multitude of cases. In order to limit the analysis, I will refer in detail only to those shifts in relative influence among the Fund's most powerful members that have led to changes in the Fund's hierarchy of influence or that have been of sufficient magnitude to almost precipitate such a change. In order to establish the occasions on which such important changes have taken place, I have plotted the shifting hierarchy of IMF influence from the Fund's establishment until 1995 in a series of diagrams.

Figure 6 is the most general of the diagrams and represents changes in relative voting power among the Fund's most influential members since the establishment of the Fund. Its purpose is to demonstrate two things: First, that the shares of total votes of both the United States and Britain have fallen dramatically - in the case of the US from 34 percent in 1946 to under 18 percent in 1995 and in the British case from 16 percent to 5 percent - and, second, that the once relatively predominant British position has been completely eroded.

Figure 7 (magnification 1) covers the same period as figure 6 but zooms in on the lower portion of the latter - i.e., that portion from 16 percent of total votes on down - in order to throw into better relief the fluctuating hierarchies in the lower portion of figure 6 and to demonstrate more clearly the decline in British influence.

Figure 8 (magnification 2), again covering the entire period of the Fund's existence, expands the very lowest portion of figure 6 in order to demonstrate as clearly as possible the changing relative influence of all Executive Director-appointing members apart from the United States and, partially, the UK.

In order to represent as clearly as possible the web of fluctuating hierarchies in figure 8, figures 9, 10, 11 and 12 - all magnification 2 - stretch figure 8 into more manageable proportions: Figure 9 covers the period from the Fund's establishment until the end of the 1950s, figures 10 and 11 cover a decade each and figure 12 covers the final period from the beginning of the 1980s until 1995, the cut off date for this analysis.

States' relative positions of influence during each year of this period are joined by lines in all figures in order better to represent fluctuations in relative influence and thus help detect not only shifts in the relative influence of the Fund's most influential members but also to pinpoint actual changes in the uppermost portion of the Fund's hierarchy. Intersecting lines in figures 9 through 12 represent such hierarchy changes and, for this analysis, constitute the most significant periods of the Fund's development. Lines that come close to intersecting or that deviate from a common trajectory with other lines are also interesting in this regard, however. A brief look at figures 9 through 12 reveals the most important periods to be analysed. They are: France's attempt to bypass China in 1946, China's demotion and Germany's promotion under the first general review of 1959, the de-coupling of Germany's quota from that of France under the fourth quintennial review of 1965, the rise of Japan under fifth general review of 1970, the closing of the gap with Britain under the eighth general review of 1983 and, most significantly of all, the fundamental shake-up of the Fund's hierarchy that took place under the ninth general review begun in 1990.

First Evidence of Positional Conflict

It did not take long after the commencement of Fund activities for positional forces to become evident in the IMF. Since quotas agreed at Bretton Woods had been arrived at as a result of negotiation between the Fund and the individual members concerned, many members remained dissatisfied with the quota originally assigned to them. At the end of the Bretton Woods conference, four countries - Australia, India, Iran and France - entered their dissatisfaction with the size of their respective quotas into the official record (Proceedings, 1948: 1045, 1088-90). Many more remained dissatisfied but thought it prudent not to have their dissatisfaction officially recorded.

One of the first tasks facing the Executive Board when it began operations in 1946, therefore, was to review requests from such members to increase their quotas. The French, basing their argument on figures generated by the Mikesell formula, demanded that their quota be increased from the $450 million set at Bretton Woods to $675 million, an amount that would have surpassed the Chinese quota of $550 million. China, in response, submitted a request that its quota be increased to $715 million, enough to retain its fourth-place ranking were the French request to be successful. The Board of Governors, however, mindful of the promise made to China by the US during the negotiations leading up to the Bretton Woods conference, decided to grant only part of the increase requested by France. The French quota was increased to $525 million - $25 million less than the Chinese quota - and, since the threat to its place on the Fund's hierarchy was thereby dissolved, China withdrew its request for a quota increase. The resultant relative increase in France's influence in the IMF is shown in figure 4 (1946-47).

Thus, at the very outset of the Fund's operations we see a perfect

Positionality, Tension and Stability in the International Monetary Fund 191

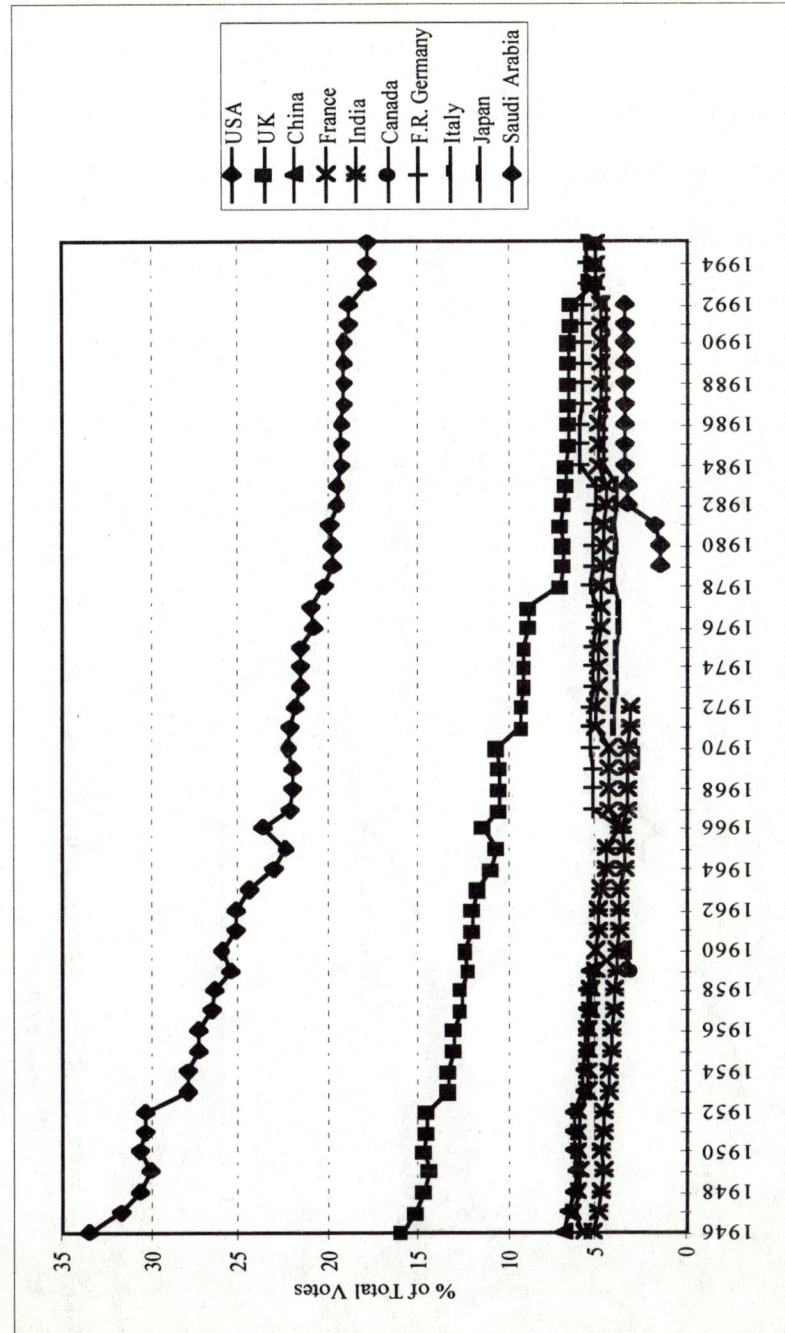

Figure 6 IMF Voting Power 1946-1995
Source IMF Annual Reports

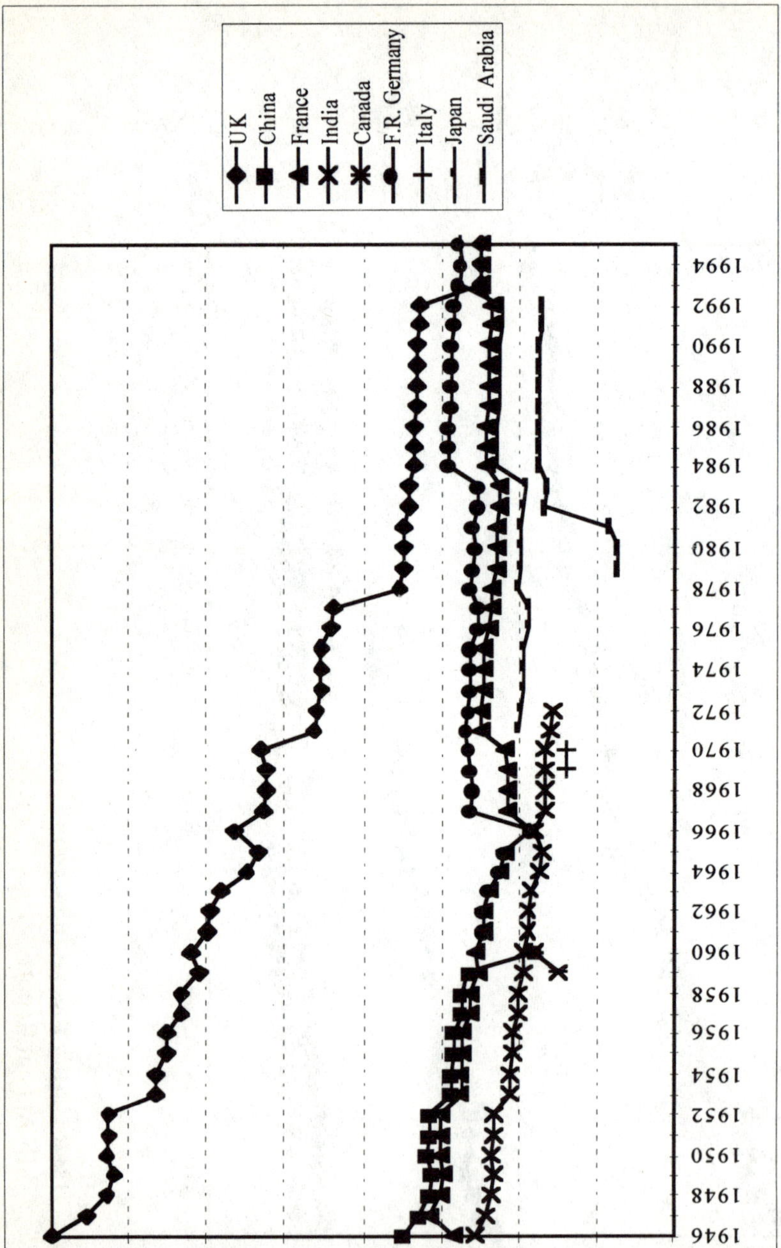

Figure 7   **IMF Voting Power 1946-1995 (Magnification 1)**
Source   IMF Annual Reports

Positionality, Tension and Stability in the International Monetary Fund 193

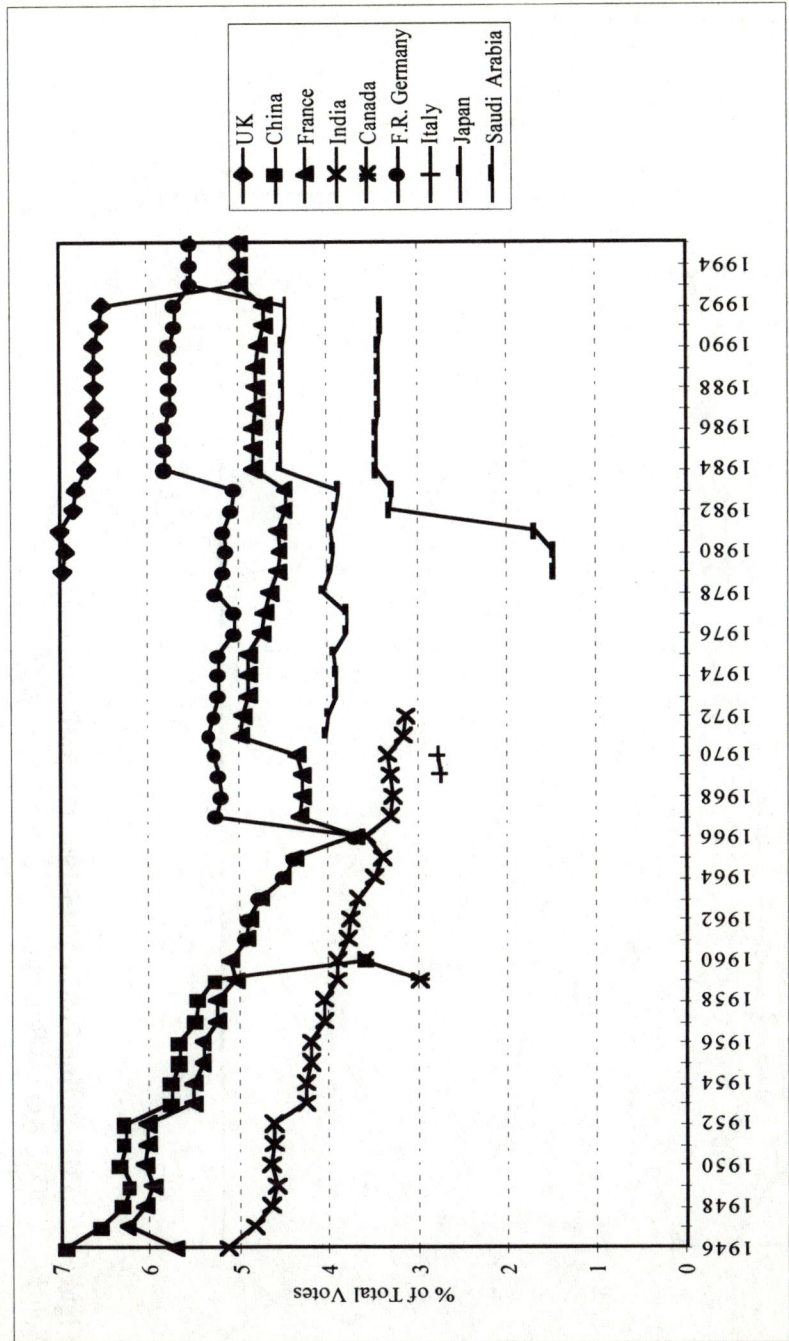

Figure 8 IMF Voting Power 1946-1995 (Magnification 2)
Source   IMF Annual Reports

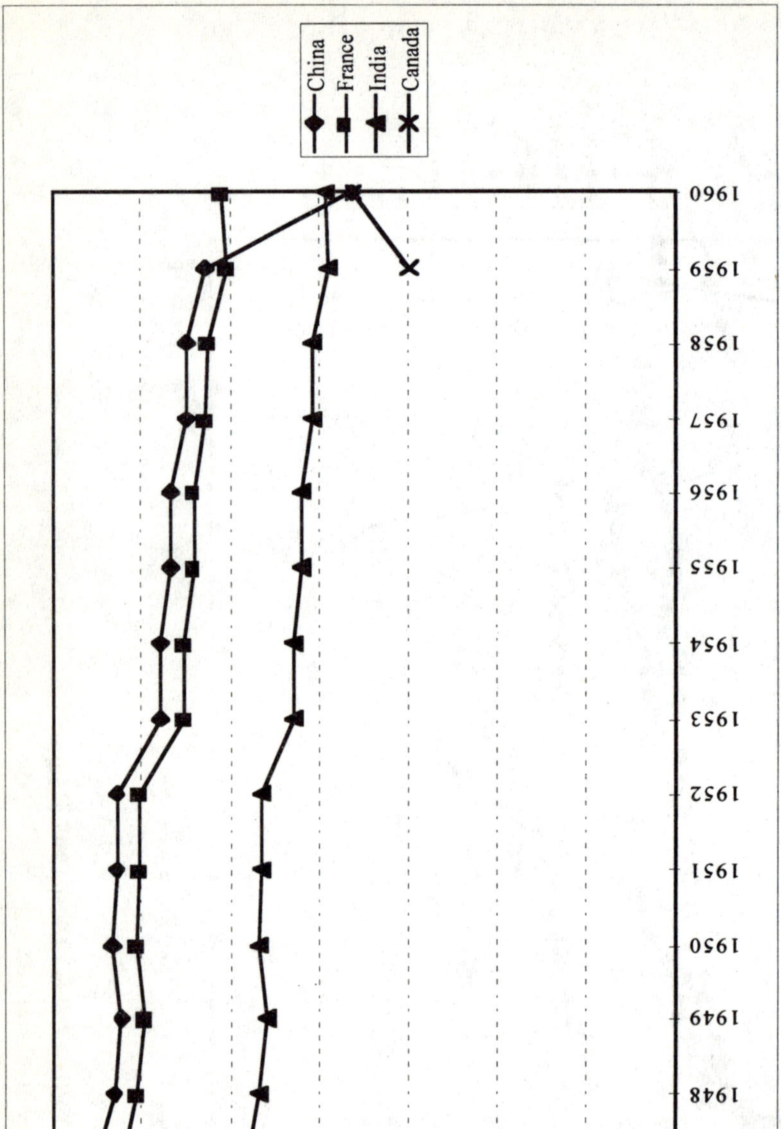

194 *Hierarchy and Flexibility in World Politics*

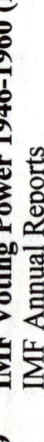

Figure 9 IMF Voting Power 1946-1960 (Magnification 2)
Source   IMF Annual Reports

Positionality, Tension and Stability in the International Monetary Fund 195

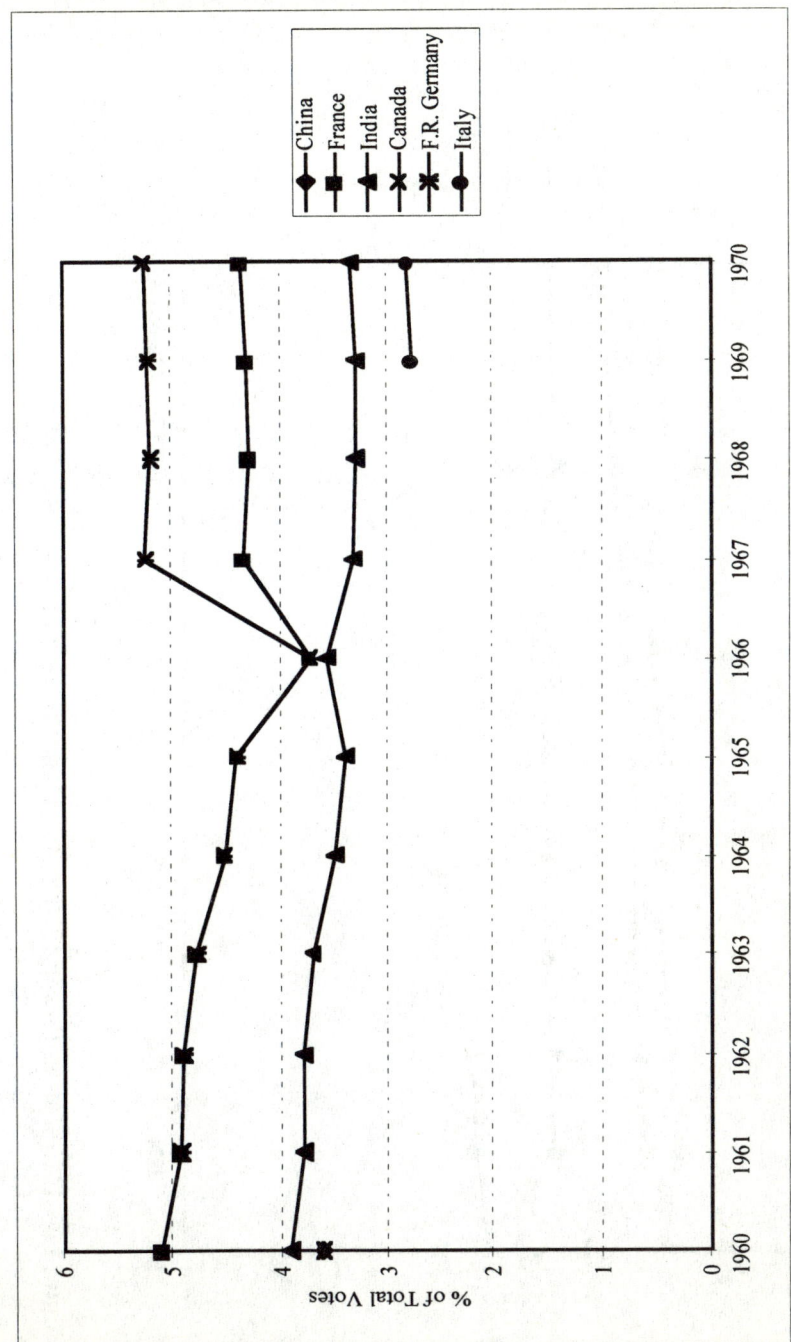

Figure 10 IMF Voting Power 1960-1970 (Magnification 2)
Source   IMF Annual Reports

196 *Hierarchy and Flexibility in World Politics*

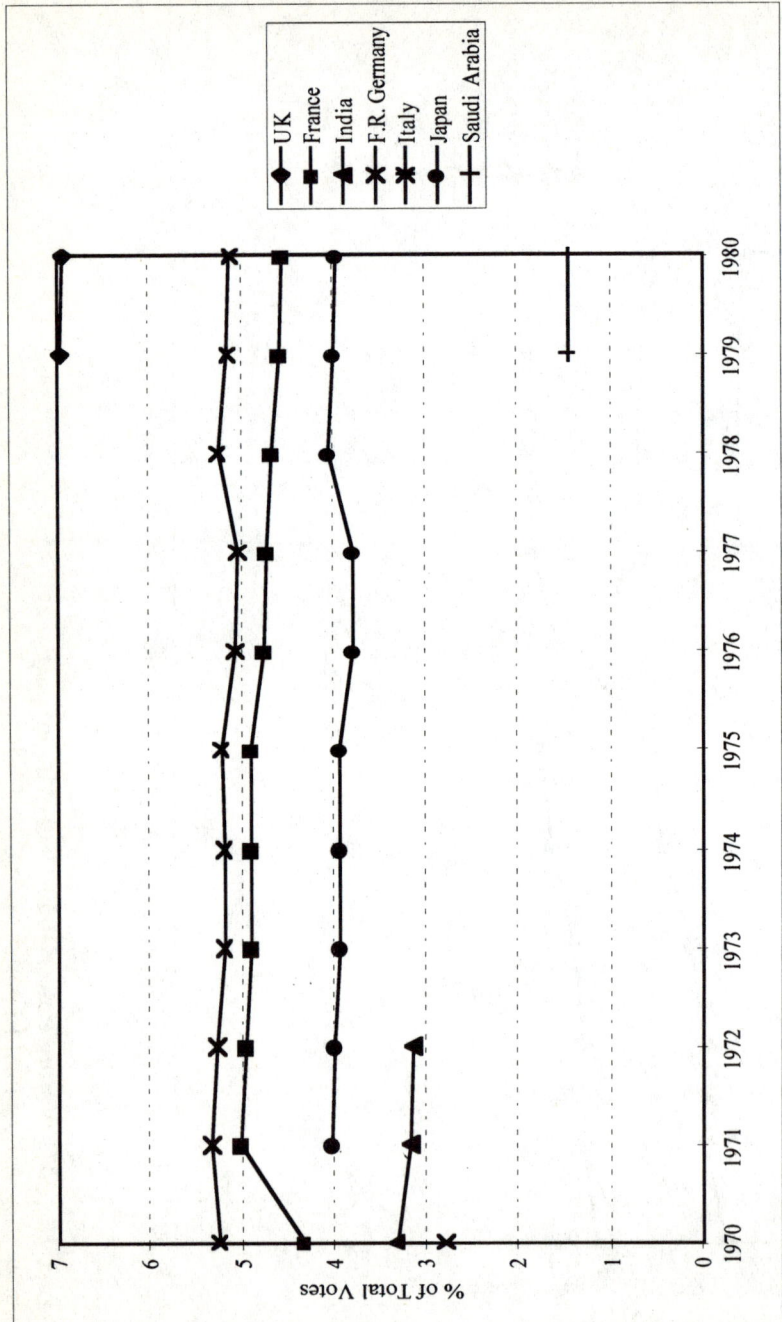

Figure 11 IMF Voting Power 1970-1980 (Magnification 2)
Source   IMF Annual Reports

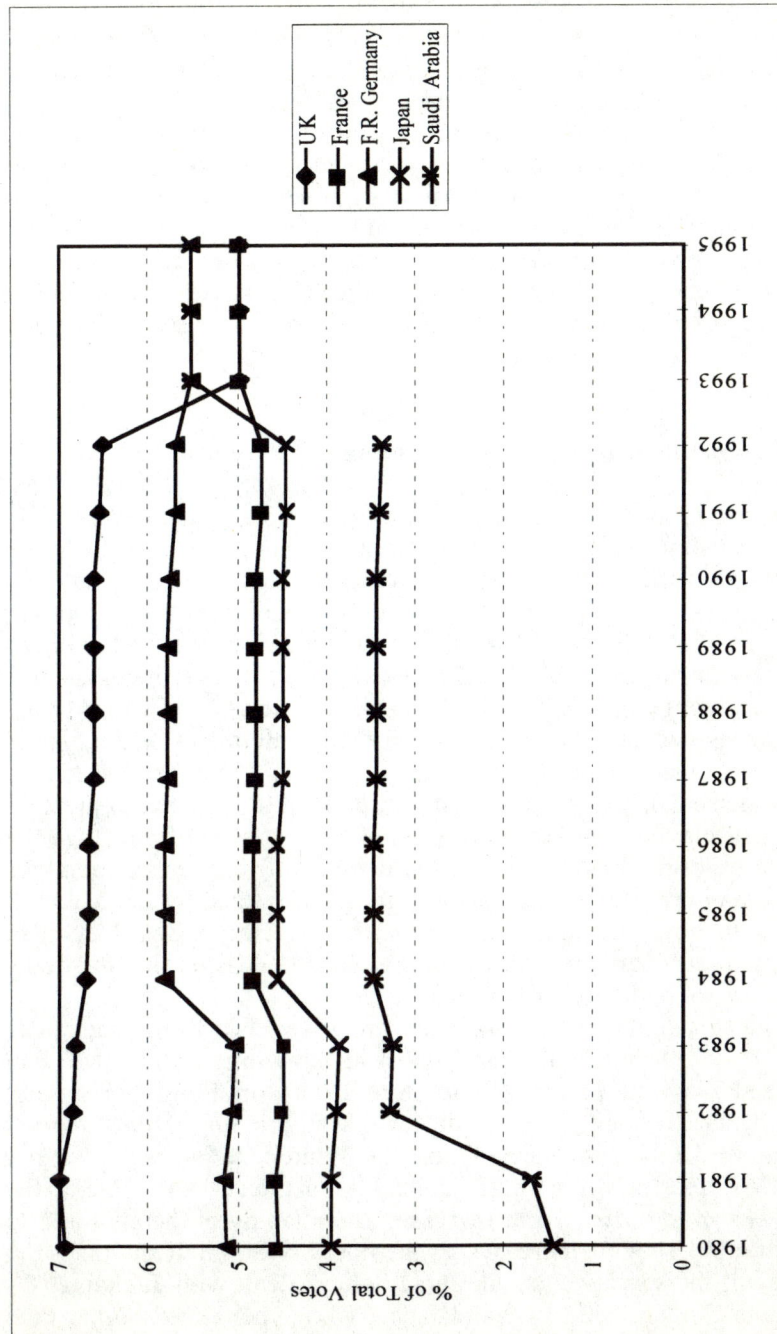

Figure 12 IMF Voting Power 1980-1995 (Magnification 2)
Source   IMF Annual Reports

case of the interplay of upward and downward positionality. France, convinced that its position in the institutionalised hierarchy of governance was not compatible with its actual capabilities, sought to improve upon that position at the expense, inevitably, of another state. China, despite having gained its position mainly as a result of political considerations, sought to defend its position at all costs, even if it meant increasing its quota by $165 million. That this illustrates immense determination on the part of China to retain its fourth-place ranking is evidenced by the fact that, in all subsequent general reviews of quotas until Chinese participation in the IMF was taken over by the government of the People's Republic in 1980, China never once consented to an increase in its quota (Jacobson & Oksenberg, 1990).

The Demotion of China and the Promotion of Germany

It was not long, however, before the resolve and resources necessary to maintain the Chinese position waned. China maintained its number three ranking through the first and second quintennial reviews - in 1950 and 1955 respectively - simply because no quota increases were proposed under these reviews due to the fact that the Fund's resources had not been widely used during its first decade of existence. Nevertheless, some pressure for change had built up prior to both reviews. Prior to the first quintennial review, a staff committee advised that all quotas be doubled in order to reflect the general economic growth of Fund members. Between the first and second reviews, a staff report pointed to the need to increase the quotas of eleven members whose trade had increased faster than the overall increase in world trade as well as those of three more members whose quotas bore little resemblance to those calculated by the Mikesell formula. On both occasions, however, the Executive Board decided against any quota increases, noting on the second occasion that the quota structure was not badly distorted.

The first sign that the Fund's resources were becoming inadequate came in 1957. During that year, almost all drawings on the IMF had necessitated waivers of the quantitative limits on Fund borrowing, suggesting that the aggregate quota level was too low. Staff reports concluded in 1958 also warned that the Fund's resources were not sufficient to meet possible future demands on them. As a result, the Board of Governors decided to increase all quotas by 50 percent and to grant additional special increases to members with small quotas - the beginnings of the so-called "small quota policy" dealt with in chapter 8 - as well as to Canada, Germany and Japan, who experienced higher than average economic growth in the post-war period and to 14 other countries whose Bretton Woods quotas were initially based either on inaccurate or unavailable data.

These changes did alter the upper echelons of the Fund's hierarchy of influence partly by design and partly as a result of China's refusal to accept the 50 percent increase offered it. Because China declined its increase, it relinquished to Germany the right to appoint an Executive Director. Germany's quota had been increased by almost 130 percent as a result of the review. Consequently, its share of total votes had also increased from 3.3 percent in 1959 to 5.1 percent in 1960. As a consequence of this massive increase in influence, Germany also bypassed India in the Fund's pecking-order and took up position on the same step of the hierarchy as occupied by France; each country controlling exactly 8,125 votes.

China's behaviour in this instance reveals a marked departure from the precedent set by its spirited defence of its position in the face of French upward positionality in 1946. Had it accepted the quota increase offered it, it could have retained its position as an Executive Director-appointing state and would have forced India, instead, to be relegated from the top five. However, the fact that Nationalist China would have to have paid 25 percent of its quota increase in gold had become a sufficient preoccupation by the end of the 1950s for China to forego its increase.

India did accept the quota increase offered it and, because of China's demotion and Germany's promotion, retained its position as the smallest Fund member entitled to appoint an Executive Director (see figure 10). Because it accepted the increase, it was largely powerless to oppose being by-passed in the Fund's hierarchy by Germany and since it retained its overall position in the hierarchy, there was little reason to protest. In any case, Germany's phenomenal growth in the post-war years provided sound economic reasons as to why Germany should be promoted above India and, unlike the case of the attempted French promotion in 1946, no compelling political considerations existed that would have served to support India in a display of downward positionality. For all of these reasons, it is not difficult to understand why the promotion of Germany above India in the Fund's hierarchy of influence did not generate palpable tension within the organisation.

The German promotion elicited a more positional response from France, however, whose ranking in the Fund's hierarchy was directly threatened by Germany's rise in prominence. The fact that both countries' quotas were increased to exactly the same amount and that, following the first general increase in quotas, both disposed of exactly the same voting power, indicates that a good deal of bargaining took place between the two prior to the increase in order to reach agreement on the quota-level to which both could agree. The French strategy was guided by the interplay of two main concerns; the maintenance of its relative influence within the Fund and the avoidance of demotion in the hierarchy of influence. France succeeded in its first aim. Its relative influence in the Fund actually increased marginally - from 5.06 to 5.11 percent of total votes. It also managed to maintain its position in the Fund's hierarchy although it consented to share that position with Germany. All of this indicates that France successfully pursued a downward positional policy that prevented Germany from by-passing it in the Fund's hierarchy of influence.

The De-coupling of German and French Quotas

It was only a matter of time, however, before Germany's strong upward positionality overcame France's attempt to contain it. Concern about the level of international liquidity again prompted the Executive Board to commence a review of quotas in 1964, even though the fourth quintennial review was not due to begin until the following year. A staff report concluded in March of 1964 argued that international liquidity would benefit most from a general increase in quotas in the order of 50 percent combined with selective increases for certain members. As a result of intensive debate among the Executive Directors, however, it was agreed to increase all quotas by 25 percent and to grant special increases to 16 members.

Among the members to whom special increases were offered, three are significant from the point of view of the present analysis of positionality; namely, Germany, Canada and Japan. While significant special increases were undoubtedly appropriate for these three countries as a result of their strong economic performance since the previous quota review, considerations of hierarchical positioning also played an important role in determining the quota increases accepted by all three. On the one hand, Canada and Japan surpressed any upward positional tendencies they might have had. Both accepted special quota increases that were smaller than those to which they would have been entitled had reference been made solely to their respective relative economic growth. They did so specifically in order not to displace India as an Executive Director-appointing state (Horsefield, 1969): Canada increased its quota to $740 million and Japan increased its to $725 million. India, which was not offered a special increase and, therefore, only took advantage of the general 25 percent increase, increased its quota to $750 million and, thus, retained its fifth-place ranking.

Germany, on the other hand, gave vent to its upward positionality: France had opposed the quota increases proposed under the fourth quintennial review all along and was sceptical about the means being proposed to increase international liquidity. As a result, it was not prepared to accept a special increase in its quota although it did accept the 25 percent general increase. This "made it difficult for Germany... to accept as large an increase as the data warranted" (Horsefield, 1969: 583) but presented it, nonetheless, with a choice; it could refuse to accept the special increase offered it and, by accepting only the general increase, keep its quota linked to that of France, or it could make full use of its allowance for an increase and by-pass France in the Fund's hierarchy. It chose the latter course of action and took up position as the Fund's third most influential member behind the US and Britain (see figure 10, 1966-67).

Thus, under the fourth quintennial review there is evidence of both restraint and ambition. Japan and Canada, on the one hand, did not display upward positionality even though they both had the opportunity to improve upon their respective positions in the Fund's hierarchy. Germany, on the other hand, chose to improve upon its position even though it had the choice of maintaining its link with the French quota. What accounts for this divergence in behaviour? On the one hand, the behaviour of Japan and Canada may be explained at least in part by the fact that Fund quotas involve both costs and benefits for the states that hold them. While a state's influence in the Fund and the extent of its access to Fund resources are dependent upon its quota-level, higher quotas also required higher gold and capital transfers to the Fund. Since neither Japan nor Canada had made great use of the Fund's resources prior to the fourth quintennial review, they had little incentive greatly to increase their quotas in order to have access to more of those resources. The same reasoning was not followed by Germany, however, who perceived advantage in improving upon its relative influence in the Fund.

The Rise of Japan

Following the completion of the fourth quintennial review, positionality concerns increased among Fund members, especially those situated close to the top of the hierarchy of influence. From the latter half of the 1960s, "[m]embers became more concerned about their relative voting positions in the Fund" (De Vries, 1976: 287). This was due in large part to the fact that the allocation of Special Drawing Rights (SDR), then under discussion, were to be made on the basis of members' quotas; more SDRs to be allocated to members with higher quotas. That members' heightened concern with their relative influence in the IMF was linked to considerations of SDR distribution is evidenced by the fact that the Executive Board decided to begin the fifth general review a little early - in mid 1969 - so that it would coincide with discussions of the SDR distribution. Also, negotiations leading to the completion of the fourth quintennial review had taken almost two years to complete and the Executive Directors sensed in advance that "[t]he fifth general review was likely to raise more intractable questions" (ibid.) due to the renewed interest of members in maintaining or improving upon their position in the Fund's hierarchy of influence.

Early in the negotiations, some of the Fund's largest members indicated their intention to seek substantial special increases in their quotas "in order to bring [them] more into line with their stronger economic positions in the world" (De Vries, 1976: 290). There was an early realisation that "the upcoming quota review would affect not only the total size of the Fund but also the relative positions of members within the Fund, with resulting consequences for voting power and for representation on the Executive Board" (ibid.).

Agreement on an upper limit to the aggregate increase in quotas was reached outside the Fund among the Group of Ten (G-10). They stipulated that the Fund's resources should be increased by approximately 33 percent when both general and special increases were taken into account. This agreement acted as a framework within which further discussion took place in the Fund itself, a significant element of which revolved around persuading as many members as possible to accept smaller increases in their quotas than had been calculated for them so that the overall increase in the Fund's resources could remain within the range indicated by the G-10. G-10 members had limited success, however, in persuading other members - especially other industrial and non-industrial developed members - to accept smaller quota increases since these were adamant that their relative positions within the Fund should not be adversely affected by the solution reached. As a result, the brunt of scaled-down increases necessary to keep the overall increase close to the G-10-imposed limit had to be absorbed by G-10 members themselves, many of whom accepted quota increases that were well below those due to them under the Fund's calculations.

The quota increase finally agreed upon by the Executive Board raised the Fund's resources by 35.4 percent, a figure that was acceptable to the G-10 as a whole. This increase consisted of a 25 percent equiproportional increase and various special increases distributed unevenly among members. Of these special increases, the following are the most significant to this analysis: The United Kingdom accepted an overall quota increase of only 14.8 percent, i.e., not even the full amount of the general increase granted to all members. As a result, its relative position in the Fund dropped significantly, its share of total votes falling from 10.5 percent to 9.4 percent (see figure 7, 1970-71).

Germany agreed to increase its quota by 33 percent while France consented to an increase of 52 percent - the fourth largest quota increase overall. This increase allowed France to gain ground on Germany but was not sufficient to by-pass Germany in the Fund's hierarchy (see figure 11, 1970-71). The largest increase of all, however, was reserved for Japan who increased its quota by all of 65 percent and, in doing so, increased by almost a full percentage point its share of total Fund votes. This increase made Japan's quota the fifth largest in the Fund and automatically entitled it to appoint an Executive Director. As a result, India was relegated from this position in the Fund's hierarchy and took up its new standing at number eight below Canada and Italy, whose quotas, as a result of the large increases accepted by them, also surpassed that of India.

Unchanging Hierarchy

Following the fifth general review of quotas, the hierarchy of influence among the Fund's most powerful members remained unchanged until the ninth general review took place in the early 1990s (see figures 11 and 12, 1971-1992). During this time, however, shifts did take place in the relative power of these members that are significant enough to warrant a brief examination. First, the relative influence of Britain continued to decline dramatically. In 1979 its share of total Fund votes fell below 7 percent (registering for the first time under magnification 2 of figure 11) and, for the first time, its position in the IMF hierarchy became vulnerable. Second, in the same year, Saudi Arabia, as a major creditor country, appointed its first Director to the Executive Board. Finally, the influence of Germany and Japan increased relative to all other Executive Director-appointing states as a result of both the sixth and eighth general reviews (see figure 11, 1977-78 and figure 12, 1983-84).

Among the Fund's most influential members, the period between the fifth and ninth general reviews was again characterised by high levels of tension generated by the interplay of upward and downward positionality. As a result of the first amendment to the Fund's Articles of Agreement - completed in conjunction with the fifth general review in the late 1960s - quota levels were to be used, in addition to their other functions, to determine the extent of members' access to SDRs. Because of this increase in the importance attributed by the Fund to quota levels, "every member was vitally interested in the size of its quota both in absolute terms and relative to the quotas of other members" (De Vries, 1985: 511). Characteristic of this renewed emphasis on positionality was the fact that, of the equiproportional and special quota increases that took place between the fifth and ninth reviews, it was the specific increases - i.e., those that had the potential of altering the relative influence of members in the Fund - that provoked most debate (ibid.).

Countries and groups of countries - i.e., G-10 members, other developed industrialised members, developed non-industrialised members, major oil-exporting developing members and other developing members - became increasingly concerned with their relative position in the Fund. Those who had demonstrated robust economic performance since the previous review asserted their upward positionality: Prior to the sixth general review begun in 1976, Germany and Japan both initiated vigorous campaigns to increase their quotas, basing their arguments on the steadily increasing volume of their international trade. Likewise, the major oil-exporting countries made reference to the large payments surpluses they had accumulated as a result of dramatic oil price increases to support their contention that their quotas should be substantially augmented. Finally, other developing members, demanding the establishment of a New International Economic Order (NIEO) and, pushing for stronger influence in all international fora in which they were involved, demanded that their collective IMF quota be increased (Ferguson, 1988).

On the other hand, those members who could not make reference to such criteria in order to support demands for special increases in their quotas, displayed strong downward positionality. They were "reluctant to see any reduction in their relative shares [of total quotas] because changes in quotas had direct consequences for voting power in the Fund and for representation on the Executive Board" (De Vries, 1985: 512). The tension - or "conflicts of interest" as De Vries calls it - caused by the interplay of these positional forces made the sixth, seventh and eighth reviews of quotas particularly difficult to execute.

The question that dominated the negotiations constituting the sixth general review was who should pay - through a relative decline in influence - for the large quota increase that was due to the major oil-exporting developing countries. At the first meeting of the Committee of the Whole dealing with the review in April 1974, non oil-exporting developing members made it clear that they were not willing to bear the brunt of such an increase and demanded that their relative influence, as a group, not be adversely affected by the sixth quota review. The US suggested that the burden of the increase be shared proportionally between all OECD countries except Britain, who had already made clear that it was willing to let its relative influence drop disproportionately.

Germany and Japan were not satisfied with this suggestion, however, pointing out that their economic advances since the previous review had been the highest in the Fund and that, therefore, their quotas should be increased more than other industrialised countries. In making this argument, Japanese officials called attention to the "imbalance between the quota structure of the Fund and the relative economic strength of members" (De Vries, 1985: 520), a clear reference to a gap perceived by the Japanese to be opening up between the institutional hierarchy of the Fund and the de facto hierarchy of international economic affairs.

In the face of such strong upward positionality from Japan and Germany, many other industrialised countries also expressed concern about maintaining, or improving upon, their relative position in the Fund. As an added complication, the US was not willing to see its share of total votes fall below the 20 percent that guaranteed it a veto over the most important decisions of the Fund. Although an 85 percent majority had been introduced for certain categories of decisions in the first amendment to the Articles of Agreement adopted in 1969, many important decisions continued to be taken by an 80 percent majority. The US favoured a buffer of one or two percent above the vital 20 percent level. In 1977, its share of total votes stood at just over 21 percent (IMF Annual Report, 1977: 120). This figure gave little room for downward manoeuvre.

After much discussion and "behind the scenes activity" (De Vries, 1985: 523), especially between industrialised countries, agreement was eventually reached to increase quotas by SDR 10 billion - the equivalent of an increase in the Fund's resources of 32.5 percent. It was agreed that the quotas of the group of major oil-exporting developing countries would be doubled and that the relative influence of the group of other developing countries would be maintained. Only after a last-minute accord was reached between industrial members, however, did the final shape of the review become clear. Under the agreement, the overall share of votes held by industrialised members fell from 63 to 59 percent, enough to compensate for the increased influence of the oil-exporters. Within the industrial group, influence shifted from the US, Britain and France toward Germany and Japan. The US, in return for an amendment to the Articles of Agreement that made an 85 percent majority necessary to pass all of the Fund's most important decisions, agreed to allow its voting share to drop dangerously close to the 20 percent mark. Britain accepted a drop in voting share of over one and a half percent. Germany and Japan, on the other hand, improved upon their relative position while France's share of total votes fell slightly (see figure 11, 1977-78).

Because of the heightened interest of states in their relative position in the Fund, negotiations for the sixth general review were intense and protracted. The Executive Board had failed to reach agreement on the review before February 1975, the deadline implied in the Articles of Agreement, and was forced to continue negotiations well beyond that date, the final version of the review being adopted by the Board of Governors one year later. Members were also slow to ratify the review once it had been adopted (De Vries, 1985). All this is indicative of the increasing positionality concerns of members.

The seventh general review also raised similar problems, demonstrating that "the expansion of the Fund's resources through increases in quotas was becoming politically much more difficult than it had been in the past" since "the question of relative distribution of quotas among individual members... was raised much more sharply in the sixth and seventh general reviews of quotas than in the three decades since Bretton Woods" (De Vries, 1985: 535-36).

Once more, the interplay of upward and downward positional forces was clearly evident. During the course of the seventh review, the US asserted that there should be no change in the relative position of members and that only equiproportional increases based on existing quotas should be granted. Germany and Japan, on the other hand, argued that special upward adjustments should be granted to those members whose quotas were "seriously out of line with their relative positions in the world economy" (De Vries, 1985: 531); a category that included many oil-exporting countries and, naturally, Japan and Germany themselves. Most other developed countries, however, opposed disproportionate increases for Japan and Germany (ibid. : 533). As a result, the Executive Board failed to reach agreement on the seventh general review and referred the issue to the Interim Committee, the Fund's decision-making body that serves the function of resolving politically sensitive questions.

Eventually, and somewhat surprisingly, agreement was reached by the Fund's Interim Committee to go along with the suggestion of the Fund's new Managing Director, J. de Larosière, to increase all quotas by 50 percent and to grant special increases only to 11 developing members. Since, under the seventh general review, no special increases were granted to industrialised members, their influence in the Fund relative to one another was not altered.

The eighth general review also did not alter the Fund's hierarchy of influence but did modify the relative influence of certain members.

The review took place as the Fund was considering a $5 billion package to rescue Mexico from a major financial crisis. A prominent concern of the review negotiations, therefore, was that the Fund should have adequate resources to deal with similar future cases. A study released by the Washington-based Institute of International Economics in August 1982 warned that, without a substantial increase in the Fund's resources, the IMF would not be able to cope with future crises similar to that experienced by Mexico (Rowen, 25.08.1982). Similarly, the Fund's Interim Committee, meeting in Helsinki in May 1982, reaffirmed their conviction that the IMF "must be strong enough, and have adequate resources, to be able to cope effectively with the problems it may face in the 1980s" (IMF Survey, 16.08.1982: 249).

Although the developing debt crisis may have constituted the overarching theme of the eighth review, substantial consideration was also given to the problem of adjusting the Fund's hierarchy of influence. At its Helsinki meeting, the Interim Committee observed that "the present quotas of a significant number of members [did] not reflect their relative positions in the world economy and... enlargement of the Fund under the Eighth General Review should be used to bring the quotas of these members more in line with their relative positions..." (IMF Survey, 16.08.1982: 250). By the time of the next Interim Committee meeting in Toronto in September 1982, however, little agreement had been reached on the details of the review. The delay was caused in large part by US resistance to the large quota increase - 50-100 percent - being sought by most other members.[1] Nevertheless, the Committee re-iterated its commitment to adapt the Fund's hierarchy to that existing in the world economy.

The question of how an increase in resources should be distributed among Fund members in the form of selective quota increases generated "an animated exchange of views" on the Executive Board (IMF Survey, 04.10.1982: 328). Both upward and downward positionality were clearly evident in the arguments made. One of the most openly upwardly positional members was Japan, whose Finance Minister, Michio Watanabe, argued that "an extensive adjustment of quota shares among member countries would be an indispensable precondition in implementing the eighth quota increase" (ibid.). Similarly, the representative of the Arab members, Sheikh Al Maktoum, emphasised that any quota increase agreed upon under the eighth review "should include significant selective adjustment in actual quotas so as to bring them better in line with the changing relative positions of members in the world economy" (ibid.).

Downward positionality was displayed mainly by less developed countries who feared that their relative influence in the Fund would decline as a result of the large selective increases being sought by some industrialised and oil-exporting members. The group of Latin American countries and Spain, for example, suggested that quota increases should be granted to groups of states so as to preserve their relative influence. Other non oil-exporting developing countries argued that a large percentage of the quota increase agreed upon under the eighth general review should be equiproportional and that only a small proportion of it should be dedicated to selective quota increases.

Of the almost SDR 30 billion quota increase[2] agreed upon by the Interim Committee at its Washington meeting in February 1983, however, only 40 percent was earmarked for equiproportional distribution. The remaining 60 percent was made available for selective increases in the quotas of members whose relative influence in the Fund had drifted out of line with their actual influence in the world economy. The extent of this drift was determined by reference to the difference between members' calculated and actual quotas. Of the Fund's five Executive Director-appointing members, three - Germany, France and Japan - increased their relative influence in the organisation (see figure 12, 1983-84). Of these three, Germany and Japan increased their share of total Fund votes by twice the amount of France's increase, resulting in a decline in the influence of France relative to both countries (see figure 12, 1983-84).

A Hierarchy Transformed

Of all the quota reviews undertaken by the IMF, the ninth general review has been the most significant from the point of view of altering the Fund's hierarchy of influence. A glance at figure 12 (1992-93) shows the drastic hierarchy changes wrought by this review. Lines intersect a total of five times, completely transforming the upper echelons of the Fund's hierarchy from one characterised by the independent spacing of states across a relatively wide range (from 4.5 to 6.5 percent of total votes) to one characterised by the tight spacing of states (from 5 to 5.55 percent) and the sharing of positions in the hierarchy.

The ninth general review also resulted in one major demotion and one major promotion: After almost fifty years of declining influence in the Fund, Britain finally relinquished its number two position in the hierarchy and was demoted below both Germany and Japan to share joint fourth place with France. Japan, on the other hand, after years of outspoken upward positionality, was promoted above both Britain and France to share joint second place with Germany. These changes came as a result of political deals struck between states displaying upward positionality, on the one hand, and those displaying downward positionality, on the other. They were necessary in order to relieve the significant amount of tension that had built up in the Fund since the eighth general review and they demonstrate, better than any of the other reviews, the difficulties involved in altering Fund hierarchies.

Although work on the ninth general review of quotas began in 1987, it was not until June of 1990 that the Board of Governors adopted a resolution to increase IMF quotas by 50 percent. This delay was due in large part to US reluctance to increase its quota while it was trying to win congressional approval for a substantial increase in World Bank resources. It was also due in some part to delays incurred by conflicts of interest between those demanding promotion and those attempting to avoid demotion. Between 1987 and 1990, however, the volume and intensity of behind-the-scenes activity set the scene for the major changes to follow.

As early as the IMF/IBRD annual meeting in Berlin in 1988, predictions were being made that Britain would lose its number two position in the Fund's hierarchy to Japan (Stephens, 23.09.1988), who was actively seeking promotion by pursuing the principles of the "Miyazawa Plan," named after the then Finance Minister. Japan's campaign for a stronger voice in Fund decision-making was initially opposed, however, by the US who, according to the Chairman of the Interim Committee, H.O. Rudding, was reluctant "to have its power diluted by larger Japanese contributions to organisations such as the IMF (FT, 08.02.1989). Rudding also pointed out that Britain, France and Germany "didn't like" the idea of being by-passed by Japan (NYT, 12.02.1989; see also Lord, 11.09.1989) while another source pointed to "Mrs. Thatcher's known dislike of having Britain concede anything in international affairs" (Norman, 26.09.1989).

US opposition to the promotion of Japan in the ranks of the IMF disintegrated, however, when Japan supported US Treasury Secretary Brady's third-world debt-relief plan with a contribution of over $2 billion. Japan was the only government to make such a contribution. In return for this support, the Bush administration accepted that Japan should be given a bigger say in international economic decision-making (Riddell, 13.03.1989). Two other factors also played an important role in the US policy-reversal. First, US support for the promotion of Japan in the Fund's hierarchy of influence was compatible with the overarching US policy of developing closer relations with Japan and other Pacific-rim states. Second, due to a worsening of the situation in Latin America - riots in Venezuela, pressure on the Salinas government in Mexico, etc. - the debt issue had become one of national security for the Bush Administration. The US did not have the resources to deal with this problem alone and was, therefore, willing to involve Japan in the solution, even at the price of increasing Japan's influence in the IMF and, as a result, seeing its own influence decline.

Nevertheless, through the latter half of 1989 the US continued to oppose a large increase in quotas on the grounds, first, that a persuasive case had not been made that a large increase was necessary and, second, that the Fund was not taking sufficient measures to ensure that arrears owing to it were collected on time. In September, the US was one of only three members of the 22-member Executive Board that continued to oppose a large quota increase; the other two being Britain and Saudi Arabia.

During an Interim Committee meeting in September 1989, Japanese Finance Minister, Ryutaro Hashimoto, re-iterated Japan's desire to be promoted to the number two position in the Fund's hierarchy arguing that quotas "should accurately reflect each member country's economic realities" (Lord, 27.09.1989). He was opposed, however, by the British Chancellor of the Exchequer, Nigel Lawson, who argued that no case could be made for more than a modest increase in Fund resources. Lawson supported a 20 percent increase in quotas - one that would not have allowed Japan to displace it from its niche in the hierarchy. He also made it clear that the UK was not willing to discuss changes in the pecking order of the most influential members until agreement had been reached on a quota increase. The Interim Committee, unable to reach agreement, postponed a decision on increasing quotas until the end of 1989.

Faced with this opposition, Japanese officials warned that, if it did not achieve the promotion it desired, its government might experience difficulties in securing legislative support for international lending agencies such as the IMF and the World Bank. The governing Liberal Democratic Party, Japanese officials argued, had been weakened by recent electoral losses and expected to have trouble passing appropriation bills if it could not show that it was being successful in having its growing economic influence reflected in increased institutional influence (Rowen, 26.09.1989).

This manoeuvring by Britain and Japan sparked a "lively internal debate" (ibid.) on who would move up and down in the Fund's hierarchy of influence and caused those states most likely to be leap-frogged by Japan to set in motion a series of face-saving measures, despite the fact that an Italian official continued to maintain that "to drop the Brits from number two to number five would be asking a little much" (ibid.).

At this stage, a possible diplomatic solution to the problem at hand began to crystallise. It was suggested that Japan and Germany share joint second place in the hierarchy of influence above Britain and France who would share the next position. This potential solution introduced an important additional consideration, however, i.e., the willingness of the states in question to share a hierarchy ranking with another state. At the time, although Japan believed it deserved to occupy the number two position on its own, IMF sources indicated that Japan would not oppose sharing the position with Germany (Rowen, 26.09.1989).

The proposal that Britain and France share a spot on the Fund's hierarchy turned out to be significantly more problematic, however. French Finance Minister, Pierre Beregovoy, had stated that France was "willing to be on the same level as Great Britain if it [would] make things easier" (ibid.), suggesting that France deserved to occupy a position above Britain but was willing to consent to an equal ranking for the sake of convenience. Britain, for its part, was unwilling to contemplate occupying a position below France on the Fund's hierarchy and was just as adamant in claiming that, whatever year's data were used in the calculation, Britain deserved to occupy a position above France. A similar argument was later also used by France in sustaining a quarrel that would seriously delay and almost disrupt agreement on the ninth general quota review.

In late November 1989, the deadline for a decision on increasing IMF quotas was again postponed until the end of March 1990 mainly because the US and other Fund members could not reach agreement on the size of the increase. The US indicated that it was willing to support a 35 percent quota increase whereas most other members favoured at least a 50 percent increase. The increase supported by the US would likely not have been sufficient to dislodge Britain from the number two position unless a substantial special increase for Japan was incorporated within it. If such a special increase was included, Japan could have moved to number two but Britain's position would have slipped only one notch to number three, remaining above both Germany and France, who would have been demoted to the fourth and fifth positions respectively (Lord, 04.12.1989).

By the end of 1989, Britain began to concede that it would have to relinquish its place in the Fund's hierarchy to Japan, whose arguments in support of promotion were based upon irrefutable indicators of extraordinary economic growth and whose campaign for promotion had won general acceptance and, more importantly, the favour of the US.

During a series of G-7 meetings in late 1989 and early 1990, agreement was reached that the UK would move down the Fund's hierarchy and that Japan would be promoted to the number two position.

Britain attempted to make a virtue of this necessity by portraying itself as an unselfish benefactor, more concerned with maintaining the influence of developing countries in the Fund than with maintaining its own position in the Fund's hierarchy (see Ryder, 22.03.1990). In the words of the British ambassador to the United States; "the United Kingdom has in fact helped provide a solution to this problem by offering to give up some of its own voting rights, thus enabling Japan's share of the votes to increase without reducing the voting rights of the developing countries" (Acland, 07.03.1990). Britain essentially argued that its demotion was a precondition for Japanese promotion not because of its faltering economic performance but because of the need to maintain the relative influence of developing countries in the Fund in the face of the large increase in influence to be granted to Japan (Norman, 03.01.1990).

Following quickly on the heels of this accord came agreement that, under the ninth general review, quotas should be increased by 50 percent.[3] However, the persistence of an additional positionality conflict delayed implementation of the review. Under the proposed solution for the ninth review, Germany and Japan would occupy joint second place in front of Britain and France, who would occupy joint fourth. While Germany and Japan were willing to accept this solution, Britain and France were not. Both claimed the right to occupy fourth position in the Fund's hierarchy of influence and, initially, neither was willing to yield to the other. When a trip to Europe in late February by US Treasury Secretary Brady failed to result in a solution to the stand-off, the Executive Board was once more forced to extend the deadline for agreement on the ninth review - this time until the end of June 1990.

Britain argued that it had already made an important concession in allowing its share of Fund votes to drop so that Japan could be promoted and added that it was not willing to make a similar additional concession in order to share fourth place with France. France was adamant, however, that it was not willing to occupy fifth place behind Britain (Torday, 07.05.1990). At a G-7 meeting in Washington in May of 1990, both countries came under pressure to reach agreement so that the ninth general review could proceed. Once more, Japan threatened detrimental consequences for its foreign-aid spending if its promotion to the Fund's number two position was not expedited (Joseph, 04.05.1990).

Responding to this pressure, Britain and France engaged in what one participant described as "horse-trading" and succeeded in reaching a compromise agreement under which, for the foreseeable future, both would share joint fourth place in the Fund's hierarchy. Under the terms of the agreement, Britain lent a small percentage of its quota to France in order to allow the latter to increase its voting share to equal that held by Britain. In order to make the agreement long-term and thus to postpone the re-emergence of a similar positional conflict, they further agreed that, should Britain's economic weight fall below that of France, France would return the initial favour by lending Britain part of its quota in order to keep their voting power at the same level. In return for this concession from Britain, France agreed to site the headquarters of the European Bank for Reconstruction and Development in London albeit on the understanding that the presidency of the Bank would go to Jaques Attali, President Mitterrand's economic adviser (Norman, 08.05.1990). Following this agreement, no further obstacles stood in the way of proceeding with the ninth general review, which was duly adopted by the Board of Governors on June 28, 1990, some three years after work on the review had begun.[4]

This examination of the numerous quota reviews undertaken by the IMF since its foundation illustrates three important things: First, the Fund's most influential members are highly concerned about their respective positions in the institutional hierarchy and, accordingly, display both upward and downward positionality. Second, despite the tension generated by the interplay of these positional forces, the Fund's hierarchy of influence has, on numerous occasions, been changed to more accurately reflect the distribution of economic capabilities in the international system. Finally, the procedures followed in order to make these changes have normally only partly conformed with the formal operating procedures of the Fund and have, especially in the case of the ninth general review, often involved the use of "ad hoc" methods of adjustment (Roncesvalles & Tweedie, 1991: 29) arrived at as a result of political bargaining.

Conclusion

Since its establishment, the IMF has been largely successful in maintaining a close fit between its institutional hierarchy of governance and the de facto distribution of economic power in the international system. In doing so, it has not only taken into consideration objective measures of its members' economic capability but also the desire of individual members to move upward or downward in its hierarchy of influence. It would be wrong, however, to attribute this stability to the largely technical function that the IMF fulfils and thereby to argue that the Fund is stable largely because it is not subject to the same intensity of positional competition that may be detected in international institutions involved in traditionally more "political" issue-areas. This chapter has demonstrated that states are extremely concerned with their respective positions in the IMF's hierarchy of influence and have tended to become even more so since the introduction of the SDR facility in 1969 increased the significance of relative quota levels. In short, this chapter has shown that upward and downward positionality have played extremely important roles in determining the outcomes of the Fund's numerous quota reviews.

If the Fund's stability may not be adequately explained by reference to the technical nature of its activities, how, then, may it be explained? The answer lies in the formal rules and informal procedures that govern the adjustment of the Fund's hierarchy of influence. First, the formal provision that quotas be reviewed at least every five years, and more often if necessary, decouples the initiation of debate on reform from the level of tension in the organisation. Thus, the development of a high level of positional tension is not a prerequisite for debate on reform to occur in the IMF. Since the initiation of such debate is provided for di jure, the chances that even low levels of tension will be diffused are greatly increased.

Second, the same formal rules and informal procedures undermine downward positionality and, as a consequence, bolster upward positionality. It is difficult, on the one hand, for states to maintain their positions in the Fund's hierarchy of influence once they have experienced relative economic decline and easier, on the other hand, for rising states to translate superior economic performance into greater decision-making influence within the organisation. This is the case for a number of reasons: Apart from the United States, no IMF member state exercises a veto over decisions to reform the Fund's hierarchy of influence. The ultimate tool of downward positionality is only available, therefore, to the United States. Also, regular reviews of quotas increase the pressure on declining states to relinquish their positions to rising states. Finally, the ability to manipulate the formula used in determining promotions and demotions in the IMF's hierarchy of influence makes it possible to incorporate political as well as economic considerations into reform decisions.

Despite having to cope with opposing positional forces driven by both political and economic developments, therefore, the IMF succeeds in diffusing the tension generated by their interplay by regularly adapting its hierarchy of influence in line with shifts in the actual distribution of economic power in the international system. While the means by which it achieves this may at times appear ugly and involve a good deal of "horse-trading," it is nonetheless evident that the IMF may serve as a model against which the stability of other international institutions may be judged.

Notes

1. For details of the increases sought by other members, see *IMF Survey* of October 4, 1982: 327-328.
2. Under the eighth general review, Fund quotas rose from about SDR 61.03 billion to SDR 90 billion - an increase of 47.5 percent. In addition, however, the resources provided by G-10 members under the General Arrangements to Borrow (GAB) were also substantially increased - from SDR 6.4 billion to SDR 17 billion - and their use extended to all Fund members. As a result of both increases, the resources made available to the Fund were almost doubled.
3. The US agreed to the 50 percent increase - up from its earlier ceiling of 35 percent - in return for assurances that the Fund would proceed more vigorously against states who had fallen into arrears. Also, US officials recognised that the upheavals in Eastern Europe would likely lead to an increase in the demand for Fund resources and that, therefore, a 50 percent increase in quotas was most appropriate.
4. In December 1994, the Executive Board decided that the quota increase under the ninth general review had provided the Fund with adequate resources to enable it to carry out its functions and, although a staff report pointed to continuing discrepancies between the actual and calculated quotas of some members (Treasurers Department, 1995: 33), the Executive Board decided to conclude the tenth general review without an increase in quotas.

10 Reviewing (and Restating) the Hypotheses

Introduction

A theory of stability having been elucidated, a methodology specified, and empirical analyses conducted, all that remains to be done before general conclusions may be drawn from this entire enterprise is to examine the state of the original hypotheses in the wake of the empirical analysis. This is the purpose of this penultimate chapter. It measures the extent to which each of the hypotheses presented in chapter 3 has been supported or undermined by the empirical examination of the UN Security Council and the International Monetary Fund. It argues that the hypotheses have been strongly supported despite the fact that some behaviour was recorded that did not comply with the specific predictions inherent in the hypotheses.

The Strategy of Analysis

With regard to the analysis of case study data, Yin asserts that "[t]he first and more preferred strategy is to follow the theoretical propositions that led to the case study" (Yin, 1994: 103) in order to establish if they do, in fact, correspond with each case examined. In analysing the case studies of the UN Security Council and the International Monetary Fund and in determining the extent to which they corroborate or undermine the theory of stability developed in chapter 3, therefore, I will rely on matching the original hypotheses with the realities of each case.

In this context, Yin argues further that "one of the most desirable strategies is to use a pattern-matching logic [that] compares an empirically based pattern with a predicted one (Yin, 1994: 106).[1] Simply put, if the pattern predicted by a theory coincides with the case study results obtained, the theory will be supported; if not, it will be undermined.

The theory of stability developed in chapter 3 is composed of specific predictions regarding the behaviour of states involved in systems of international governance. These predictions have been made specific in chapter 4. Furthermore, thanks to the use of process tracing in conducting the case study research, it has been possible to compile a rich set of data on both the Security Council and the IMF that allows causal chains to be specified between the identified variables. For these reasons, both the general strategy of focusing on the theoretical propositions made at the outset of this study and, within this framework, of using the specific technique of pattern matching to assess the accuracy of theory, are particularly suited to analysing the case studies conducted in the previous five chapters.

On Reorganisation and Institutionalisation

The first hypothesis presented in chapter 3 states that: "The most powerful states to emerge from system-wide conflict establish and institutionalise a hierarchy of influence atop which they install themselves and through which they attempt to govern the post-war international system." Later in the same chapter, the single hierarchy assumption is relaxed allowing for the establishment of hierarchies of influence in various issue-areas considered by powerful states to be important enough to warrant governance.

This hypothesis closely describes the attempts by the victorious powers to manage international security and monetary affairs following World War II. Even before the cessation of hostilities - in the case of the IMF, even before it was at all sure who would emerge victorious from the war - detailed plans for post-war international security restructuring and for the regulation of the post-war international economy were being developed and discussed by those states who hoped to exert the strongest influence over the governance of the post-war international system. Such plans became the cornerstones of the post-war international security and monetary systems.

In the area of security, the core group of the US, Britain and the USSR determined the shape of the post-war order through their discussions in Moscow in 1943, at Dumbarton Oaks in 1944, and at Yalta in 1945. The sub-grouping of the US and Britain also discussed and co-ordinated policies bilaterally in order to produce the Atlantic Charter in 1941 and, on Malta in early 1945, to prepare for their meeting with the USSR at Yalta. The conclusions of the deliberations of this triad were tested on China and, to a much lesser extent, on France but neither was afforded much influence in the deliberative process. By the time that the United States invited other states to attend the "United Nations Conference on International Organization" in San Francisco in 1945, the structure and voting procedure of the Security Council - including the identity of the permanent members and their right of veto - had already been largely determined. During the course of the conference, the Security Council was presented to the remaining 45 delegations as a fait accompli.

Likewise, in the area of monetary cooperation, the influence of a core group of major powers on the reordering of the post-war system was even more pronounced. In this instance, the United States and Britain determined between them how post-war monetary policies would be regulated. Drawing lessons from the inter-war period, the US was convinced that post-war economic cooperation at a global level was vital if another disastrous war was to be avoided. Britain, on the other hand, although sharing the same sentiments in principle, was worried that it might be forced to resort to more restrictive economic and trade practices following the war. By using the negotiation leverage it had gained as a result of the lend-lease agreement, however, the US was successful in imposing its convictions on Britain, thus keeping it on the path towards a liberal post-war economic order.

British and US economic expertise played a most vital role in establishing an institution to support a liberal post-war international trading order. John Meynard Keynes' plan for an International Clearing Union and Harry Dexter White's plan for an International Stabilisation Fund merged into the "Joint Statement by Experts on the Establishment of an International Monetary Fund," the Document that formed the basis for negotiation at Bretton Woods. The principle of weighted voting in the Fund was also suggested by both Keynes and White in their respective early proposals and the related hierarchical organisation of the IMF was determined largely by the US and Britain in a set of political deals made before negotiators took their places around the table at Bretton Woods.

Thus, despite the impressive spectacle of the large-scale, inclusive conferences held at San Francisco and Bretton Woods, the UN Security Council and the International Monetary Fund did not come into existence as a result of the combined will of the international community of states nor did they assume their hierarchical structure from agreement reached at these mass meetings. On the contrary, the decision to create the Security Council and the IMF and the decision to organise these institutions in a particular hierarchical manner was taken by the most powerful states to emerge from the Second World War - in decreasing order of importance, the United States, Britain, Russia, China and, to a lesser extent, France.

The influence exerted by these states on the reorganisation of the post-war security and monetary systems was by no means equal, however. In both instances, the US took the lead in conceptualising, designing and bringing to fruition the institutions that would regulate these issue-areas.

US experts produced the first draft of the UN Charter and, together with British experts, produced the document that formed the basis for negotiation at Bretton woods. The large-scale conferences that founded both the Security Council and the IMF were held on US soil, with the US government being the main sponsoring nation on each occasion.

The second most influential state in post-war reorganisation was Britain. Its role in creating the IMF rivalled that of the United States. The intellectual leadership and inspiration provided by Lord Keynes was second to none, even if the United States did manage, by dint of the political influence generated by the size of its "money-bags," and the decided lack of same on the British side, to substitute some of Keynes' most central ideas with those of his main intellectual rival, Harry Dexter White.[2]

In the bilateral and small scale negotiations that led up to the San Francisco conference, Britain, along with Russia, also played an important role, although the influence exerted by these two states on the final form of the Security Council did not match that of the United States. China did take an active part in discussing the form and membership of the Security Council although its contribution in this regard was more peripheral than that of Russia and certainly than that of Britain. Although China was an original signatory of the Moscow Declaration, for example, it did not exert a strong influence on its drafting. Furthermore, although China did take part in the second round of negotiations held at Dumbarton Oaks, the most significant decisions had already been taken during the first round of negotiations at which only the US, Britain and Russia were present (Fox, 1946: 116).

Finally, France exerted the least influence of all among the states listed above as being the main shapers of the post-war international system in the areas of international security and money. In the negotiations leading up to the Bretton Woods conference and the creation of the IMF, its only input took place during the medium-scale consultations that the US and Britain organised in Washington in May and June of 1943, prior to the large-scale coming together at Bretton Woods two years later. France's recommendations at this meeting, however, did not exert any appreciable influence on the design of the IMF (Horsefield, 1969). Likewise, France played a peripheral role in the negotiations leading up to the San Francisco conference and the creation of the Security Council. It was not present at the pivotal negotiations held in Moscow, Dumbarton Oaks or Yalta nor was it a sponsor of the San Francisco Conference. It was drafted into the group of permanent members of the Security Council as a result of considerations of prestige, moral and political weight, and its potential to become a regional power

(Lee, 1947; Briggs, 1945).
  Not only did these states collude in deciding to create these institutions and to distribute decision-making influence unequally within them, they also installed themselves on top of each institution's hierarchy of influence. In the Security Council, the Big Five achieved this by granting themselves permanent membership and individual veto power over all substantive decisions. In the IMF, the same Big Five granted themselves the largest quotas - and, therefore, the largest influence - even though the quotas granted to Russia and China could not be justified by reference to the supposedly objective formula that had been devised to allocate quotas. Russia subsequently decided not to become an original member of the IMF, thereby making it possible for India, as holder of the fifth largest quota, to appoint an Executive Director. If Russia had joined, however, the states occupying the upper echelons of the Fund's hierarchy of influence would have been the same as those enjoying permanent membership on the Security Council.

On Differential Growth

The second hypothesis presented in chapter 3 posits that "the differential growth of states causes inconsistencies to emerge between the distribution of power in the international system and the hierarchy of influence created following system-wide war." Since differential growth is treated as an exogenous variable and a perennial characteristic of international politics, little more need be said in this respect. It is clear that states have grown at different rates since 1945. Therefore, it is necessarily the case that this differential growth has caused disjunctures to emerge between the distribution of power in the international system following the reorganisation stage, on the one hand, and the distribution of influence institutionalised during the organisation stage, on the other.

On Upward Positionality

The third hypothesis presented in chapter 3 states that "dissatisfaction caused by inconsistencies between the hierarchy of influence and the distribution of power lead rising states to seek to improve their position in the hierarchy of influence." This hypothesis describes the phenomenon of upward positionality - the action that results from a desire to move upward in a hierarchy of influence - strong evidence for which, but also exceptions to which, have been found in the analysis of both the Security

Council and the IMF.

In the Security Council, upward positionality is more evident in the contemporary debate on Security Council reform than it was during the reform debate of the early 1960s that led to addition of two extra non-permanent seats on the Security Council. The 1965 reform of the Security Council did not result from pressure generated by upward positionality as such. Although it is true that the rank and file UN membership sought to increase their representation on the Security Council through the addition of extra non-permanent seats - and succeeded in this attempt - they did not seek to improve their position in the Security Council's hierarchy of influence by insisting upon the extension of the right of permanent membership and veto power. Nevertheless, to the extent that this reform campaign was driven by a desire to improve the representation of the general UN membership - especially developing countries - and to undermine, however slightly, the decision-making influence of the permanent members of the Security Council, upward positionality did play a small role in reforming the Security Council in 1965.

Upward positionality is to the forefront, however, in the current debate on Security Council reform. It has two main sources. The first is identical to that which characterised the reform debate of the early 1960s; i.e., a large increase in the number of developing countries in the UN and the resulting desire of these countries to increase their representation on the Security Council. The second source of upward positionality stems from the phenomenal growth since 1945 of Japan and Germany, both of which have initiated vigorous campaigns for permanent seats on the Security Council.

These two sources of dissatisfaction with the UN's institutionalised hierarchy of influence have combined in an interesting way. Since Germany and Japan need the support of developing countries in order to ensure the success of their respective campaigns, and since developing countries rely on the German and Japanese campaigns in order to maintain the momentum of the current reform debate, these agitators for reform have reached a compromise whereby developing countries agree to support the German and Japanese campaigns and, in return, Germany and Japan agree to argue for the addition of at least one developing country to the permanent membership of the Security Council. The result of this amalgamation of interests is that both developing countries, on the one hand, and Japan and Germany, on the other, are actively demonstrating upward positionality since they all wish to improve their respective positions in the UN's hierarchy of influence - Germany and Japan on an individual basis and developing countries on a bloc basis, since even the presence of one developing country in a permanent Security Council seat would have significant consequences for the discussion at the highest level of issues affecting all developing countries.

Upward positionality has been perhaps less visible, but no less palpable in the IMF. On numerous occasions throughout its history, Fund members have made it adequately clear, through words and actions, that they were dissatisfied with their position in the Fund's pecking order. On the commencement of Fund operations in 1946, France tried, but failed, to bypass China in the Fund's hierarchy of influence. As a result of the fourth quintennial review of quotas, Germany managed to de-couple its quota from that of France and move above it in the hierarchy. During the course of negotiations on the fifth general review, Japan petitioned for a significant promotion in order to bring its position within the Fund in line with its economic stature in the international economy and, as a result, succeed in appointing its first Director to the Executive Board. In the period between the fifth and ninth general reviews of quotas, Germany and Japan, along with the oil-exporting countries, were at the forefront in demanding increases in their institutional influence and in the ninth review of quotas, Japan succeeded in its attempt to significantly improve upon its position in the Fund's hierarchy of influence.

On the negative side, the empirical analysis of the IMF also uncovered two cases in which a state did not improve upon its position in a hierarchy of influence even though the way had been made clear for it to do so. These two cases refer to the behaviour of Japan and Canada during the fourth quintennial review of quotas conducted in 1964 during which both suppressed any upward positional tendencies they might have had by accepting special quota increases that were smaller than those to which they would have been entitled had reference been made solely to their respective relative economic growth. They did so specifically in order not to displace India from its fifth-place ranking in the Fund's pecking order (Horsefield, 1969). As chapter 9 has pointed out, however, neither Canada nor Japan had a strong incentive to increase their quotas since they were not in need of the increased access to Fund resources that this implied.

For each of these two cases of obvious non-upward positionality, however, many more have been uncovered in the analysis of the IMF and the Security Council that conform with the predictions inherent in hypothesis 3. In general, therefore, strong support is found in the empirical analysis for this hypothesis. In the majority of cases examined, states whose capabilities have been growing at a higher-than-average rate have become dissatisfied with their position in the hierarchy of influence and have attempted to improve their position therein.

The insight provided by the two deviant cases does call for a slight modification of this hypothesis, however. It would seem, logically, that a state that does not stand to gain significantly - either in terms of prestige or material benefit - from improving upon its position in a hierarchy of influence, may not take the opportunity to do so when it presents itself. Hypothesis 3 may, therefore, be usefully restated as follows: "Dissatisfaction caused by inconsistencies between the hierarchy of influence and the distribution of power lead rising states who stand to benefit from such action to seek to improve their position in the hierarchy of influence."

On Downward Positionality

Hypothesis 4, presented in chapter 3, states that "attempts by rising states to improve their position in the hierarchy of influence are opposed by states whose position therein is threatened by these attempts." This hypothesis describes the phenomenon of downward positionality - the action that results from an aversion to moving downward in the hierarchy of influence. In the analysis of the Security Council and the IMF, strong evidence for the existence of downward positionality was found, although some behaviour was also encountered that does not conform to the predictions inherent in hypothesis 4.

In the case of the Security Council, the most striking example of downward positionality was presented by the initial responses of France and Britain to the German and Japanese campaigns for permanent membership thereof. Both France and Britain were quick to denounce such a development, stressing that any change in the membership of the Security Council that might adversely affect its decision-making effectiveness was unacceptable. Furthermore, in opposing the suggestion of permanent membership for Japan and Germany, neither Britain nor France shirked from pointing to the highly dubious correlation that exists between the status of permanent member of the Security Council and the status of declared nuclear power.

This response is a clear indication of downward positionality on the parts of Britain and France and is fully in accordance with the predictions inherent in hypothesis 4. Of all the permanent members, Britain and France are most threatened by the ascension to institutional prominence of Germany and Japan since they have the weakest justification for holding onto their permanent seats. Of course, their position as permanent members is secure even if Germany and Japan are successful in gaining permanent representation since their veto power makes it impossible to relieve them of their seats without their consent. Nevertheless, the presence of Germany and Japan as permanent members of the Security Council would put increased pressure on France and Britain to relinquish their seats.

The subsequent acquiescence by Britain and France to the necessity of reforming the Security Council does not represent a significant decrease in their downward positionality. This shift in emphasis in British and French policy was a necessary response to a difficult political situation. Continuing to oppose openly the general will of UN members - which is in favour of reforming the Security Council - could have precipitated all sorts of problems. Instead, Britain and France chose to make the best of a bad lot by supporting the permanent membership of Japan and Germany, countries with which they enjoy good relationships in any case. They have not extended their support to the idea of granting a permanent seat to a developing country, however, and France still harbours reservations about the extent of Japan's international military responsibility. The change in British and French policy on Security Council reform resulted not because they thought that reform had become a good idea, but because such a shift had become politically necessary. Britain and France - and, to a lesser extent, Russia and China - are reluctant collaborators in a reform process driven by the ambitions of rising states.

Russia and China did not openly oppose at the outset the addition of Germany and Japan as permanent members although their support for such a development was also conspicuously absent. Both have opted for the strategy of ultra-cautious acceptance of the necessity of extending the permanent membership of the Security Council, insisting, however that any such momentous alteration should be approached with great care and only implemented when the widespread agreement of UN members has been secured. China's position is particularly conservative in this respect. As well as foreseeing a long and laborious reform process, it insists that the decision to add permanent members to the Security Council should require the unanimous agreement of UN members - a highly unlikely development.

The initial US reaction to the German and Japanese campaigns for permanent membership, on the other hand, did not correspond to the behaviour to be expected of a downwardly positional state. From the very beginning of these campaigns in the early 1990s, the US has openly supported adding Germany and Japan as permanent members of the Security Council and it may be supposed that earlier US support encouraged both Japan and Germany to initiate their formal campaigns in the first place. One explanation for this deviant behaviour is that the

United States is more secure in its status as a permanent member than are, for example, France and Britain and, therefore, is not as threatened by the rise to permanent member status of Japan and Germany. Another explanation is that granting additional decision-making influence to such like-minded, rich states as Japan and Germany is a convenient way for the United States to underwrite its declining hegemony. Nevertheless, the deviation of US behaviour from that predicted by hypothesis 4 will necessitate a slight reformulation of the hypothesis to the effect that only states that are most threatened by rising states will display downward positionality.

Strong evidence for the presence of downward positionality was also found in the analysis of the IMF. No sooner had the Fund commenced operations in 1946, France and China were embroiled in a positional conflict which China won by asserting its downward positionality, thus retaining its third-place ranking in the IMF's hierarchy of influence. Likewise, during the first general review of 1958, France succeeded in preventing Germany from bypassing it in the hierarchy of influence by agreeing to link its quota with that of Germany. This success was relatively short-lived, however. During the fourth quintennial review of 1964, French downward positionality was no longer a match for a rising Germany who succeeded in de-coupling its quota from that of France and moving above it in the Fund's hierarchy.

During the period immediately preceding and following the introduction of the SDR facility in 1969, IMF members, especially those occupying the upper levels of its hierarchy of influence, became increasingly defensive of their relative positions. Since quota-levels also determined the extent of access to SDRs, states were more determined than ever to ensure that they retained or improved upon their relative influence in the Fund. This was especially evident during the period of the "unchanging hierarchy" - i.e., between the fifth and the ninth general reviews. During this time, reviewing and adjusting quota-levels was particularly troublesome since no state, with the exception of Britain (see below), was willing to pay, through a relative decline of its own quota-level, for the relative increases due to the oil-exporting countries and demanded by Japan and Germany.

The turbulent ninth general review also provides striking examples of downward positionality in the IMF. Against the strong upward positionality of Japan, the United States was originally reluctant to countenance a dilution of its decision-making influence and, therefore, opposed the promotion of Japan. The resolve of the US's downward positionality was subsequently softened, however, by a large Japanese contribution to Treasury Secretary Brady's Third-World debt-relief plan.

The other main example of downward positionality provided by the ninth general review of quotas concerns Britain's final descent, after almost fifty years of gradual decline, from its number two ranking in the Fund's hierarchy of influence. Although Britain had accepted its decline over this long period of time, and even contributed to it by not always accepting in full the quota increases offered it, the ninth general review represented the first time that Britain's place in the Fund's hierarchy was under threat by upwardly positional states. It put up a spirited final defence of its position and its last stand bears all the trademarks of downward positionality.

Britain was at first unwilling to accept as large an increase in quotas as was being demanded by Japan, arguing instead that a 20 percent increase would suffice to fulfil the needs of the Fund. Such a relatively small increase would have made it impossible for Japan to displace Britain from its number two ranking. Faced with increasing pressure for reform, however, and the Japanese threat that both its financial support of the Bretton Woods institutions and the level of its foreign-aid might decline if its demands for promotion were not met, Britain conceded its replacement by Japan as the most influential Fund member behind the United States. In doing so, however, Britain stressed that its demotion was necessary if developing countries were to retain their influence in the Fund, preferring this argument to one that focused on its relative decline as an economic power.

Britain's downward positionality did not stop there, however, but rather came again to the surface over the question of how it and France would be ranked in the Fund's hierarchy of influence. France was of the opinion that, as well as falling below Japan and Germany, Britain should also be demoted below it but, in a rather condescending manner, conceded that it was willing to occupy the same rank as Britain if for no other reason than to simplify matters. Britain, on the other hand, originally refused to accept such a solution, maintaining that any objective measurement of the relative sizes of the British and French economies justified its inclusion above France in the IMF's pecking order. This disagreement intensified over the course of the ninth general review and was only resolved when enormous pressure was brought to bear on both countries to end the dispute; an occurrence that required the significant side-payment by France to Britain of the siting of the European Bank for Reconstruction and Development in London.

As well as these numerous examples of downward positionality in the IMF, however, the empirical analysis of this institution also uncovered a deviation from the predictions inherent in hypothesis 4. China's dogged downward positionality during the Fund's first year stands in sharp contrast to its passive acceptance of its demotion as a result of the first general review of quotas. How can this later behaviour be explained? China's ability to sustain its original strong downward positionality was undermined over the course of the first decade of the Fund's existence by the unwillingness of the nationalist Chinese government to pay the rising price of its high status within the institution. When the first general review of 1958 offered China the possibility of increasing its quota by 50 percent, it declined. As a result, it fell below France and India in the Fund's hierarchy of influence and, in 1961, out of the upper strata of the Fund's pecking order. China's failure to display in the late 1950s the same extent of downward positionality it had displayed in the mid 1940s may be attributed, therefore, to a growing unwillingness to foot the bill demanded by its position.

Also, Britain's acquiescence to the gradual decline of its decision-making influence within the IMF - especially its refusal to accept the full extent of the quota increases offered it as a result of the fifth and sixth general reviews - would seem contrary to the behaviour to be expected from a state attempting to maintain its position in a hierarchy of influence. The fact is, however, that during most of this long-drawn-out period of decline, Britain did retain its position in the Fund's hierarchy of influence. Even though Britain's decision-making influence within the Fund has been in constant decline since the outset, the extent of its original influence - over twice that of its nearest rival - allowed Britain to acquiesce in its own decline and, at the same time, retain its second place ranking. It is not at all surprising, therefore - nor does it contradict hypothesis 4 - that Britain did not do everything it could to maintain its level of influence within the fund during the period 1946-1983. Britain's position was simply not under threat during this time. However, when its position did come under threat after the increase in the relative influence of Germany in 1984, Britain immediately displayed downwardly positional tendencies.

Overall, the empirical support found for hypothesis 4 far outweighs the deviant Chinese case and the apparently deviant British case. As a result mainly of the deviant behaviour of the United States with regard to the proposed promotion of Japan and Germany to permanent membership of the Security Council, however, the hypothesis may usefully be re-stated as follows: "Attempts by rising states to improve their position in the hierarchy of influence are opposed by those states whose position therein is most threatened by these attempts."

On Tension

Hypothesis 5 stated that "As a result of the interplay of upward and downward positionality, tension is generated in the international system. Significantly more tension is generated when the hierarchy of influence is rigidly institutionalised than when it is flexibly institutionalised." The discovery of state behaviour that may be classified as upwardly and downwardly positional in both of the case studies conducted improves the likelihood that hypothesis 5 will also be supported. Indeed, strong support is found for this hypothesis in both the UN Security Council and the IMF.

In the Security Council, tension is generated by the interplay of upward and downward positionality along three main fissures: (1) The urgency with which various states view the necessity of reforming the Security Council, (2) the acrimonious debate on the future of the veto, and (3) the major disagreements over how many permanent and non-permanent seats should be added to the Council and who should fill them. The positions occupied on these issues by various states largely correlate with the direction of their positional tendencies.

On the question of how much urgency is attributed to reforming the Security Council, downwardly positional states tend to prefer a slow, cautious approach while, on the other hand, upwardly positional states tend to prefer a quick resolution of the question. The United States constitutes somewhat of an exception in this regard since it has been a consistent supporter of a quick solution to the problem of reforming the Security Council. As has been outlined above, however, since the US position as a permanent member is not threatened by the proposed promotion of Japan and Germany but stands instead to gain greatly from such a development, we should not expect that it will display the characteristics typical of a downwardly positional state. In this light, the urgency attached by the US to resolving the question of Security Council reform does not seem so exceptional.

The lines of battle with regard to the question of the veto are somewhat different, however. The rank and file UN membership opposed the principle of granting veto power to the Big Five in 1945 and have not changed their positions since. They continue to call for either the phasing out or the outright abolition of the veto and vehemently oppose the extension of veto rights to Japan and Germany, should they succeed in becoming permanent members of the Security Council. Germany and Japan, naturally enough, persist in demanding the full rights and privileges of permanent membership and their demands are largely supported by the present permanent members who wish to avoid the degeneration of the status of the veto that would occur if Germany and Japan were not successful in obtaining it.

Finally, the tension that surrounds the question of whom to add to the membership of the Security Council centres on the issue of how to increase the representation of developing countries. Understandably, developing countries argue that any reform of the Council should improve upon their representation therein, preferably through the addition of developing countries as permanent members. As a result of their alliance with many developing countries on the question of Security Council reform, Germany and Japan are not opposed to the addition of at least one developing country to the permanent membership of the Council. States displaying upward positionality, therefore, also tend to support the creation of a developing country permanent seat on the Security Council. The present permanent members, however, while indicating general support for the improvement of developing country representation on the Council, do not extend their support to the idea of granting permanent representation to a developing country. Interestingly, the United States does not constitute an exception in this regard, as it has on other aspects of downward positionality, but rather displays the same preferences as do the other permanent members. On the question of adding a developing country as a permanent member of the Security Council, the US recognises a sufficient threat to the decision-making efficiency of the institution to oppose such a development.

Since upward and downward positionality have also been identified in the empirical analysis of the IMF, tension has also been evident there. It has taken the form of disagreements that arise when particular states make reference to their strength in the international economy in order to support their demands for promotion in the Fund's hierarchy of influence but are opposed by other states who wish to maintain their relative influence in the Fund. Such tension was particularly palpable during the struggle between France and China in 1946, the rise of Japan beginning with the fifth general review of quotas, and the final decline of Britain from the mid-1980s.

Tension in the IMF has sometimes been accompanied by specific threats - as when Japan threatened to reduce its financial support for the Bretton Woods institutions as well as the level of its foreign-aid if its promotion in the ninth general review of quotas was not expedited - and has sometimes required side-payments in order to be diffused - as when France agreed to site the headquarters of the European Bank for Reconstruction and Development in London in return for the loan of some of the British quota during the same review.

It is generally the case, however, that tension has tended to build up less in the IMF - which has a flexibly institutionalised hierarchy of influence - than in the Security Council - which has a rigidly institutionalised hierarchy of influence. In the IMF, formal rules exist that prescribe the regular review of its hierarchy of influence with the result that tension tends to be diffused at low levels. In the Security Council, on the other hand, no such formal rules exist. Instead, an ad-hoc approach to hierarchy adjustment is taken which, because of its relative ineffectiveness, tends to allow tension to build up to much higher levels.

Another important difference between the way in which tension develops within the IMF, on the one hand, and in the Security Council, on the other, concerns the level of tension that is necessary in order to initiate debate on how to diffuse it. In the IMF, the presence of tension is not necessary in order for the issue of hierarchy review to be debated by Fund members. Even at times when no significant dissatisfaction exists among members with regard to their relative positions in the Fund's hierarchy of influence, the rule concerning periodic review of the hierarchy of influence ensures that the issue of review is raised in any case. Furthermore, as a result of the amendment to Article III, Section 2 (a) of the Articles of Agreement adopted in 1969, quota reviews may be held whenever it is deemed that the level of tension within the Fund is reaching a worrying level and are not, therefore, restricted to being held only every five years, as the original version of the Articles stipulated.

The situation in the Security Council is quite different, however. There is no provision made in the UN Charter for the regular review of the Security Council's hierarchy of influence. As a result, debate on such review does not arise automatically. Instead, a high level of tension must first exist in the organisation before the question of hierarchy review is debated by UN members. In sum, it is not only true that tension tends to be diffused at lower levels in the IMF than in the Security Council, it is also the case that debate on hierarchy reform tends to be initiated at lower levels of tension in the IMF than in the Security Council. A flexibly institutionalised hierarchy of influence has two main advantages, therefore: It aids in the diffusion of tension at relatively low levels and makes the level of tension existing in an institution independent of the decision to initiate debate on reform. A rigidly institutionalised hierarchy of influence, on the other hand, not only allows tension to rise to a higher level, but also makes the existence of such a high level of tension a prerequisite for the initiation of debate on reform.

On Conflict

The two final hypotheses presented in chapter 3 link the presence of tension in an international system of governance to its ability to persist in ordering and managing international affairs. Hypothesis 6 stated that "if the tension generated by the interplay of upward and downward positionality is not diffused but continues to increase, conflict is likely to occur" while hypothesis 7 added that "an international system in which the hierarchy of influence is flexibly institutionalised is less likely to experience conflict than is an international system in which the hierarchy of influence is rigidly institutionalised." These hypotheses are based on the assumption that conflict is more likely to occur when tension within a system of governance is allowed to rise to a high level.

With regard to issue-specific systems of international governance such as the Security Council and the IMF, "conflict" implies the gradual decline or sudden breakdown of such systems precipitated by unresolvable conflicts of interest. It does not imply that the occurrence of an international war is necessary in order to reorganise the distribution of influence within such systems. Since conflict in the former sense has not yet been observed in either of the systems of governance under investigation, hypotheses 6 and 7 cannot be directly supported by empirical observations. Their accuracy may only be judged, therefore, from the plausibility of supposing that decline or breakdown is more likely in systems of international governance experiencing sustained high levels of tension than in those experiencing intermittent low levels of tension.

If this argumentation is correct, it leads to the necessary conclusion that the future of the IMF looks significantly brighter than does the future of the UN Security Council. Because, in the IMF, tension is regularly diffused at low levels, the organisation is less likely to be paralysed by internal disagreements over relative influence. Since in the UN Security Council, on the other hand, tension must necessarily rise to high levels before debate on hierarchy reform may take place, and since the initiation of such debate offers no guarantee that tension will be diffused, it is more likely that the persistence and intensity of internal disputes over relative influence in the Security Council will have a detrimental effect upon the work of the institution. Furthermore, the impossibility of demoting any of the present permanent members against their wills makes any reduction of tension by the addition of extra permanent members at best a temporary solution that will lead, in the longer term, to serious problems of effectiveness.

Restating the Hypotheses

Based on the level of support that has been found for the hypotheses originally presented in chapter 3, and the modifications that have been made to two of these hypotheses, they may be re-stated as follows:

(1) The most powerful states to emerge from system-wide conflict establish and institutionalise a hierarchy of influence atop which they install themselves and through which they attempt to govern the post-war international system.

(2) The differential growth of states causes inconsistencies to emerge between the distribution of power in the international system and the hierarchy of influence created following system-wide war.

(3) Dissatisfaction caused by inconsistencies between the hierarchy of influence and the distribution of power lead rising states who stand to benefit from such action to seek to improve their position in the hierarchy of influence.

(4) Attempts by rising states to improve their position in the hierarchy of influence are opposed by those states whose position therein is most threatened by these attempts.

(5) As a result of the interplay of upward and downward positionality, tension is generated in the international system. Significantly more tension is generated when the hierarchy of influence is rigidly institutionalised than when it is flexibly institutionalised.

(6) If the tension generated by the interplay of upward and downward positionality is not diffused but continues to increase, conflict is likely to occur.

(7) An international system in which the hierarchy of influence is flexibly institutionalised is less likely to experience conflict than is an international system in which the hierarchy of influence is rigidly institutionalised.

Conclusion

The set of inter-related hypotheses that constitutes the theory of international stability presented in chapter 3 has been strongly supported by the empirical analysis carried out on the Security Council and IMF in chapters 5 through 9. To the extent that examples were found that did not accord with hypotheses 3 and 4 - those concerning upward and downward positionality - slight modifications were made to these hypotheses in order to bring them more into line with the empirical evidence. In both cases, the modifications made restricted the scope of the hypotheses in question. In hypothesis 3, the focus was reduced from states in general to states that stand to benefit from moving upward in a hierarchy of influence and, in hypothesis 4, the focus was reduced from states threatened by the upward positionality of rising states to those most threatened by such upward positionality.

Since these hypotheses were restricted in scope as a result of a comparison with empirical evidence, the new more restricted versions cannot be held to be true until they have been tested against new empirical evidence (King, Keohane & Verba, 1994). This new evidence should not, obviously, be taken from the domain which necessitated the restriction in the first place; i.e., not from the analysis of the Security Council or the International Monetary Fund. This methodological consideration does not significantly undermine the status of the original versions of hypotheses 3 and 4, however. In the empirical analysis, these hypotheses were strongly supported although some deviant cases were uncovered. Furthermore, the restrictions necessary in order to make them comply better with the empirical evidence are minimal.

The theory of international stability presented in chapter 3, therefore, has withstood the test of two detailed empirical analyses that have, in turn, suggested ways in which the theory may be improved by further exposure to empirical testing.

Notes

[1] For more on the technique of pattern-matching, see Trochim (1989).
[2] A witty but revealing ditty penned by a participant at Bretton Woods informs us that;
In Washington Lord Halifax
Once whispered to Lord Keynes:
"It's true *they* have the money bags
But *we* have all the brains
(Gardner, 1980: xiii).

Lord Halifax was the British ambassador to the United States during the negotiations leading up to the establishment of the International Monetary Fund.

11 Conclusion

In concluding this study, it is useful to recall the question posed at the outset: What do we mean when we say that an international system is stable? Chapter 2 demonstrated that we - i.e., students of international relations - have meant many things at various times and that, following the end of the Cold War, we are even more at a loss to agree upon a standardised definition. Stability, "that much overburdened word with unstabilized definition" (Ashby, 1979 [1956]: 73), continues to be interpreted in different ways by people occupying different standpoints.

The aim of this book has been to aid in rectifying this situation by suggesting a conceptualisation of international stability that, in theory at least, may be interpreted in a positive manner by all observers of international politics; be they relatively detached academics or partisan states people. Chapter 3 set out the details of such a conceptualisation. It argued, in essence, that for an international system to be stable, it must be capable of attributing to rising states ever greater roles in the governance of the international system. It identified the main barrier to achieving stability to the institutionalisation of relative influence that takes place following major international conflicts. Such institutionalisation, although intended to create "systems of peace," may, in fact, be one of the most fundamental "causes of war" (Betts, 1992).

The case study conducted in chapters 5 through 7 demonstrated that the UN Security Council is a typical example of an unstable system of international governance. The institutionalisation of relative military influence that took place following World War II still determines the relative decision-making influence of states on the Council, despite the fact that significant differential growth in the ability of states to contribute to the maintenance of international peace and security has taken place since 1945.

The case study conducted in chapters 8 and 9, on the other hand, showed that the International Monetary Fund constitutes a model example of a stable system of international governance. Throughout its history, the IMF has been successful in allaying the dissatisfaction of its rising members by granting them increasing levels of decision-making influence. Equally important, it has been successful in subtracting decision-making influence from members whose relative economic capabilities have declined.

Two alternative explanations for this variation in stability were suggested in chapter 4 and tested in both case studies. The first, based on the conceptualisation of international stability presented in chapter 3, attributed the variance in stability to the way in which the respective hierarchies of influence of the Security Council and the IMF were initially institutionalised. It hypothesised that a flexibly institutionalised hierarchy of influence would make for more stability than would a rigidly institutionalised one. The second explanation, chosen for its obvious plausibility, attributed the variance in stability to the difference in the technical nature of the activities undertaken by the Security Council and the IMF. It argued that the IMF constitutes a more stable system of international governance because its activities are, in general, more technical and the relative capabilities of its members more quantifiable than those of the Security Council and that, therefore, it is easier in the IMF to determine who deserves to be promoted and demoted in the hierarchy of influence.

The analysis of the IMF undermined the explanatory power of this latter hypothesis by demonstrating, first, that the criteria applied by the IMF in determining its hierarchy of influence are not as objective as it might seem at first glance and that, second, the positional behaviour of states in the IMF is just strong as it is in the Security Council.

The ranking of states in the upper echelons of the Fund's original hierarchy of influence was not determined by the results obtained from plugging economic indicators into pre-defined formulas. On the contrary, the original formulas utilised by the Fund had the purpose of justifying a hierarchy of influence that had already been agreed upon in a series of political deals. Thus, rather than being a case of a pre-conceived formula determining the hierarchy, it was, in fact, a case of a pre-conceived hierarchy determining the formula.

Likewise, during the subsequent development of the Fund's hierarchy of influence, the objectivity implied by the use of mathematical formulas has consistently taken a back seat to the subjectivity implied by political necessity. Formulas have twice been adjusted so that the quotas they calculated would correspond more closely with the existing positions of states in the Fund's hierarchy of influence - another case of an existing hierarchy determining the composition of formulas and not vice-versa. Furthermore, the use of multiple formulas in order to generate a range of values for members' quotas has demonstrated the important role that negotiation between the Fund and member states plays in determining relative influence.

In short, chapters 8 and 9 demonstrate that the IMF is as subject to political wrangling when it comes to establishing and modifying a pecking order as is the UN Security Council. The existence of objective economic indicators and of formulas in which to incorporate them does give the impression that the position of a state in the Fund's hierarchy of influence, as well as its promotion and demotion therein, is determined in a political vacuum. Nothing, however, could be further from the truth. In determining the Fund's original hierarchy of influence and in subsequently modifying it, subjective, political considerations have played a more important role than have objective, economic ones.

If the difference between the stability of the IMF and the Security Council cannot be explained by reference to the differences in the technical nature of the issue-areas in which they operate, how, then, can it be explained? The empirical analysis undertaken in this book shows that it can best be explained by reference to the way in which the original hierarchies of influence in the issue-areas of security and money were institutionalised following World War II.

The processes of institutionalisation that resulted in the creation of the IMF and the Security Council are similar in one important respect. In both cases, the most influential states to emerge from World War II colluded in creating a hierarchy of influence atop which they installed themselves and through which they intended to govern the international system in the issue-areas of money and security, respectively. The similarity stops there, however. The way in which these states institutionalised the hierarchy of influence embodied in each organisation differed in one important respect.

In the IMF, on the one hand, the hierarchy of influence was institutionalised in a flexible manner. A rule was enshrined in the Fund's constitution specifying that the relative influence of states within the organisation must be regularly reviewed. Equally important, however, no specific criteria were identified regarding the way in which such reviews were to be carried out. In this way, a legal impetus was provided for regular reviews of the Fund's hierarchy of influence while, at the same time, sufficient ambiguity was created to allow the criteria used in carrying out such reviews to adapt in line with political necessity.

This flexible institutionalisation of the hierarchy of influence in the area of international money in the aftermath of World War II has aided the stability of the IMF in two ways. First, under normal circumstances, it has made the decision to initiate revisions of the Fund's hierarchy of influence independent of the amount of dissatisfaction that exists with regard to relative levels of decision-making influence. A process of influence re-distribution is initiated *de jure* whether or not states believe that such a re-distribution is necessary. In special circumstances, however, reviews may also begin if support for a re-distribution of influence grows to a sufficient level before the time specified for such a review to begin has arrived. The result is that dissatisfaction with relative influence levels within the organisation tends to be diffused at low levels.

Second, the rule regarding the conduct of regular reviews, as well as the possibility of developing various criteria for carrying out such reviews, undermine the natural tendency of states to attempt to maintain their relative position in a hierarchy of influence even after their capabilities have declined relative to other states. In the terminology used in the book, downward positionality is undermined in the IMF as a result of the flexible way in which its hierarchy of influence was institutionalised. Even though, in general, states do their best to avoid demotion in the Fund's hierarchy of influence, they are hindered in doing so by institutional rules.

In the UN Security Council, on the other hand, the hierarchy of influence was institutionalised in a rigid manner. No rules were included in the UN Charter to provide for the review, regular or otherwise, of the distribution of decision-making influence within the Security Council. Instead, provisions were included that rendered this distribution exceedingly difficult to amend. Permanent members were granted veto power over all of the most important decisions of the Security Council as well as the right to determine what constituted an important decision. In this way, they were granted the ability to defend indefinitely their privileged position in the Security Council's hierarchy of influence.

This rigid institutionalisation of the hierarchy of influence in the area of international security in the aftermath of World War II has provided for the instability of the UN Security Council in two ways. First, it has made the build-up within the organisation of a large amount of dissatisfaction with levels of relative decision-making influence a prerequisite for the initiation of debate on the reform of the Council's hierarchy of influence. As a result, serious reform debates have only taken place twice since the foundation of the Security Council; once in the early 1960s - which resulted in the addition of two extra non-permanent members - and one, begun in the early 1990s - which is still ongoing and is likely to result in the extension of permanent membership of the Council.

Second, the rules governing the structure and membership of the Security Council aid states in their attempt to avoid demotion in its hierarchy of influence. The fact that permanent members possess a veto on any decision to reform the Council means that they may not be divested of their membership privileges without their consent. While it may be possible, therefore, for rising states to improve upon their positions in the Security Council's hierarchy of influence by gaining permanent membership, for example, it is very unlikely that such a development will be accompanied by a corresponding demotion of a current permanent member. In the longer run, this does not augur well for decision-making effectiveness on the Security Council.

By showing that differences in the way in which hierarchies of influence in the areas of security and money were institutionalised following World War II - as opposed to differences in the technical nature of the activities undertaken in these two issue-areas - best explain the variation in stability detected in the UN Security Council and the International Monetary Fund, the theory of international stability set out in chapter 3 has been supported. The central argument of the theory - that an international system of governance with a flexibly institutionalised hierarchy of influence will be more successful in incrementally adapting to shifts in the international distribution of power, thereby avoiding conflict and system breakdown - has been strengthened.

Are these findings at all important? Is it not obvious that an international institution designed to take into account the occurrence of differential growth in the international system should be more successful in adapting to the constantly changing architecture of relative state power than one not designed to do so? Viewed at this level, the findings of this book are indeed dull and completely in accordance with intuition. Viewed at the level of generality at which this book posed its research questions, however, they become significantly more interesting and open up all sorts of avenues for further enquiry. Two questions are of particular importance, however. First, what role does agency play in determining the stability of an issue-area of international governance? Second, why are systems of governance still created by rigidly institutionalising hierarchies of influence? I will briefly deal with each of these questions in turn.

This book has shown that variations in the technical nature of issue-areas of governance do not alter the upward and downward positional tendencies of states. In both technical and non-technical issue-areas, rising states strive to improve upon their position in the hierarchy of influence and, in doing so, are opposed by those states they wish to displace. The IMF, therefore, has the same *potential* for tension build-up as does the Security Council. The only reason that tension is regularly diffused in the former and allowed to build to high levels in the latter is that individuals made different choices when originally institutionalising each hierarchy of influence.

The role of agency, therefore, is central to the understanding of international stability promoted by this book. One of the arguments of chapter 3 was that the conceptualisation of stability developed therein has a great deal of policy relevance since international stability, as there defined, could be aided, or indeed created, by the foresight and creativity of human beings. Foresight is necessary in order to recognise that the differential growth of states will shift the distribution of power in the international system and cause dissatisfaction to grow among rising states. Creativity is necessary in order to devise institutional mechanisms that allow hierarchies of influence to adapt to such shifts by attributing to these states ever higher levels of decision-making influence. The designers of the IMF seem to have developed a particularly ingenious way of solving the problems presented by differential growth - create a rule that stipulates regular hierarchy review but remain silent on the criteria according to which such reviews are to be carried out. The designers of the Security Council, on the other hand, were far less successful in this respect. What accounts for this difference?

Was it more difficult in 1945 to recognise that differential growth would take place in the capability of states to contribute to the maintenance of international peace and security than it was to recognise that differential economic growth would take place? It seems not. The designers of the Security Council took the effects of differential growth into account when they included France and China among its permanent members. Following the war, as chapter 5 has pointed out, these two countries were considered second-class members of the P-5 group. They were included in this group, however, because their potential to become regional powers was recognised by the Big Three of the United States, Russia and Britain. However, this is hardly a case of flexibly institutionalising a hierarchy of influence. Rather, it is a case of rigidly institutionalising a hierarchy of influence that is likely to become current in the near future.

Was it more difficult, then, to devise means to flexibly institutionalise the hierarchy of influence in the area of security than it was to devise means to do so in the area of money? This explanation is also not convincing. The case of the IMF demonstrates that flexibly institutionalising a hierarchy of influence need not be a complicated affair. States themselves will see to it that a hierarchy of influence is maintained in line with changes in the distribution of power if they are spurred to do so by a legal rule but allowed the maximum of discretion in deciding upon how it should be achieved.

Should it not have been possible, therefore, for the designers of the Security Council to come up with an equally innovative solution as that devised by the designers of the IMF? Of course, the insistence of the permanent members of the Security Council on veto power over all important decisions complicated matters, but it is difficult to believe that this insistence precluded the possibility of finding an innovative solution to the problem posed by differential growth in the area of international security.

Would not the Security Council have been rendered more stable, for example, if the proposal, made at San Francisco, had been accepted that permanent members not be named in the Charter, but rather their identities decided upon at intervals of ten years (Bentwich & Martin, 1969)? This, I contend, would at least have been a beginning. To be effective, it would have had to be supplemented by provisions that facilitated the demotion of permanent members despite their veto power but surely the articulation of such provisions is not beyond the capabilities of human ingenuity.

The explanation for differences in institutionalisation in the areas of security and money that took place following World War II does not lie, therefore, in a lack of foresight on the part of the designers of the Security Council nor in appreciable differences in the difficulty involved in devising appropriate institutional provisions. Rather, the explanation lies in differences between the will of the designers of the Security Council, on the one hand, and those of the IMF, on the other, to innovate in the face of differential growth.

The principal designers of the IMF - John Meynard Keynes and Harry Dexter White - were expert academic economists first and statesmen second. As such, they were more concerned with providing for the continuing relevance of the Fund's hierarchy of influence than they were with ensuring that particular states would continue to prevail indefinitely in decision-making within the organisation. Had Keynes, for example, been more concerned with preserving the influential position of Britain in the Fund's hierarchy than with ensuring the general stability of the Fund, he would not have proposed that the relative influence of all Fund members be reviewed at regular intervals. It was this process of review, after all, that led to the eventual demotion of Britain from its position as second most influential state behind the United States to a position as joint-fourth most influential state behind the US, Germany and Japan.

On the other hand, the principal designers of the Security Council - primarily officials in the US Department of State and, to a lesser extent, British and Russian statesmen - were more concerned with ensuring that UN-sponsored collective action could not be taken against any major power than they were with ensuring that the hierarchy of influence of the institution they were designing would be capable of adapting to shifts in the distribution of power. The issue of stability was subordinated to the necessity of ensuring that great powers could not be marginalised within the Security Council, even though it is quite possible that this primary aim could have been achieved while at the same time providing for the adaptability of the Security Council's hierarchy of influence.

The difference in stability between the Security Council and the IMF, therefore, may best be explained by reference to the determination of their respective designers to creatively offset the detrimental effects of differential growth. Both sets of designers recognised that differential growth could have adverse effects on the operation of the institution being designed. However, only one set invented institutional rules to deal with this problem. The other set focused all its attention on ensuring that the institution would be effective at the outset and was satisfied when it succeeded in devising a means of achieving this aim. The fact remains, however, that just as both institutions have the same potential for the build-up of tension within them, they also, in principle, have the same potential for diffusing this tension at relatively low levels. That the IMF realised this potential and the Security Council not, may be attributed to the agency of their respective designers.

If the findings of this book still seem rather dull, consider the recent development of the European Union (EU). It would seem that in utilising weighted- and qualified majority voting in many areas of decision-making on the Council of Ministers, the EU's institutional designers are making the same mistakes made by the designers of the Security Council over fifty years ago - i.e., they are not taking into consideration the detrimental effect that differential growth may have on the acceptability to states of institutionalised hierarchies of influence.

Since the establishment of the European Community, member states have been allocated differential voting power on the Council of Ministers that either "takes some account of its weight in the Community" (Henig, 1980: 25), "reflect[s] differences in size" (Brams & Affuso, 1985: 137), or "reflect[s] their varying populations" (Johnston, 1995: 245). That voting power on the Council of Ministers reflects differences in population size is hardly the case, however, since there are huge differences in the per capita influence of various nationalities on the Council.[1] The fact is that there are no set criteria governing the allocation, or revision, of decision-making influence on the Council of Ministers. Up until now, members have simply agreed through a process of negotiation on how much influence each should exercise.[2]

It is possible that this situation may lead to a build-up of tension in the European Union as differential growth causes some states to become dissatisfied with their relative decision-making influence in the Council of Ministers. Since no institutional rules are in place that would aid in diffusing such tension at low levels, the same kind of positional conflict now being observed in the Security Council could conceivably develop in the Council of Ministers. I do not intend to delve into this issue further but simply to point out that the lessons that may be drawn from a comparative analysis of the UN Security Council and the International Monetary Fund are not being heeded by the institutional designers of the European Union.

The theoretical elucidation and empirical analysis contained in this book constitute only the beginning of a general research programme that points in the direction of more case studies and, consequently, theoretical refinement. Much more work remains to be done in this area. In particular, one major shortcoming of the conceptualisation of stability promoted by this book needs special attention. In arguing for the attribution to rising states of ever higher levels of formal decision-making influence over the governance of the international system, this study completely eschews ethical considerations. It focuses on proposing an understanding of international stability and in identifying its necessary conditions with sole reference to the relations between states rather than to the nature of relations within them. Michael David Wallace has correctly pointed out, however, that:

> By granting attributed status (and the rewards that accompany it) on the basis of capability, we would be overlooking the fact that there are often very pressing ethical reasons for *not* granting such status. The clearest examples are those nations which are governed by regimes which practice totally abhorrent and morally unacceptable policies within their borders, such as Nazi Germany and South Africa. In such cases, the danger of war which may result from withholding attributed status must surely be balanced against the great harm that may be caused by lending support and sanction to such regimes (Wallace, 1973).

Despite this, and many other shortcomings, however, this book has achieved the goal set for it in its title. It has made a contribution towards revitalising the concept of international stability; a concept that has been abused throughout the history of post-war international relations. It has proposed an alternative, dynamic meaning of international stability that is, I contend, more useful than those that have existed before it. Whether this meaning, refined as it needs to be through further research, becomes generally accepted or not remains to be seen. However, if this analysis at least encourages students of international relations to think consciously about what they mean by international stability and to criticise the conceptualisation thereof promoted by this book, it will have achieved a lot.

Notes

1. Every 200,000 Luxembourgers, for example, have one vote on the Council of Ministers. The corresponding number for France is 5.75 million. Germany, since unification, has one vote for every 9.06 million of its population. For a full list of member states' per capita influence on the Council of Ministers, see Johnston (1995).

2. The present distribution of votes on the Council of Ministers is as follows: France, Germany, Italy and Britain have 10 votes each. Spain has 8 votes. Belgium, Greece, The Netherlands and Portugal have 5 votes each. Sweden and Austria have 4 votes each. Denmark, Ireland, and Finland have 3 votes each. Luxembourg has 2 votes.

Bibliography

Acland, A. (07.03.1990), "Britain's Place in the IMF," *Washington Post*. Letter to the Editor by the British Ambassador to the United States, Anthony Acland.
Agence Europe (05.10.1994), "United Nations: Mitterrand States Japan should become Permanent Member of Security Council," *Agence Europe*. Brussels.
Agence France (10.03.1995), "China Expresses Qualified Support for UN Reform," *Agence France Presse*.
__ (27.09.1993), "Hosokawa Pledges Greater International Role for Japan," *Agence France Presse*.
Aitkin, D. (1977), *Stability and Change in Australian Politics*. Canberra: Australian National University Press.
Albright, M. K. (03.02.1995), *Briefing, Albright, the United Nations* [gopher: // dosfan. lib. uic.edu: 70/0F-1% 3A19376%3A95/02/03%20 Albright].
Altenburg, G. (1994), "Deutschland auf dem Prüfstand: Die nichtständige Mitgliedschaft im Sicherhietsrat der Vereinten Nationen," *Europa Archiv* (24): 693-700.
Altman, O. L. (1956), "Quotas in the International Monetary Fund," *Staff Papers (International Monetary Fund)*, 5 (2): 129-150.
Alvarez, J. E. (1993), *A Global Agenda: Issues Before the 48th General Assembly of the United Nations*. Lanham / New York / London: University Press of America.
Ashby, W. R. (1979 [1956]), *An Introduction to Cybernetics*. London: Methuen.
__ (1952), *Design for a Brain*. New York: Wiley.
Atkinson, R. (1-2.07.1995), "Germans Vote to Send Unit and Planes," *International Herald Tribune*. Bologna: 1.
Attiná, F. (1991), "Organisation, Competition and Change of the International System," *International Interactions* 16 (4): 317-333.
Auswärtiges Amt (18.10.1995), *Deutschland ist bereit zur wieteren Stärkung seines Engagements in den Vereinten Nationen*. Statement

of the German Foreign Office [http://www.auswaertiges-amt.government.de/de/auss_pol/pr1910 95.htm].

— (28.09.1995), *Welche Rolle Deutschland in der UNO Spielt; der Weg zur Mitgliedschaft Deutschlands.* Statement of the German Foreign Office (Auswärtiges Amt, Abt. VNMH) [http://www.auswaertigesamt.government.de/de/int_kont/uno.htm].

Axelrod, R. (1990), "The Concept of Stability in the Context of Conventional War in Europe," *Journal of Peace Research* 27 (3): 247-254.

Bailey, S. D. (1988), *The Procedure of the UN Security Council.* Second Edition. Oxford: Clarendon Press.

Barber, L. (09.03.1995), "EU Backs Japan for UN Role: Brussels Supports Tokyo's Campaign for Security Council Seat," *The Financial Times.* London: 4.

Bauer, F. (1995), "Security Council Reform Will Wait," reprinted from 'Frankfurter Allgemeine Zeitung', April 4, 1995; The UN at 50 cover story. *World Press Review* 42 (6): 20.

BBC (14.11.1994), "Malaysia; Jiang Zemin Abjures Force in International Disputes, Criticizes Hegemonism," *The British Broadcasting Corporation; BBC Summary of World Broadcasts.*

— (16.12.1992), "Japan Welcomes UN Resolution on Security Council; Looks Forward to New Role," *British Broadcasting Corporation Summary of World Broadcasts.*

Bellamy, C. (04.01.1994), "Big Five Nuclear Powers Braced for Move to Ban Bomb," *The Independent.* London: 8.

Bellman, R. (1953), *Stability Theory of Differential Equations.* New York: McGraw-Hill.

Bentwich, N. & Martin, A. (1969), *A Commentary on the Charter of the United Nations.* Second Edition. London: Routledge & Kegan Paul.

Bernhardt, B. (1992), "Der Sicherheitsrat der Vereinten Nationen: Geschichte, Gegenwart - Zukunftsperspektiven und Modelle," *Österreichische militärische Zeitschrift* 5: 424-430.

Bertrand, M. (1993), "The Historical Development of Efforts to Reform the UN," in A. Roberts & B. Kingsbury (eds.), *United Nations, Divided World; The UN's Roles in International Relations.* Oxford: Clarendon Press.

— (1988), "Can the United Nations be Reformed?," in A. Roberts & B. Kingsbury (eds.), *United Nations, Divided World: The UN's Role in International Relations.* Oxford: Clarendon Press.

— (1988a), "Some Reflections on Reform of the United Nations," in P. Taylor & A.J.R. Groom (eds.), *International Institutions at Work.* London: Pinter.

Besteliu, R. M. (1977), "The Procedure of Consensus in the Adoption of Decisions by the International Monetary Fund and the International Bank of Reconstruction and Development," *Revue Roumaine d'Etudes Internationales* 11 (4): 517-526.

Betts, R. K. (1992), "Systems for Peace or Causes of War," *International Security* 17 (1): 5-43.

Bevins, A. (20.12.1991), "Hurd Hints at Backing Moscow over UN Seat," *The Independent*. London: 12.

Blum, Y. Z. (1992), "Russia Takes Over the Soviet Union's Seat at the United Nations," *European Journal of International Law* 3 (2): 354-361.

Bone, J. (12.05.1993), "Russia Vetoes Plan to Cut UN Cyprus Force," *The Times:* 11.

Boulding, K. E. (1956), "General Systems Theory - The Skeleton of Science," *Management Science* 2: 197-208.

Brams, S. J. & Affuso, P. J. (1985), "New Paradoxes of Voting Power on the EC Council of Ministers," *Electoral Studies* 4 (2): 135-139.

Brecher, M. & James, P. (1989), "Polarity, Stability, Crisis: The Debate over Structure and Conflict Twenty-five Years Later. I. State of the Art and New Directions," in M. Brecher & J. Wilkenfeld, *Crisis, Conflict and Instability*. Oxford: Pergamon Press.

Brecher, M. & Wilkenfeld, J. (1989), *Crisis, Conflict and Instability*. Oxford: Pergamon Press.

Bremer, S. A. (1992), "Dangerous Dyads - Conditions Affecting the Likelihood of Interstate War, 1816-1965," *Journal of Conflict Resolution* 36 (2): 309-341.

Bretton Woods Commission (1994), "Bretton Woods: Looking to the Future: Commission Report, Staff Review, Background Papers," Washington, D.C.: The Commission.

— (1994a), "Bretton Woods: Looking to the Future: Conference Proceedings," Washington, D.C.: The Commission.

Briggs, H. W. (1945), "Power Politics and International Organization," *American Journal of International Law* 39 (4): 664-679.

Brodie, B. et al. (1983), *National Security and International Stability*. Cambridge, MA: Oelgeschlager, Gunn & Hain Publishers.

Brown, C. (01.07.1993), "Defence Cuts 'Threat to UN Seat'," *The Independent*. London: 8.

Browne, M. A. (1988), *United Nations Reform: Issues for Congress*. Washington, D.C.: Library of Congress. Congressional Research Service.

Buerstedde, S. (1964), *Der Ministerrat im konstitutionellen System der europäischen Gemeinschaften*. Bruges: De Tempel, Tempelhof.

Bundesverfassungsgericht (12.07.1994), "Das Urteil des Bundesverfassungsgerichts vom 12. Juli 1994," *Europa Archiv* (15): D427-D431.
Burton, J. W. (1965), *International Relations: A General Theory*. Cambridge: Cambridge University Press.
Canadian Committee For The Fiftieth Anniversary Of The United Nations (1994), *Canadian Priorities for United Nations Reform: Proposals for Policy Changes by the United Nations and the Government of Canada*. Ottawa: The Committee.
Canavan, G. H. (1994), "Traditional Notions of Deterrence - Stability in a Multipolar, Proliferated Environment," *Comparative Strategy* 13 (1): 147-154.
Carlsson, I. (1995), "The UN at 50: A Time to Reform," *Foreign Policy* 100 (Fall): 3-18.
Caron, D. D. (1993), "The Legitimacy of the Collective Authority of the Security Council," *American Journal of International Law* 87 (4): 552-588.
Carr, E. H. (1964 [1946]), *The Twenty Years' Crisis; An Introduction to International Relations*. New York: Harper.
Carter, J. & Vance, C. (1978), *Reform and Restructuring of the UN System. President's Report and Secretary's Report*. Washington, D.C.: Department of State [International Organization and Conference Series 135].
C.G.G. (1995), *Our Global Neighbourhood: The Report of the Commission on Global Governance*. Oxford/New York: Oxford University Press.
Chauvancy, F. (1995), "Actions internationales: Le Japan et le Conseil de securité de l'Onu; Chroniques," *Defense nationale* 51 (1): 145-148.
Childers, E. &. Urquhart, B. (1994), "Renewing the United Nations System," *Development Dialogue* 1.
Christopher, W. (25.09.1995), "Address by U.S. Secretary of State Warren Christopher at the United Nations General Assembly," *Federal Information Systems Corporation; Federal News Service*. State Department Briefing.
Ciechanski, J. (1994), "Restructuring of the UN Security Council," *International Peacekeeping* 1 (4): 413-431.
Clark, G. & Sohn, L. B. (1966 [1958]), *World Peace Through World Law*. Cambridge, MA: Harvard University Press.
Clark, I. (1989), *The Hierarchy of States: Reform and Resistance in the International Order*. Cambridge: Cambridge University Press.
Claude, I. L. (1966), "Collective Legitimization as a Political Function of the UN," *International Organization* 20: 267-279.

Claude, I. L. Jr. (1991), "The Management of Power in the Changing United Nations," in R.A. Falk, S.S. Kim & S.H. Mendlovitz (eds.), *The United Nations and a Just World Order*. Boulder/San Francisco/Oxford: Westview Press.
Coate, R. A. & Puchala, D. J. (1990), "Global Policies and the United Nations System," *Journal of Peace Research* 27: 127-140.
Collier, D. (1995), "Trajectory of a Concept: 'Corporatism' in the Study of Latin American Politics," in P.H. Smith (ed.), *Latin America in Comparative Perspective: New Approaches to Method and Analysis*. Boulder: Westview Press.
__ (1995a), "Translating Quantitative Methods for Qualitative Researchers: The Case of Selection Bias," *American Political Science Review* 89 (1): 1-6.
__ (1993), "The Comparative Method," in Finifter, A. W. (ed.), *Political Science: The State of the Discipline II*. Washington, D.C.: American Political Science Association.
Collier, D. & Levitsky, S. (1994), "Democracy 'With Adjectives': Finding Conceptual Order in Recent Comparative Research," revised version of a paper presented at the Annual Meeting of the American Political Science Association, New York City, September 1-4, 1994.
Collier, D. & Mahon, J. E. Jr. (1993), "Conceptual 'Stretching' Revisited: Adapting Categories in Comparative Analysis," *American Political Science Review* 87 (4): 845-855.
Conybeare, J. A. C. (1980), "International Organization and the Theory of Property Rights," *International Organization* 34: 307-334.
Cox, R. W. & Jacobson, H. K. (1973), "The Framework for Inquiry," in R.W. Cox & H.K. Jacobson (eds.), *The Anatomy of Influence; Decision Making in International Organization*. New Haven / London: Yale University Press.
Crawshaw, S. (03.02.1993), "Kinkel Backtracks as Bonn Policy Wavers," *The Independent*. London: 8.
Czempiel, E. O. (1994), "Funktion und Reformbedarf des Weltsicherheitsrats," *Blätter für deutsche und internationale Politik* 39 (11): 1330-1341.
Daily Mail (19.02.1993), "UN Chief Beckons Japan to 'Top Table'," *Daily Mail*. Associated Newspapers Ltd.
Daily Yomiuri (30.09.1994), "Britain and France Reaffirm Support for Permanent Membership for Germany and Japan," *The Daily Yomiuri*: 2.
__ (26.08.1993), "Coalition Discord Affects Drafting of UN Speech," *The Daily Yomiuri*: 3.

Daley, T. (1992), *Russia's "Continuation" of the Soviet Security Council Membership and Prospective Russian Policies toward the United Nations.* Santa Monica, CA: Rand [P-7778-RGS].

Dam, K. W. (1982), *The Rules of the Game: Reform and Evolution in the International Monetary System.* Chicago: University of Chicago Press.

De Gara, J. (1989), *Administrative and Financial Reform of the United Nations: A Documentary Essay.* Hanover, N. H.: Academic Council on the United Nations System, Reports and Papers, 1989-2.

De Mesquita, B. B. (1978), "Systemic Polarization and the Occurrence and Duration of War," *Journal of Conflict Resolution* 22 (2): 241-267.

___ (1975), "Measuring Systemic Polarity," *Journal of Conflict Resolution* 19 (2): 187-216.

De Vries, M. G. (1986), *The IMF in a Changing World, 1945-85.* Washington, D.C.: International Monetary Fund.

___ (1985), *The International Monetary Fund, 1972-1978: Cooperation on Trial.* Washington, D.C.: International Monetary Fund.

___ (1976), *The International Monetary Fund, 1966-1971: The System Under Stress.* Washington, D.C.: International Monetary Fund.

De Vries, M. G., Horsefield, J. K. et al. (1969), *The International Monetary Fund 1945-1965; Twenty Years of International Monetary Cooperation.* Volume II: Analysis. Washington, D.C.: International Monetary Fund.

Delli Carpini, M. X. (1986), *Stability and Change in American Politics.* New York: New York University Press.

Deutsch, K. W. (1969), *The Analysis of International Relations.* New Jersey: Prentice Hall (Foundations of Modern Political Science).

___ (1963), *The Nerves of Government.* London: Collier-Macmillan Ltd.

Deutsch, K. W. & Singer, J. D. (1964), "Multipolar Power Systems and International Stability," *World Politics* 16 (3): 390-406.

Di Maggio, P. J. & Powell, W. W. (1991), "Introduction," in P.J. Di Maggio & W.W. Powell (eds.), *The New Institutionalism in Organizational Analysis.* Chicago: University of Chigago Press.

Diehl, O. (1993), "UN-Einsätze der Bundeswehr," *Europa Archiv* 8: 219-227.

Diesing, P. (1971), *Patterns of Discovery in the Social Sciences.* Chicago: Aldine-Atherton.

Dodd, M. (05.05.1993), "Japanese UN Policeman Killed in Cambodia: Dutch Commandos Wounded in Second Day of Khmer Rough Attacks," *The Independent.* London.

Doyle, L. (26.06.1993), "Rift with France Adds to Bonn's Troubles," *The Independent*. London: 8.
___ (28.01.1993), "Hurd Warning Over 'Slide into Disorder': Foreign Secretary Backs Imperial UN and Defends Britain's Global Role to Justify Permanent Security Council Seat," *The Independent*. London: 1.
___ (10.12.1991), "Moscow May Lose Seat at UN Top Table," *The Independent*. London: 9.
Doyle, L. & Brown, C. (01.02.1992), "UN to Fight Spread of Nuclear Weapons," *The Independent*. London: 1.
Dreyer, J. & Schotter, A. (1980), "Power Relationships in the International Monetary Fund: The Consequences of Quota Changes," *Review of Economics and Statistics* 62 (1): 97-106.
Drifte, R. (1994), "Japan: von der wirtschaftlichen zur politischen Supermacht," *Europa Archiv* (2): 53-60.
Eagleton, C. (1945), "The Charter Adopted at San Francisco," *The American Political Science Review* 39 (1): 934-942.
East, M. A. (1971), "Status Discrepancy and Violence in the International System: An Empirical Analysis," in Rosenau, J. N., Davis, V. & East, M. A. (eds.), *The Analysis of International Politics*. New York: Free Press.
Eckstein, H. (1992), *Regarding Politics: Essays on Political Theory, Stability, and Change*. Berkeley: University of California Press.
___ (1975), "Case Study and Theory in Political Science," in Greenstein, F. I. & Polsby, N. W. (eds.), *Strategies of Enquiry*. Reading, Mass.: Addison-Wesley (Handbook of Political Science, Vol. 7).
Economist (02.12.1995), "Dodging Bullets by Dodging Issues," *The Economist*: 31.
___ (18.11.1995),"The Decline of Faith and Discipline," *The Economist*: 40.
___ (21.10.1995), "United Nations; To Bury or to praise," *The Economist*: 23-27.
___ (01.07.95), "Germany and Bosnia: Time to move on, if not in," *The Economist*: 25.
___ (24.06.1995), "UNhappy Birthday," *The Economist*: 15-16.
___ (01.10.1994), "The Trouble with Japan," *The Economist*: 17-18.
___ (17.09.1994), "Japan and the UN; Big Ambitions," *The Economist*: 62.
___ (29.08.1992), "Open the Club," *The Economist*: 14.
Eggan, F. (1954), "Social Anthropology and the Method of Controlled Comparison," *American Anthropologist* 56 (October): 743-763.

Eisenhammer, J. (11.01.1992), "Kohl Rebuts Mighty Germany's Critics," *The Independent.* London: 6.

Eitel, T. (13.11.1995), Statement by Ambassador Tono Eitel, Permanent Representative of Germany to the United Nations, to the United Nations' 50th General Assembly. Agenda item 47: Question of equitable representation on and increase in the membership of the Security Council and related matters. New York: Permanent Mission of Germany to the United Nations.

Europa Archiv (1994), "Das Urteil des Bundesverfassungsgerichts vom 12. Juli 1994," *Europa Archiv* (15): D-427-D431.

__ (1993), "Dokumene zur Reform des Sicherheitsrats der Vereinten Nationen," *Europa Archiv* 48 (19): D379-D396.

__ (1955), "Probleme einer Änderung der Charta der Vereinten Nationen; Stellungnahme einer deutschen Studienkommission," *Europa Archiv* 10 (3): 7263-7278.

Falk, R. A., Kim, S. S. & Mendlovitz, S. H. (1991), *The United Nations and a Just World Order.* Boulder/San Francisco/Oxford: Westview Press.

Fawcett, E. & Newcombe, H. (eds.) (1995), *United Nations Reform: Looking Ahead after Fifty Years.* Toronto/Heddington/Oxford/Niagara Falls, N.Y.: Science for Peace, distributed by Dundurn Press.

FAZ (27.06.1995), "Kabinett stimmt Einsatz deutscher Soldaten in Bosnien zu," *Frankfurter Allgemeine Zeitung.* Frankfurt: 1-2.

__ (14.06.1995), "Bonn wartet auf einen Entschluß des UN-Sicherheitsrats," *Frankfurter Allgemeine Zeitung.* Frankfurt: 1.

__ (14.06.1995a), "Gedämpfter Eifer beim Werben um einen Ratssitz in New York: Japan und die Vereinten Nationen," *Frankfurter Allgemeine Zeitung.* Frankfurt: 3.

__ (30.01.1995), "Kinkel: Bonn unterstützt Reformkurs Jeltzins," *Frankfurter Allgemeine Zeitung:* 1.

Fearon, J. D. (1990), "Counterfactuals and Hypothesis Testing in Political Science," *World Politics* 43: 169-195.

Fedotov, Y. V. (15.11.1995), *Statement by Deputy Permanent Representative of the Russian Federation to the United Nations, Yuri V. Fedotov, at the Meeting of the UN General Assembly on the Question of Equitable Representation and Expansion of the Security Council, November 15, 1995.* New York: Russian Federation, Permanent Mission to the United Nations [Press Release No. 33 (Nov. 16, 1995; Unofficial Translation)].

Ferguson, T. (1988), *The Third World and Decision Making in the International Monetary Fund: The Quest for Full and Effective Participation.* London/New York: Pinter.

Feste, K. A. (ed.) (1990), *American and Soviet Intervention: Effects on World Stability*. New York/Washington/London: Crane Russak.
Finkelstein, L. S. (1991), "What is International Governance?" Paper presented to the annual meeting of the International Studies Association, Vancouver, March 21, 1991.
___ (1989), "What War in Europe - The Implications of Legitimate Stability," *Political Science Quarterly* 104 (3): 433-446.
___ (1955), "Reviewing the United Nations Charter," *International Organization* 9 (2): 213-231.
Fisher, A. G. B. (1968), "Relative Voting Strength in the International Monetary Fund," *The Banker* 118: 334-339.
Fox, W. T. R. (1946), "The Super-Powers at San Francisco," *The Review of Politics* 8: 115-127.
Friauf, K. (1960), *Die Staatenvertretung in supranationalen Gemeinschaften*. Marburg: N.G. Elwert Verlag.
Fromuth, P. J. (1993), "The Making of a Security Community; The United Nations After the Cold War," *Journal of International Affairs* 46 (2): 341-336.
Fruchtbaum, H. (1995), "Yalta and the 'Voting Formula'," *UN Chronicle* (March): 92.
___ (1994), "Conversations dans un manoir: La conception de l'ONU," *Chronique ONU* (September): 76.
FT (30.03.1995), "Britain in the World," *Financial Times*. London: 19.
___ (27.01.1995), "World Statesmen Urge Reform of UN and Other Global Bodies," *Financial Times*. London: 8.
___ (08.02.1989), "Japan 'Wants Bigger Voice at the IMF'," *Financial Times*. London: 4.
Fuchs, G. (28.09.1994), "Debats Nations Unies: pour une réforme de l'ONU," *Le Monde*. Paris: 2.
Funabashi, Y. (1991), "Japan and the New World Order," *Foreign Affairs* (Winter).
Gaddis, J. L. (1986), "The Long Peace - Elements of Stability in the Postwar International System," *International Security* 10 (4): 99-142.
Gallarotti, G. M. (1991), "The Limits of International-Organization - Systematic Failure in the Management of International-Relations," *International Organization* 45 (2): 183-220.
Galtung, J. (1964), "A Structural Theory of Aggression," *Journal of Peace Research* 2 (2): 95-119.
Gardner, R. N. (1980), *Sterling-Dollar Diplomacy in Current Perspective: The Origins and Prospects of our International Economic Order*. New York: Columbia University Press.

Gardner, R. N. & Gati, T. T. (19.12.1991), "Russia Deserves the Soviet Seat," *The New York Times.* New York: 2.
Garrett, G. (1995), "From the Luxembourg Compromise to Codecision: Decision Making in the European Union," *Electoral Studies* 14 (3): 289-308.
Geertz, C. (1973), "Thick Description: Toward an Interpretative Theory of Culture," in Geertz, C. (ed.), *The Interpretation of Cultures.* New York: Basic Books.
Geller, D. S. (1993), "Power Differentials and War in Rival Dyads," *International Studies Quarterly* 37 (2): 173-193.
George, A. (1993), "Japan Participation in UN Peacekeeping Operations - Radical Departure or Predictable Response," *Asian Survey* 33 (6): 560-575.
George, A. L. (1979), "Case Studies and Theory Development: The Method of Structured, Focused Comparison," in Lauren, P. G. (ed.), *Diplomacy; New Approaches in History, Theory, and Policy.* New York: Free Press.
George, A. L. & Mckeown, T. J. (1985), "Case Studies and Theories of Organizational Decision Making," in Coulam, R. F. & Smith, R. A. (eds.), *Advances in Information Processing in Organizations.* Vol. 2. Greenwich, Conn.: JAI Press.
Gerster, R. (1993), "Proposals for Voting Reform Within the International-Monetary-Fund," *Journal of World Trade* 27 (3): 121-136.
Gianaris, W. N. (1990/91), "Weighted voting in the International Monetary Fund and the World Bank," *Fordham International Law Journal* 14 (4): 105-132.
Gilpin, R. (1981), *War & Change in World Politics.* New York: Cambridge University Press.
Gladwyn, Lord (03.02.1993), "Change in the Security Council," *The Independent.* London: 18.
Glass, D. S. (1990), "The UN Security Council II: Perceptions of Bias," *The World Today* 46 (12): 217-218.
Gochman, C. S. (1980), "Status, Capabilities, and Major Power Conflict," in Singer, J. D. (ed.), *The Correlates of War: II; Testing Some Realpolitik Models.* New York: The Free Press.
Gold, J. (1984), "Some Impressions of the Early Fund," *Finance & Development* 21 (1): 23-25.
___ (1981), "The Origins of Weighted Voting Power in the Fund," *Finance & Development* 18 (1): 25-28.

___ (1980), "Symmetry as a Legal Objective of the International Monetary System," *New York University Journal of International Law and Politics* 12 (3): 423-477.

___ (1978), *The Second Amendment of the Fund's Articles of Agreement.* Washington, D.C.: International Monetary Fund [IMF Pamphlet Series, no. 25].

___ (1977), *Voting Majorities in the Fund: Effect of Second Amendment of the Articles.* Washington, D.C.: International Monetary Fund [IMF Pamphlet Series, no. 20].

___ (1974), *Membership and Nonmembership in the International Monetary Fund; A Study in International Law and Organization.* Washington, D.C.: International Monetary Fund.

___ (1974a), "Weighted Voting Power: Some Limits and Some Problems," *American Journal of International Law* 68 (4): 687-708.

___ (1972), *Voting and Decisions in the International Monetary Fund; An Essay on the Law and Practice of the Fund.* Washington, D.C.: International Monetary Fund.

___ (1969), *The Reform of the Fund.* Washington, D.C.: International Monetary Fund.

___ (1968), *Interpretation by the Fund.* Washington, D.C.: International Monetary Fund.

Goldmann, K. (1988), *Change and Stability in Foreign Policy.* Princeton, N.J.: Princeton University Press.

Goodrich, L. M. & Hambro, E. (1946), *Charter of the United Nations.* Boston: World Peace Foundation.

Gordon, W. (1994), *The United Nations at the Crossroads of Reform. Studies in Institutional Economics.* Armonk, N.Y.: M. E. Sharpe.

Gornostayev, D. (02.11.1994), "Kozyrev is Busy; Russian Foreign Minister Continues to Participate in UN General Assembly," first published in the *Nezavisimaya Gazeta*, October 5, 1994, *Current Digest of the Post-Soviet Press* 46 (40): 27.

Gott, R. (1992), "The UN Cannot be Reformed," *Third World Resurgence* (32): 30-32.

Gow, D. (16.09.1992), "Brandt Urges Stronger UN to Guarantee World Peace," *The Guardian:* 6.

Gowa, J. (1989), "Bipolarity, Multipolarity, and Free-Trade," *American Political Science Review* 83 (4): 1245-1256.

Graefrath, B. (1994), "Die Vereinten Nationen im Übergang; Die Gratwanderung des Sicherheitsrates zwischen Rechtsanwendung und Rechtsanmaßung," in Klaus Hüfner (ed.), *Die Reform der Vereinten Nationen: Die Weltorganisation zwischen Krise und Erneuerung.* Opladen.

Graf Zu Rantzau, D. (13.10.1994), Statement by Ambassador Detlev Graf zu Rantzau, Permanent Representative of Germany to the United Nations, to the United Nations' 49th General Assembly. Agenda item 33: Question of equitable representation on and increase in the membership of the Security Council. New York: Permanent Mission of Germany to the United Nations.

___ (16.03.1994), Statement by Ambassador Detlev Graf zu Rantzau, Permanent Representative of Germany to the United Nations, to the Open-Ended Working Group on the Question of Equitable Representation on and Increase in the Membership of the Security Council at the United Nations, New York. New York: Permanent Mission of Germany to the United Nations.

Grieco, J. M. (1993), "Anarchy and the Limits of Cooperation: A Realist Critique of the Newest Liberal Institutionalism," in Baldwin, D. A. (ed.), *Neorealism and Neoliberalism; The Contemporary Debate.* New York: Colombia University Press.

Gross, E. A. (1954), "Revising the Charter; Is it Possible? Is it Wise?" *Foreign Affairs* 32 (January): 203-216.

Günsche, K. L. (27.06.1995), "Ein überlastetes Guburtstagskind: Die UNO wird 50 - Interne Krisen - Millionenverluste durch Korruption," *Die Welt.*

Guzzini, S. (1994), "Robert Gilpin: The Realist Quest for the Dynamics of Power," *EUI Working Paper SPS.* No. 94/7.

Haas, E. B. (1990), *When Knowledge is Power; Three Models of Change in International Organizations.* Berkeley/Los Angeles/Oxford: University of California Press.

Haas, M. (1970), "International Subsystems: Stability and Polarity," *American Political Science Review* 64 (1): 98-123.

___ (1967), "Types of Asymmetry Within Social and Political Systems," *General Systems* 12: 69-79.

Hartley, J. F. (1994), "Case Studies in Organizational Research," in Cassell, C. & Symon, G. (eds.), *Qualitative Methods in Organizational Research; A Practical Guide.* London: Sage.

Hayek, F. A. (1952), *The Counter-Revolution of Science.* Glencoe, Illinois: The Free Press.

Heberlein, H. (1994), "Rechtliche Aspekte einer ständigen Mitgliedschaft Deutschlands im UN-Sicherheitsrat," *Zeitschrift für Rechtspolitik* 27 (9): 358-365.

Helm, S. & Mc Carthy, T. (31.01.1992), "Japan Expected to Seek Security Council Seat," *The Independent.* London: 12.

Henig, S. (1980), *Power and Decision in Europe; The Political Institutions of the European Community.* London: Europotentials Press.

Henze, G. (17.05.1994), *Modalities for Bringing Change into Effect and Consideration of Related Charter Amendments.* New York: Permanent Mission of Germany to the United Nations [Statement by Ambassador Dr. Gerhard Henze, Acting Permanent Representative of Germany to the United Nations, to the Open-Ended Working Group on the Question of Equitable Representation on and Increase in the Membership of the Security Council at the UN, New York].

Herman, E. S. (1993), *Beyond Hypocrisy: Decoding the News in an Age of Propaganda.* Boston: South End Press.

Hexner, E. (1964), "The Executive Board of the International Monetary Fund: A Decision-making Instrument," *International Organization* 18 (1): 74-96.

Hindell, K. (1990), "The UN Security Council I: Filling the Gaps," *The World Today* 46 (12): 216-217.

Hintze, P. (24.06.1995), "Die UNO muß gestärkt werden," *Die Welt.*

Hiscocks, R. (1973), *The Security Council: A Study in Adolescence.* London: Longman.

Hodgson, G. (18.07.1991), "World Voice or US Puppet?: After Years of Antagonism, America Suddenly Likes the United Nations," *The Independent.* London: 23.

Hoffmann, S. (1977), "An American Social Science: International Relations," *Dædalus* 1 (Summer): 41-60.

Hoffmann, W. (1994), *United Nations Security Council Reform and Restructuring.* Livingston, N.J.: The Center for UN Reform and Education [Monograph # 14].

Holbrooke, R. (1991), "Japan and the United States: Ending the Unequal Partnership," *Council on Foreign Relations* (Winter).

Holsti, K. J. (1992), "Governance Without Government; Polarchy In Nineteenth-Century International Politics," in J.N. Rosenau & E. O. Czempiel (eds.), *Governance Without Government: Order and Change in World Politics.* Cambridge: Cambridge University Press.

___ (1991), *Peace and War: Armed Conflicts and International Order 1648-1989.* Cambridge: Cambridge University Press.

Holt, R. T. & Turner, J. E. (1970), "The Methodology of Comparative Research," in Holt, R. T. & Turner, J. E. (eds.), *The Methodology of Comparative Research.* New York: Free Press.

Hopf, T. (1993), "Polarity and International Stability - Response," *American Political Science Review* 87 (1): 177-180.

___ (1991), "Polarity, the Offense-Defense Balance, and War," *American Political Science Review* 85 (2): 475-493.

Hopf, T. & Gaddis, J. L. (1993), "Correspondence: Getting the End of the Cold War Wrong," *International Security* 18 (2): 202-210.

Horsefield, J. K. (1969), *The International Monetary Fund, 1945-1965: Twenty Years of International Monetary Cooperation.* Volume I: Chronicle Washington, D.C.: International Monetary Fund.

___ (1969a), "Derivation and Significance of the Fund's Resources," in M.G. De Vries, J. K. Horsefield et al. *The International Monetary Fund, 1945-1965: Twenty Years of International Monetary Cooperation.* Volume II: Analysis Washington, D.C.: International Monetary Fund.

___ (ed.) (1969b), *The International Monetary Fund 1945-1965; Twenty Years of International Monetary Cooperation.* Volume III: Documents Washington, D.C.: International Monetary Fund.

Hosli, M. (1996), "Coalitions and Power: Effects of Qualified Majority Voting in the Council of the European Union," *Journal of Common Market Studies* 34 (2): 255-273.

Hovet, T. & Hovet, E. (1986), *Annual Review of United Nations Affairs; A Chronology and Fact Book of the United Nations 1941-1985.* Seventh Edition. Dobbs Ferry, New York: Oceana Publications.

Huth, P., Bennett, D. S. & Gelpi, C. (1992), "System Uncertainty, Risk Propensity, and International Conflict Among the Great Powers," *Journal of Conflict Resolution* 36 (3): 478-517.

Huth, P., Gelpi, C. & Bennett, D. S. (1993), "The Escalation of Great Power Militarized Disputes - Testing Rational Deterrence Theory and Structural Realism," *American Political Science Review* 87 (3): 609-623.

Huysmans, J. (1992), "Discourse-Knowledge-Practice: Reinterpreting the Polarity-Stability Debate," Paper presented to the Workshop "Conceptual Theory" at the Inaugural pan-European Consortium for Political Research, Heidelberg, Germany, 16-20 September, 1992.

IMF (1993), *Articles of Agreement.* Washington, D.C.: International Monetary Fund.

___ (1990), *Proposed Third Amendment of the Articles of Agreement of the International Monetary Fund: Report of the Executive Board to the Board of Governors.* Washington, D.C.: International Monetary Fund.

___ (1976), *Proposed Second Amendment to the Articles of Agreement of the International Monetary Fund: A Report by the Executive Directors to the Board of Governors.* Washington, D.C.: International Monetary Fund.

Independent (26.05.1994), "UN Chief Wants Japan in Council," *The Independent*. London: 13.
___ (27.01.1994), "Germany Wants UN Seat," *The Independent*. London: 11.
___ (05.07.1993), "Hurd 'Cautious' on German Seat," *The Independent*. London: 9.
___ (10.05.1993), "Cambodia's Test of United Nations' Effectiveness," *The Independent*. London: 15.
___ (08.05.1993), "UN Troops Hurt," *The Independent*. London: 10.
___ (28.01.1993), "An Anachronism that Works," *The Independent*. London: 26.
___ (31.01.1992), "An International Interest," *The Independent*. London: 20.
Independent Working Group On The Future Of The United Nations (1995), *The United Nations in Its Second Half-Century*. New York: Ford Foundation.
Inter Press (03.08.1993), "United Nations: 'Big Five' Split Over Security Council Reforms," *Inter Press Service*.
Interviews, New York (5-7.02.1996), Personal interviews with senior officials of the US, UK, French, Russian, German, Japanese and European Union Permanent Missions to the United Nations, New York, February 5-7, 1996.
Intrilligator, M. D. & Brito, D. L. (1986), "Arms Races and Instability," *Journal of Strategic Studies* 9 (4): 113-125.
I.P.A. & Stanley Foundation (1994), *Reform of the Security Council*. Memorandum submitted to the president of the UN General Assembly; Chair of the Open-ended Working Group on the Question of Equitable Representation on and Increase in the Membership of the Security Council, from the International Peace Academy and The Stanley Foundation.
Isaka, S. (13.06.1994), "Bid for UN Seat Clarified," *The Nikkei Weekly*. Nihon Keizai Shimbun, Inc.
___ (29.11.1993), "Officials Urge Clear Stand on UN Security Seat Issue; Tokyo's Position Called Confusing," *The Nikkei Weekly*. Nihon Keizai Shimbun, Inc.
Italian Proposal (1996), *A Revised Proposal for the Enlargement of the Security Council of the United Nations*. Proposal presented by the Permanent Mission of Italy to the United Nations to the Open-Ended Working Group on the Question of Equitable Representation on and Increase in the Membership of the Security Council, January 1996 [http://www.undp.org/missions/italy/proj 96.htm].

I.W.G. (1995), *The United Nations in its Second Half-Century*. Yale University: The Report of the Independent Working Group on the Future of the United Nations [http://www.library.yale.edu/un/unhome.htm].

Jackson, R. G. A. (1969), *A Study of the Capacity of the United Nations Development System*. Geneva: United Nations [UN Doc. DP/5 1969].

Jackson, T. (16.09.1991), "Japan and Britain: Perplexities of a New Role," *The Independent*. London: 26.

Jacobson, H. K. & Oksenberg, M. (1990), *China's Participation in the IMF, the World Bank, and GATT; Toward a Global Economic Order*. Ann Arbor: University of Michigan Press.

James, P. & Brecher, M. (1988), "Stability and Polarity - New Paths for Inquiry," *Journal of Peace Research* 25 (1): 31-42.

JEI Report (25.03.1994), "Japan Pursues Leadership Role in the United Nations," *Japan Economic Institute of America* 199 (12).

Jervis, R. (1993), "Arms-Control, Stability, and Causes of War," *Political Science Quarterly* 108 (2): 239-253.

Jianxiong, L. (08.10.1993), "Nations Push for Security Council Reform," *Xinhua General Overseas News Service*.

Jiji Press (05.09.1994), "Foreign Min. Suggests Rotating UNSC Membership," *Jiji Press Ticker Service*.

__ (09.06.1994), "UNSC Seats to Only Japan, Germany Said Unlikely," *Jiji Press Ltd*. Jiji Press Ticker Service.

__ (17.03.1994), "Takemura Plays Down Bid for More Say in U.N.," *Jiji Press Ltd*. Jiji Press Ticker Service.

Johnston, R. J. (1995), "The Conflict over Qualified Majority Voting in the European Union Council of Ministers: An Analysis of the UK Negotiating Stance Using Power Indices," *British Journal of Political Science* 25 (2): 245-288.

Joseph, J. (04.05.1990), "Japan Ready to Slow Foreign Aid Over Issue of IMF Rank," *The Times*. London: 29.

Kahler, M. (1990), "The United Nations and the International Monetary Fund: Declining Influence or Declining Interest?," in Karns, M. P. & Mingst, K. A. (eds.), *The United States and Multilateral Institutions: Patterns of Changing Instrumentality and Influence*. Boston: Unwin Hyman.

Kaiser, K. (1993), "Die ständige Mitgleidschaft im Sicherheitsrat; Ein berechtigtes Ziel der neuen deutschen Außenpolitik," *Europa Archiv* 19: 541-552.

Kallen, R. M. Jr. (compiler) (1992), *A UN Revitalized: A Compilation of UNA-USA Recommendations on Strengthening the Role of the United*

Nations in Peacemaking, Peacekeeping, and Conflict Prevention. New York: United Nations Association of the United States of America.

Kaplan, M. A. (1967), "Systems Theory," in Charlesworth, J. C. (ed.), *Contemporary Political Analysis.* New York: Free Press.

___ (1963), "A Brief Note on Needed Research in the Systems Framework," *Background* 7 (3): 131-132.

___ (1957a), *System and Process in International Politics.* New York: Wiley.

___ (1957b), "Balance of Power, Bipolarity and other Models of International Systems," *American Political Science Review* 51 (3): 684-695.

Katzenstein, P. J. (1996), "Culture, Norms, and Japanese Security," *Social Science Japan* (August): 9-11.

Kaufmann, J. (1991), "Developments in Decision Making in the United Nations," in R.A. Falk, S.S. Kim & S.H. Mendlovitz (eds.), *The United Nations and a Just World Order.* Boulder/San Francisco/Oxford: Westview Press.

___ (1988), "Developments in Decision Making in the United Nations," in J. Harrod & N. Schrijver (eds.), *The UN Under Attack.* Aldershot: Gower.

Kegley, C. W. & Raymond, G. A. (1992), "Must We Fear a Post-Cold-War Multipolar System," *Journal of Conflict Resolution* 36 (3): 573-585.

Keller, G. (1992, 4e trimestre), "La France et le Conseil de securité," *Le Trimestre du monde* (20): 41-51.

Kellner, P. (25.01.1991), "Britain's UN Sacrifice for a 'New World Order'," *The Independent.* London: 21.

Kennedy, P. (01.11.1995), "Ausmisten reicht nicht," *Die Zeit.* Hamburg: 6.

___ (1987), *The Rise and Fall of the Great Powers; Economic Change and Military Conflict from 1500 to 2000.* New York: Random House.

Kennedy, P. & Russett, B. (1995), "Reforming the United Nations," *Foreign Affairs* 74 (5): 56-71.

Keohane, R. O. (1993), "Institutionalist Theory and the Realist Challenge After the Cold War," in Baldwin, D. A. (ed.), *Neorealism and Neoliberalism; The Contemporary Debate.* New York: Columbia University Press.

___ (1989), *International Institutions and State Power; Essays in International Relations Theory.* Boulder/San Francisco/London: Westview Press.

Kim, W. & Morrow, J. D. (1992), "When do Power Shifts Lead to War?" *American Journal of Political Science* 36 (4): 896-922.

King, G., Keohane, R. O. & Verba, S. (1994), *Designing Social Enquiry; Scientific Inference in Qualitative Research*. Princeton, N.J.: Princeton University Press.

Kinkel, K. (01.11.1995), *Deutschland und Japan; Verantwortung in einer Welt im Wandel*. Rede des Bundesministers des Auswärtigen, Dr. Klaus Kinkel, vor der Yomiuri International Economic Society, Tokyo [http://www.auswaertiges-amt.government.de/de/auss_pol/1135.htm].

— (25.10.1995), Regierungserklärung des Bundesministers des Auswärtigen, Dr. Klaus Kinkel, aus Anlaß des 50-jährigen Bestehens der Vereinten Nationen im Deutschen Bundestag.

— (18.10.1995), *Zum 40. Geburtstag der Bundeswehr*. Rede des Bundesministers des Auswärtigen, Dr. Klaus Kinkel, anläßlich seines Truppenbesuchs beim Jägerregiment 57 aus Anlaß des 40-jährigen Bestehens der Bundeswehr am 18. Oktober 1995 in Schneeberg, Erzgebirge [http://www.auswaertiges-amt.government.de/de/auss_pol/bw.htm].

— (1992), "Rede des deutschen Außenministers, Klaus Kinkel, vor der 47. Generalversammlung der Vereinten Nationen in New York am 23. September 1992," *Europa Archiv* (20): D597-D604.

Kohl, H. (1992), "Rede von Bundeskanzler Helmut Kohl über die Aufgabe der Bundeswehr im vereinten Deutschland, gehalten auf der 33. Kommandeurtagung der Bundeswehr in Leipzig am 12. Mai 1992 (gekürzt)," *Europa Archiv* (13): D445-D448.

Kono, Y. (26.09.1995), Statement by Japanese Foreign Minister Yohei Kono at the 50th Session of the UN General Assembly [http://www.nttls.co.jp/infomofa/press/fm/ 92850th.html].

— (24.04.1995), Anonymous interview of Japanese Foreign Minister, Yohei Kono [http://www.nttls.co.jp/infomofa/press/fm/interview.html#2].

— (05.01.1995), "A Path for the Future of Japan's Foreign Policy," [Translation from the Japanese] *Gaiko Forum*, January [http://www.nttls.co.jp/infomofa/ f_m/path.html].

— (27.09.1994), Statement of the Japanese Deputy Prime Minister and Minister for Foreign Affairs, Yohei Kono, before the 49th Session of the UN General Assembly, New York, on September 27, 1994 [http://www.nttls.co.jp/infomofa/ f_m/49.html].

Krock, A. (24.10.1944), "In the Nation," *New York Times*. New York.

Kühne, W. (1994), "Erweiterung und Reform des UN-Sicherheitsrats: keine weltpolitische Nebensache," *Europa Archiv* (24): 685-692.

___ (1991), "Der Einsatz der Bundeswehr außerhalb Europas: Ein Beitrag zur Diskussion über deutsche Blauhelme," *Europa Archiv* 46 (22): 643-653.

Kühne, W. & Baumann, K. (1995), *Reform des VN-Sicherheitsrats zum 50Jährigen Jubiläum: Auswertung und Analyse der Stellungnahmen der Mitgliedstaaten im Überblick*. Ebenhausen/Isartal: Stiftung Wissenschaft und Politik; Forschungsinstitut für internationale Politik und Sicherheit [SWP-AP 2919].

Kyodo (12.06.1995), "Japan Calls for Reform of UNSC by September 1996," *Kyodo News Service*. Japan Economic Newswire.

___ (05.09.1994), "Ghali Less Sure About Early UN Security Council Reform," *Kyodo News Service*. Japan Economic Newswire.

___ (15.06.1994), "Kakizawa Eyes Japan as Permanent UNSC Member with Veto," *Kyodo News Service*. Japan Economic Newswire.

___ (09.07.1993), "Kohl Opposes Taking UNSC Seat Without Veto Power," *Kyodo News Service*. Japan Economic Newswire.

___ (30.01.1993), "Pyongyang Opposes UN Security Council Seat for Japan," *Kyodo News Service*. Japan Economic Newswire.

___ (09.10.1992), "Japan Aims at Permanent UNSC Seat Without Veto Power," *Kyodo News Service*. Japan Economic Newswire.

___ (07.09.1992), "Japan Hails Nonaligned Call for Security Council Reform," *Kyodo News Service*. Japan Economic Newswire.

Lambert, S. & Doyle, L. (27.01.1993), "US Plan for UN Upsets Europe," *The Independent*. London: 10.

Langguth, G. (1996), "Ein starkes Europa mit schwachen Insititutionen? Die europapolitische Agenda zur Regierungskonferenz 1996," *Aus Politik und Zeitgeschichte*. B1 (2/96): 35-42.

Lau, D. (10.02.1995), "Japan Backs Wider Expansion of UNSC," *The Daily Yomiuri*.

___ (18.03.1994), "Japanese Envoy Pushes for UNSC Seat," *The Daily Yomuiri*: 3.

Layne, C. (1994), "Kant or Cant; The Myth of the Democratic Peace," *International Security* 19 (2): 5-49.

Le Monde (30.09.1994), "Devant l'Assemblée générale des Nations unies M. Juppé réclame une plus grande participation des Etats aux dépenses de l'ONU," *Le Monde*: 3.

___ (26.09.1994), "La Réforme de l'ONU: La délicate question de l'élargissement du Conseil de sécurité ne sera pas réglée en 1995," *Le Monde*: 5.

___ (10.05.1994), "Bresil: La visite en France de Celso Amorim; Le chef de la diplomatie brésilienne plaide pour l'entrée de son pays au Conseil de sécurité," *Le Monde*: 5.

___ (29.03.1994), "L'avenir des Nations unies: Alain Juppé favorable à un droit de veto pour le Japon et l'Allemagne au Conseil de sécurité," *Le Monde.*

Lee, D. E. (1947), "The Genesis of the Veto," *International Organization* 1 (1): 33-42.

Leigh-Phippard, H. (1994), "Remaking the Security Council: The Options," *The World Today* 50 (8-9): 167-172.

Lenin, N. (1978 [1917]), *Imperialism, the Highest Stage of Capitalism.* Moscow: Progress Publishers [Seventeenth Printing].

Leopold, E. (14.11.1995), "US Says No UN Council Reform without Germany, Japan," *Reuters World Service.*

___ (27.07.1995), "'Sir Hunphrey' Quits as Britain's UN Envoy," *The Herald.* Glasgow: 8.

___ (09.06.1993), "U.S. Wants Germany and Japan on Security Council," *The Reuter Library Report.*

Lieber, R. J. (1991), *No Common Power; Understanding International Relations.* New York: Harper Collins.

Lieberson, S. (1992), "Small N's and Big Conclusions: An Examination of the Reasoning in Comparative Studies based on a Small Number of Cases," in Ragin, C. C. & Becker, H. S. (eds.), *What is a Case? Exploring the Foundations of Social Enquiry.* Cambridge: Cambridge University Press.

Lijphart, A. (1975), "The Comparable-Cases Strategy in Comparative Research," *Comparative Political Studies* 8 (2): 158-177.

___ (1971), "Comparative Politics and the Comparative Method," *American Political Science Review* 65 (September): 682-693.

Liska, G. (1963), "Continuity and Change in International Systems," *World Politics* 16 (October): 118-136.

___ (1957), *International Equilibrium: A Theoretical Essay on the Politics and Organization of Security.* Cambridge, MA: Harvard University Press.

Lister, F. K. (1984), *Decision-Making Strategies for International Organizations: The IMF Model.* Denver, CO: Graduate School of International Affairs, University of Denver.

Lord, R. (04.12.1989), "A Point of IMF Order," *The Times of London.*

___ (27.09.1989), "Japan's Frustration Grows at Failure to Gain IMF Leadership," *The Times.* London: 8.

___ (11.09.1989), "Britain Under Pressure to Relinquish IMF Rank," *The Times.* London: 23.

Luck, E. C. & Gati, T. T. (1992), "Whose Collective Security?" *The Washington Quarterly* (Spring): 45-46.

Machiavelli, N. (translated by George Bull) (1961), *The Prince.* Penguin.

Mahamedi, A. S. (1981), "Changes in Power Relations in the International Monetary System and the IMF: A Case Study of Organizational Responses to Environmental Variations," Ph.D. Thesis: University of Pennsylvania.

Major, J. (23.10.1995), *UN 50th Anniversary.* Statement by British Prime Minister, John Major, to the Special Commemorative Meeting of the General Assembly on the Occasion of the 50th Anniversary of the United Nations, at UN Headquarters, New York on October 23, 1995 [http: //www. fco. gov. uk/ current/ 1995/ oct/ 23/ major_statement-to-united-nations. txt].

Mansfield, E. D. (1992), "The Concentration of Capabilities and the Onset of War," *Journal of Conflict Resolution* 36 (1): 3-24.

Martin, A. & Edwards, J. B. S. (1955), *The Changing Charter; A Study in United Nations Reform.* London: Sylvan Press.

Masui, S. (26.10.1994), "Govt. Should be More Open on Gaining Seat in UNSC," *The Daily Yomiuri.*

Matanle, E. (1994), *Reform of the UN Security Council; Changing Seats at the Top Table.* London: The Royal Institute of International Affairs [Briefing Paper No. 15].

Matthews, R. O. (1993), "United Nations Reform in the 1990s: North-South Dimension," *Academic Council on the United Nations System. Reports and Papers* (5): 15-42.

Maull, H. W. (1994), "Japan und Deutschland: Die neuen Großmächte?" *Europa Archiv* (21): 603-610.

Mc Carthy, P.A. (1997), "Positionality, Tension and Instability in the UN Security Council," *Global Governance.* 3 (2): 147-169.

Mc Carthy, P.A. & Alexopoulos, A. (1995), "Theory Synthesis in IR; Problems and Possibilities," *EUI Working Papers*, Robert Schuman Centre No. 95/14.

Mc Carthy, T. (14.09.1994), "Japan Prepares Troops for Rwanda," *The Independent.* London: 10.

___ (26.01.1994), "Japan Rejects UN Plea for Peace-Keepers," *The Independent.* London: 11.

___ (18.01.1994), "Asia's New Great Game: Japan and China have Renewed their Struggle to Rule Asia," *The Independent.* London: 16.

___ (28.09.1993), "Japan Cautious over Security Council Role: The New Government is Divided Over the Value of a Permanent Seat," *The Independent.* London: 10.

___ (07.04.1993), "Hurd on Flying Visit to Tokyo: Courtesy Call to Shore Up Sagging 'Special Relationship' with Britain," *The Independent.* London: 12.

___ (19.02.1993), "Japanese Urged to Expand UN Role," *The Independent.* London: 12.

___ (10.01.1992), "Time to Tame an Economic Animal: Japan can no Longer Avoid the Demands of Superpower Status; it Must Adopt a Leading Role in International Affairs," *The Independent.* London: 19.

Mearsheimer, J. J. (1990), "Back to the Future - Instability in Europe After the Cold-War," *International Security* 15 (1): 5-56.

Mesjasz, C. (1993), "International Stability: What Can We Learn from Systems Metaphors and Analogies," Copenhagen: Centre for Peace and Conflict Research. Working Paper 3/1993.

___ (1992), "Systems Metaphors, Systems Analogies and Present Changes in International Relations," in R. Trappl (ed.), *Cybernetics and Systems Research '92.* London: World Scientific.

___ (1990), "International and Strategic Stability in the 1990s: Framework of Description and Analysis," Paper presented to the International Peace Research Association (IPRA) 25th Anniversary Conference / 13th General Conference, University of Groningen, The Netherlands, 3-7 July, 1990.

___ (1988), "Applications of Systems Modeling in Peace Research," *Journal of Peace Research* 25 (3): 291-334.

Meyer, J. W. & Rowan, B. (1991), "Institutionalized Organizations: Formal Structure as Myth and Ceremony," in P.J. DiMaggio & W.W. Powell (eds.), *The New Institutionalism in Organizational Analysis.* Chicago: University of Chicago Press.

Midlarsky, M. (1993), "Polarity and International Stability," *American Political Science Review* 87 (1): 173-177.

___ (1986), "A Hierarchical Equilibrium Theory of Systemic War," *International Studies Quarterly* 30 (1): 77-105.

Mill, J. S. (1974 [1843]), "On the Four Methods of Experimental Enquiry," in *A System of Logic.* Toronto: University of Toronto Press.

Moniac, R. (20.11.1995), "Deutsche Soldaten für Krisenfeuerwehr der UNO," *Die Welt.*

Morgenthau, H. (1946), *Scientific Man Versus Power Politics.* Chicago, Ill.: Chicago University Press.

Mortimer, E. (11.01.1995), "Inquiry into the UN: Critics are unhappy with the system for a variety of reasons," *The Financial Times.* London: 20.

Moul, W. B. (1993), "Polarization, Polynomials, and War," *Journal of Conflict Resolution* 37 (4): 735-748.

___ (1992), "Polarity, Balances of Power and War - Explaining Some Puzzling Correlates of War Project Results," *International Interactions* 18 (2): 165-193.

Mueller, J. (1988), "The Essential Irrelevance of Nuclear-Weapons - Stability in the Postwar World," *International Security* 13 (2): 55-79.

Müller, J. W. (1992), *The Reform of the United Nations [a volume in the series]. Annual Review of United Nations Affairs.* New York: Oceana.

Murata, R. (1993), "Die japanische Außenpolitik in den neunziger Jahren," *Europa Archiv* 20: 577-586.

Murayama, T. (22.10.1995), Statement by Japanese Prime Minister Tomiichi Murayama at the Special Commemorative Meeting of the UN General Assembly on the Occasion of the 50th Anniversary of the UN, New York, October 22, 1995 [http://www.nttls.co.jp/infomofa/f_m/pm/sp.html].

New York Times (23.10.1995), "And Now for the Next 50 Years: New Promises, Familiar Demands," *New York Times.* A6.

Newcombe, H., Young, C. & Sinaiko, E. (1977), "Alternative Pasts: A Study of Weighted Voting in the U.N.," *International Organization* 31: 579-586.

Niou, E. M. S. & Ordeshook, P. C. (1990), "Stability in Anarchic International Systems," *American Political Science Review* 84 (4): 1205-1234.

Niou, E. M. S., Ordeshook, P. C. & Rose, G. F. (1989), *The Balance of Power: Stability in International Systems.* Cambridge: Cambridge University Press.

Nodong Sinmun (11.10.1994), "Japan Must Not be Allowed to Take UN Security Council Seat," *Nodong Sinmun.* Pyongyang: BBC Summary of World Broadcasts.

Noel, D. L. (1976), "A Theory of the Origin of Ethnic Stratification," in Barclay, W., Kumar, K. & Simms, R. R. (eds.), *Racial Conflict, Discrimination and Power: Historical and Contemporary Studies.* New York: AMS Press.

Norman, P. (30.01.1995), "World Economic Forum: Value of World Institutions in the Balance," *Financial Times.* London: 4.

___ (08.05.1990), "Anglo-French Deal on New Bank Resolves IMF Rankings Dispute," *Financial Times.* London: 1.

___ (03.01.1990), "Britain May Move Down IMF Ranking," *Financial Times.* London: 2.

___ (26.09.1989), "Japanese Aspirations Place British Pride at Risk," *Financial Times.* London: 10.

Nyerere, J. K. (1974), *Stability and Change in Africa.* Dar es Salaam, Tanzania.
NYT (12.02.1989), "Larger Role for Japan in IMF," *New York Times.* I 16.
Oakley, R. (04.02.1992), "Major Defends Trident," *The Times.* London.
Officer, L. H. (1991), "Are International Monetary Fund Quotas Unfavorable to Less-Developed Countries? A Normative Historical Analysis," *Journal of International Money and Finance* 10 (2): 193-213.
Olson, M. (1982), *The Rise and Decline of Nations; Economic Growth, Stagflation, and Social Rigidities.* New Haven: Yale University Press.
Orum, A. M., Feagin, J. R. & Sjoberg, G. (1991), "The Nature of the Case Study," in Feagin, J. R., Orum, A. M. & Sjoberg, G. (eds.), *A Case for the Case Study.* Chapel Hill, N.C.: University of North Carolina Press.
Ostrom, C. W. & Aldrich, J. H. (1978), "The Relationship Between Size and Stability in the Major Power International System," *American Journal of Political Science* 22 (4): 743-771.
Owada, H. (13.11.1995), Statement to the United Nations' 50th General Assembly by H.E. Mr. Hisashi Owada, Representative of Japan, on item 47: Question of equitable representation on and increase in the membership of the Security Council and related matters. New York: Permanent Mission of Japan to the United Nations.
Panda, R. (1992), "Japan, Germany and the UN Security Council," *Journal of International Affairs* 48 (4): 51-70.
Pawlowski, T. (1980), *Concept Formation in the Human Sciences and the Social Sciences.* Dordrecht/Boston: Hingham, MA.
Petrovsky, V. (27.06.1995), Personal interview with Vladimir Petrovsky, Undersecretary General and Director General of the United Nations in Geneva, at the Palais des Nations, Geneva, on June 27, 1995.
Pfeiffer, A. (01.07.1995), "Bundeswehr unterstützt UN-Truppen: Parlament billigt Bosnien-Einsatz," *Stuttgarter Zeitung.* Stuttgart: 1.
Pfetsch, F. R. (1994), "Die Außenpolitik der Bundesrepublik Deutschland: Kontinuität oder Wandel nach der Vereinigung," *EUI Working Paper SPS No. 94/15.*
PIB (08.1994), *Urteil des Bundesverfassungsgerichts vom 12. Juli 1994 zu Auslands-einsätzen der Bundeswehr.* Bonn: Presse und Informationsamt der Bundes-regierung; Referat Außen- und Sicherheitspolitik.
___ (07.1994), *Zu Einsätzen der Bundeswehr im Rahmen der UNO.* Bonn: Presse- und Informationsamt der Bundesregierung; Referat Außen- und Sicherheitspolitik.

Pick, H. (25.09.1992), "Allies Resist German Push for Big-Power Seat at UN," *The Guardian:* 8.
Powell, R. (1993), "Absolute and Relative Gains in International Relations Theory," in D.A. Baldwin (ed.), *Neorealism and Neoliberalism; The Contemporary Debate.* New York: Columbia University Press.
Pringle, P. (21.09.1993), "UN Searches for a Brave New World," *The Independent.* London: 13.
Proceedings (1948), *Proceedings and Documents: United Nations Monetary and Financial Conference, Bretton Woods, New Hampshire, 1944.* Washington, D.C.: Government Printing Office; Department of State Publication, 2866 [International Organization and Conference Series].
Przeworski, A. & Teune, H. (1970), *The Logic of Comparative Social Enquiry.* New York: John Wiley.
Qian Wenrong (1995), "A Comparative Analysis of Proposals for Reforming the UN Security Council," in Malcolm Chalmers (ed.), *Asia Pacific Security and the UN.* West Yorks: University of Bradford Press [Chinese People's Association for Peace and Disarmament].
Ragin, C. C. (1992), "Cases of 'What is a Case?'," in Ragin, C. C. & Becker, H. S. (eds.), *What is a Case? Exploring the Foundations of Social Enquiry.* Cambridge: Cambridge University Press.
Ramcharan, B. G. (1987), *Keeping Faith with the United Nations.* Dordrecht/Boston/Lancaster: Martinus Nijhoff Publishers.
Ray, E. (1990), *Funding the IMF: Why an Increase in Quotas?* Washington, D.C.: External Relations Dept., International Monetary Fund.
Raymond, G. A. & Kegley, C. W. (1990), "Polarity, Polarization, and the Transformation of Alliance Norms," *Western Political Quarterly* 43 (1): 9-38.
Reston, J. B. (06.10.1944), "Chinese Accept Dumbarton Draft," *New York Times.* New York.
Reuters (15.06.1994), "Japan Still Wants UN Seat with Veto Power," Reuters, Limited.
___ (09.10.1992), "Japan Said to Seek Permanent UN Council Seat," The Reuter Library Report.
___ (24.09.1992), "U.S. Rules Out Quick Decisions on Expanding Security Council," The Reuter Library Report.
Richardson, L. F. (1960), *Arms and Insecurity.* Pittsburg: Boxwood Press.
___ (1960a), *Statistics of Deadly Quarrels.* Pittsburgh: Boxwood Press.

Riches, C. A. (1940), *Majority Rule in International Organisation; A Study of the Trend from Unanimity to Majority Decision.* Baltimore.

Riddell, P. (13.03.1989), "Washington Shifts Attitude to Japan's International Role," *Financial Times:* 2.

Rifkind, M. (26.09.1995), *The United Nations: The Lessons of Fifty Years.* Speech by British Foreign Secretary, Malcolm Rifkind, to the United Nations General Assembly, New York, on September 26, 1995 [http:// www.fco.gov.uk/ current/1995/sept/26/rifkind_speech_united-nations.txt].

__ (21.09.1995), *Principles and Practice of British Foreign Policy.* Speech by the British Foreign Secretary, Malcolm Rifkind, at the Royal Institute of International Affairs, Chatham House, London on September 21, 1995 [http://www.fco.gov.uk/current/1995/sept/21/ rifkind_speech_foreign-policy.txt].

RJDP (28.11.1995), "Review of Japanese Defense Policy; Contents of Japan's Defense Capability" [http://www.nttls.co.jp/infomofa/defense /contents.html].

Robinson, J. (1954), "The General Review Conference," *International Organization* 8 (3): 316-330.

Romanov, A. (10.03.1995), "Chinese Foreign Minister Suggests Reforming UN," *The Russian Information Agency ITAR-TASS.*

Roncesvalles, O. & Tweedie, A. (1991), "Augmenting the IMF's Resources; The How and Why of the Quota Increase under the Ninth General Review, which Strengthens the Role of the IMF in the International Monetary System," *Finance & Development* (December): 26-29.

Rosecrance, R. N. (1966), "Bipolarity, Multipolarity, and the Future," *Journal of Conflict Resolution* 10 (3): 314-327.

__ (1963), *Action and Reaction in World Politics.* Boston: Little, Brown.

Rosenau, J. N. (1995), "Governance in the Twenty-first Century," *Global Governance* 1 (1): 13-43.

__ (1992), "Governance, Order and Change in World Politics," in J.N. Rosenau & E. O. Czempiel (eds.), *Governance Without Governance; Order and Change in World Politics.* Cambridge: Cambridge University Press.

__ (1990), *Turbulence in World Politics: A Theory of Change and Continuity.* Princeton: Princeton University Press.

__ (1963), "The Functioning of International Systems," *Background* 7 (3): 111-118.

Rosenau, J. N. & Czempiel, E. O. (1992), *Governance Without Government; Order and Change in World Politics.* Cambridge: Cambridge University Press.

Rossbach, S. (1992), "Struckturwandel und Stabilität," in U. Nerlich et al. (eds.), *Sicherheitspolitik Deutschlands: Neue Konstellationen, Risiken, Instrumente.* Baden-Baden: Nomos.

Rowen, H. (26.09.1989), "Japanese Intensify Push for Higher IMF Ranking," *The Washington Post:* C1.

___ (25.08.1982), "Study Questions Whether IMF can Meet Needs," *Washington Post:* D7.

Russet, B., O'Neill, B. & Sutterlin, J. (1996), "Breaking the Security Council Restructuring Logjam," *Global Governance* (2): 65-80.

Ryder (22.03.1990), *Written Answers to Questions.* Answer by the Chancellor of the Exchequer to a written question by Mr. Riddick concerning negotiations on the ninth general review of quotas. Page 688.

Sabrosky, A. N. (1985), *Polarity & War: The Changing Structure of International Conflict.* Boulder, CO: Westview Press.

Salda, A. C. M. (1992), *The International Monetary Fund.* Oxford: Clio Press [International Organizations Series; Selective, Critical, Annotated Bibliographies, Vol. 4].

Saperstein, A. M. (1992), "Alliance Building Versus Independent Action - A Nonlinear Modeling Approach to Comparative International Stability," *Journal of Conflict Resolution* 36 (3): 518-545.

___ (1991), "The Long Peace - Result of a Bipolar Competitive World," *Journal of Conflict Resolution* 35 (1): 68-79.

Sartori, G. (ed.) (1984), *Social Science Concepts: A Systematic Analysis.* Beverly Hills, CA: Sage.

___ (1970), "Concept Misformation in Comparative Politics," *American Political Science Review* 64: 1033-1053.

Savill, A. (25.11.1993), "Britain off UN Budget Body," *The Independent.* London: 14.

___ (09.07.1993), "G7 Summit: Britain Starts to Bow towards the Inevitable: Hurd and Major Give First Signs of Accepting German and Japanese Claims to Seats on UN Security Council," *The Independent.* London: 10.

___ (09.07.1993a), "Japanese Win Right to Nuclear Weapons," *The Independent.* London: 10.

___ (11.06.1993), "US Backs Expansion of Security Council: Britain Resists Change that Would Dilute its Permanent Five Position," *The Independent.* London: 11.

___ (01.02.1992), "One Can Pay like a Grown-up, but not Play like a Grown-up," *The Independent.* London: 8.

___ (07.01.1992), "UK Finds a Way to Hold on to the Mother of all Seats," *The Independent.* London: 8.

Scheltema, H. (1988), "Transformations within the United Nations," in J. Harrod & N. Schrijver (eds.), *The UN Under Attack.* Aldershot: Gower.

Schild, G. (1995), *Bretton Woods and Dumbarton Oaks; American Economic and Political Postwar Planning in the Summer of 1944.* New York: St. Martin's Press.

Schmidt, M. (1994), "German UN Policy and a German Seat in the Security Council; An Analysis," *Peace and the Sciences* 25: 16-20.

Schneider, B. (1989), "Creative Instability Source of Inspiration for a New World," *Futures* 21 (2): 199-200.

Schroeder, P. W. (1989), "The Nineteenth Century System: Balance of Power or Political Equilibrium?" *Review of International Studies* 15 (2): 135-153.

Schuman, F. L. (1945), "The Dilemma of the Peace-Seekers," *The American Political Science Review* 39 (1): 12-30.

Schwelb, E. (1966), "The 1963/1965 Amendments to the Charter of the United Nations: An Addendum," *American Journal of International Law* 60 (2): 371-378.

___ (1965), "Amendments to Articles 23, 27 and 61 of the Charter of the United Nations," *American Journal of International Law* 59 (4): 834-856.

___ (1960), "Charter Review and Charter Amendment - Developments in 1958 and 1959," *International and Comparative Law Quarterly* 9 (2): 237-252.

___ (1958), "Charter Review and Charter Amendment - Recent Developments," *International and Comparative Law Quarterly* 7 (2): 303-333.

___ (1954), "The Amending Procedure of Constitutions of International Organizations," *The British Yearbook of International Law* 31: 49-95.

Sellen, K. L. (1992), "The United Nations Security Council Veto in the New World Order," *Military Law Review* 138 (Fall): 187-262.

Sheridan, M. (01.11.1993), "United Nations: What's Gone Wrong? The Limits of the Possible: The Promise of a Golden Era for the UN has Turned to Dust," *The Independent.* London: 14.

___ (01.11.1993a), "United Nations: What's Gone Wrong? Chaotic Harmony or Just Chaos? Structural Defects," *The Independent.* London: 14.

Sieg, L. (27.09.1993), "Japanese Premier Makes Oblique Bid for UN Seat," *Reuters*.
Singer, J. D. (1980), *The Correlates of War, Vol II: Testing Some Realpolitik Models*. New York: Free Press.
__ (1979), *The Correlates of War, Vol. I: Research Origins and Rationale*. New York: Free Press.
__ (1970), "From A Study of War to Peace Research; Some Criteria and Strategies," *Journal of Conflict Resolution*. 14 (4): 528-542.
Singer, J. D. and Associates (1979), *Explaining War: Selected Papers from the Correlates of War Project*. Beverly Hills, CA: Sage.
Singer, J. D. & Small, M. (1968), "Alliance Aggregation and the Onset of War, 1815-1945," in J.D. Singer (ed.), *Quantitative International Politics*. New York: Free Press.
Sohn, L. B. (1993), "Modernizing the Structure and Procedure of the Security Council," in Dupuy, R. J. (ed.), *The Development of the Role of the Security Council; Peace-keeping and Peace-building*. Dordrecht/Boston/London: Martinus Nijhoff Publishers.
__ (ed.) (1970), *The United Nations: The Next Twenty-five Years*. Dobbs Ferry, N.Y.: Oceana [Commission to Study the Organization of Peace].
__ (1944), "Weighting of Votes in an International Assembly," *The American Political Science Review* 38 (6): 1192-1208.
Southard, F. A. (1979), *The Evolution of the International Monetary Fund*. Princeton: International Finance Section, Department of Economics, Princeton University.
Stassen, H. (1994), *United Nations: A Working Paper for Restructuring*. Minneapolis, Minn.: Lerner Publications.
Stephens, P. (23.09.1988), "UK to Lose Rank to Japan," *Financial Times*. London: 20.
Storch, K. (12.07.1994), *Interview mit dem Generalsekretär der Vereinten Nationen, Boutros Boutros-Ghali, zum Urteil des Bundesverfassungsgerichtes zu Blauhelmeinsätzen der Bundeswehr*. Bonn: Presse und Informationsamt der Bundesregierung; Referat Außen- und Sicherheitspolitik [Das Interview fand im deutschen Fernsehen (ZDF) am 12.07.1994 um 22.25 statt].
Strachan, C. (08.01.1992), "Deceptive Strength," *The Independent*. London: 18.
Strange, S. (1973), "IMF: Monetary Managers," in R.W. Cox & H.K. Jacobson (eds.), *The Anatomy of Influence: Decision Making in International Organizations*. New Haven: Yale University Press.

Susumu, T. (1996), "Japan's Contribution to UN Peacekeeping," *Social Science Japan; Newsletter of the Institute of Social Science, University of Tokyo* (6): 7-10.

Sutterlin, J. S. (1992), *Enhancing the Capacity of the United Nations in Maintaining Peace and International Security: A Common Interest of Japan and the United States*. New York: United Nations Association - United States of America [Occasional Paper No. 5].

Taylor, P. (1988), "Reforming the System: Getting the Money to Talk," in P. Taylor & A.J.R. Groom (eds.), *International Institutions at Work*. London: Pinter.

Thakur, R. (1993), "The United Nations in a Changing World," *Security Dialogue* 24 (1): 7-20.

Tomlin, B. W. & Buhlman, M. A. (1977), "Relative Status and Foreign Policy; Status Partitioning and the Analysis of Relations in Black Africa," *Journal of Conflict Resolution* 21 (2): 187-216.

Tomuschat, C. (1992), "Die Zukunft der Vereinten Nationen," *Europa Archiv* (2): 42-50.

Torday, P. (07.05.1990), "Pride of Place a Key Issue in IMF Dispute," *The Independent:* 9.

Treasurer's Department (1995), "Financial Organization and Operations of the IMF," Treasurer's Department, International Monetary Fund, Washington, D.C. [Pamphlet Series No. 45, Fourth Edition].

Trochim, W. (1989), "Outcome Pattern Matching and Program Theory," *Evaluation and Program Planning* 12: 355-366.

Udechuku, E. C. (1972), "The Problem of the Veto in the Security Council," *International Relations* 4: 187-217.

UN Press Release (24.10.1995), *Press Release DH/2007*.

___ (23.10.1995), *UN Press Release DH/2006*.

United Nations (1975), *Report of Group of Experts*. New York: United Nations [E/AC 62/9].

Urquhart, B. & Childers, E. (1991), "Towards a More Effective United Nations," *Development Dialogue* 1 (2).

Van Dormael, A. (1978), *Bretton Woods: Birth of a Monetary Order*. New York: Holmes & Meier.

Van Evera, S. (1993), "What Are Case Studies? How Should they be Performed?" Unpublished Memo, Department of Political Science, MIT.

___ (1991), "Primed for Peace - Europe After the Cold-War," *International Security* 15 (3): 7-57.

Vasquez, J. A. (1987), "The Steps to War: Toward a Scientific Explanation of Correlates of War Findings," *World Politics* 40 (1): 108-145.

Verba, S. (1967), "Some Dilemmas in Comparative Research," *World Politics* 20 (1): 111-127.
Vernet, D. (01.07.95), "Les Allemands face à leurs responsabilités," *Le Monde*. Paris: 1.
Volgy, T. J. & Mayhall, S. (1995), "Status Inconsistency and International War: Exploring the Effects of Systemic Change," *International Studies Quarterly* 39 (1): 67-84.
Von Bertalanffy, L. (1955). "General System Theory," *Main Currents of Modern Thought*. 11 (March): 75-83.
__ (1950). "An Outline of General System Theory," *British Journal of the Philosophy of Science*. 1: 134-165.
Wagner, R. H. (1993), "What Was Bipolarity?" *International Organization* 47 (1): 77-106.
Wagner, W. (1993), "Der ständige Sitz im Sicherheitsrat; Wer braucht wen: Die Deutschen diesen Sitz? Der Sicherheitsrat die Deutschen?" *Europa Archiv* 19: 533-540.
Walker, M. (11.06.1993), "France Plays Nuclear Card Over UN Veto," *The Guardian:* 24.
Wallace, M. D. (1973), *War and Rank Among Nations*. Lexington, MA: D.C. Heath.
__ (1972), "Status, Formal Organization, and Arms Levels as Factors Leading to the Onset of War," in Russett, B. M. (ed.), *Peace, War, and Numbers*. Beverly Hills, CA: Sage.
Wallensteen, P. (1994), "Representing the World; A Security Council for the 21st Century," *Security Dialogue* 25 (1): 63-75.
Waltz, K. N. (1993), "The Emerging Structure of International Politics," *International Security* 18 (2): 44-79.
__ (1979), *Theory of International Politics*. New York: McGraw-Hill.
__ (1967), "International Structure, National Force and the Balance of World Power," *Journal of International Affairs* 21: 215-231.
__ (1964), "The Stability of a Bipolar World," *Daedalus* 43: 881-901.
Wanner, B. (1995), "Japan Seeks Nonpermanent UN Security Council Seat," *JEI Report* 199 (7): Japan Economic Institute of America.
Ward, G. F. Jr. (10.02.1995), *The United States and the United Nations*. Address by Assistant Secretary for International Organizations at Chapman University, Orange County, California [gopher://dosfan.lib.uic.edu:70/0F1%3A19376%3A95/02/10].
Watt, K. E. F. & Craig, P. P. (1986), "System Stability Principles," *Systems Research* 3 (4): 191-201.
WBG (1994), *Learning from the Past, Embracing the Future*. Washington, D.C.: World Bank Group.

Webb, M. C. (1991), "International Economic-Structures, Government Interests, and International Coordination of Macroeconomic Adjustment Policies," *International Organization* 45 (3): 309-342.

Wehberg, H. (1944), "Die Organisation der Staatengemeinschaft nach dem Kriege," *Die Friedenswarte* 44: 49-74.

Wellens, K. C. (ed.) (1993), *Resolutions and Statements of the United Nations Security Council (1946-1992); A Thematic Guide.* Dordrecht/Boston/London: Martinus Nijhoff Publishers.

WELT (07.12.1995), "Bundestag stimmt für Bosnien-Einsatz," *Die Welt.*

___ (29.11.1995), "Bosnien-Einsatz beschlossen," *Die Welt.*

___ (26.10.1995), "Kohl wehrt sich gegen Kritik," *Die Welt.*

___ (26.10.1995a), "Reformappell zum Ende der UN-Feier," *Die Welt.*

___ (20.10.1995), "Blockfreie fordern Mitsprache," *Die Welt.*

Wilcox, F. O. (1945), "The Yalta Voting Formula," *The American Political Science Review* 39 (1): 943-956.

Wisnumurti, N. (30.01.1996), Speech by Ambassador Nugroho Wisnumurti, Permanent Representative of Indonesia to the United Nations, at the Institute of International Studies, University of California, Berkeley, 30 January, 1996.

Wren, C. S. (24/25.06.1995), "The UN at 50: A Monument to Inefficiency and Waste," *International Herald Tribune.* Bologna: 1.

Wright, Q. (1942), *The Study of War.* Chicago: University of Chicago Press.

Xinhua (11.11.1994), "Jiang on Regional Cooperation and UN Reform," *Xinhua News Agency.*

___ (13.10.1994), "Security Council Reform Remains Arduous: China," *Xinhua News Agency.*

___ (01.07.1993), "China Calls for Prudence in Security Council Reform," *Xinhua General Overseas News Service.*

Yin, R. K. (1994), *Case Study Research; Designs and Methods.* Second Edition. Thousand Oaks: Sage.

Zamora, S. (1980), "Voting in International Economic Organizations," *American Journal of International Law* 74 (July): 566-608.

Zampaglione, A. (25.06.1995), "Onu, compleanno amaro fra critiche e troppi debiti," *La Repubblica.* Roma: 14.

___ (16.06.1995), "La Bosnia divide i Sette," *La Repubblica.* Roma: 14.

Zinnes, D. A. (1980), "Three Puzzles in Search of a Researcher," (Presidential Address to the International Studies Association) *International Studies Quarterly* 24 (3): 315-342.

___ (1967), "An Analytical Study of the Balance of Power Theories," *Journal of Peace Research* 4: 270-288.

___ (1964), "The Requisites for International Stability: A Review," *Journal of Conflict Resolution* 8 (3): 301-305.

Zinnes, D. A. & Muncaster, R. G. (1988), "The War Propensity of International Systems," *Synthese* 76 (2): 307-331.